House United, House Divided

Studies of the East Asian Institute
Columbia University

APPROACHING YEN-LIAO

HOUSE UNITED, HOUSE DIVIDED

The Chinese Family in Taiwan

Myron L. Cohen

1976
Columbia University Press
New York and London

The Andrew W. Mellon Foundation, through a Special Grant, has assisted the Press in publishing this volume.

Library of Congress Cataloging in Publication Data

Cohen, Myron L.   1937–
    House united, house divided.

    (Studies of the East Asian Institute, Columbia University)
    Bibliography
    Includes index.
    1. Ethnology—Taiwan. 2. Family—Taiwan. 3. Taiwan—
Social life and customs. I. Title. II. Series: Columbia University.
East Asian Institute. Studies.
GN635.T28C63   301.42′1   75–28473
ISBN 0–231–03849–6

To the Memory of
Maurice Freedman
1920–1975

THE EAST ASIAN INSTITUTE OF
COLUMBIA UNIVERSITY

THE EAST ASIAN INSTITUTE of Columbia University was established in 1949 to prepare graduate students for careers dealing with East Asia, and to aid research and publication on East Asia during the modern period. The faculty of the Institute are grateful to the Ford Foundation and the Rockefeller Foundation for their financial assistance.

The Studies of the East Asian Institute were inaugurated in 1962 to bring to a wider public the results of significant new research on modern and contemporary East Asia.

Contents

Illustrations appear as a group beginning on p. 104

Foreword

FOREWORDS and introductions have many purposes. Some go on much too long and infringe on the works they present, killing surprise and providing "unnecessary critical aperçus" as someone recently commented. Others are bestowed as gifts to mark friendships and reward long associations. That is true in this instance. Nevertheless, the reader is always aware that the prefatory remarks are not the responsibility of the author whose work follows them. In turn, the author should relax and enjoy the plaudits. If along the way some insight illuminates this front matter, so much the better; if not, well, I still wonder how many readers actually start with the foreword.

I start with that brilliant, blue-skied day in 1964, when Ch'en Shao-t'ing and I visited Myron Cohen in "Yen-liao." The brief journey has left only the warmest and most colorful memories of friendly people and rich landscapes and deeply informed conversations. The people of Yen-liao, if they recall it at all, may remember it differently. We did not arrive on the appointed day and thus frustrated plans for lavish hospitality. At the close of the visit, Shao-t'ing returned to his home in Tainan and I went off, everyone thought, to catch a plane from Tainan to Taipei. That flight ended in a sensational crash, which killed all aboard. The villagers were horrified. But, without speaking of my change in plans, I had gone off elsewhere, avoiding my rendez-vous with fate.

A visit to "Myron Cohen's village" was much prized among the foreign scholars living in Taiwan at that time. Even though

the people of Taiwan are known for their friendliness and cour-
tesy, word had gotten round that Cohen had achieved marvelous rapport. It seemed that everyone knew that the young anthropologist from Columbia was carrying out a truly impressive
study. Yet, since he was now friend and confidant to the village,
Cohen discouraged many attempts to drop in on him, thereby
preserving the privacy of his hosts.

Even the casual visitor to Yen-liao was struck by the mixture
of typical and atypical characteristics which, in sum, made Yen-
liao at once unique and a marvelous place for ethnographic
study by a researcher with a commitment to broader theoretical
goals. The beauty of the locale came out at first glance from the
dramatic meeting of receding plains and onrushing mountains.
A second impression flowed from the richness of the precisely
cultivated fields, from the subtle plotting of a variety of crops—
rice, sugar, banana, tobacco, and sweet potato—each yielding its
own shade of green. The architecture also stood out, from the
quite traditional forms of the town that was the gateway to the
area, to the unusual shapes of the region's most distinctive trait,
the structures in which the tobacco was cured. Tobacco also
supplied a conspicuous source of wealth here, and that affected
local social structure, the forms of domestic life and enterprise,
and, as Cohen shows so well, provided for a remarkable in-
cidence of large, joint families.

I think it is fair to say that Myron Cohen is of that new generation of social anthropologists whose specialization in Chinese
culture and society is based upon extensive competence in
Chinese languages—in his case, upon fluency in spoken Mandarin and Hakka, as well as proficiency in reading. Also, Cohen's generation was taught in classrooms, and in the literature
current when he did his graduate work, that the overwhelmingly predominant form of family organization in Chinese society was of small scale. This was a reaction to the previously
held stereotypic view that Chinese families were often very
large and joint in structure. Cohen had also been taught to asso-
ciate large joint families with the Chinese gentry. Imagine his
surprise, then, to discover a startlingly large frequency of joint

families in Yen-liao, the more so since it could hardly be argued that these were associated with or even the remnants of the old "gentry." This book has at its core Myron Cohen's exploration and explanation of this phenomenon. In the course of his analysis we see exactly how such families are organized, how new ones are formed and how they sustain themselves, how they prosper, and how they wither and decline, ultimately splitting up into small independent units. This is done neither through normalistic utterances nor by novelistic extrapolation and synthesis, but by presenting and analyzing actual data derived from existing families or from veritable historical records, often having legal status. Throughout, Cohen is intent on conveying an understanding of the larger social processes involved, for behind Cohen's alert ethnographic eye is a gifted concern for the major problems of social theory. Cohen, who since the writing of this book has traveled in the People's Republic of China, is attuned to the multiplex political and economic currents whose alternate shifts of speed and direction provide the changing conditions to which real people must adapt. Family structure is one of the primal means by which such adaptation is managed.

There are several reasons for delight with Cohen's study, even though attention is now turning toward events on Mainland China. One of the most important is that it adds to an already substantial literature, thereby enabling us to penetrate quite deeply, even if we only use the English language, into a portion of the Chinese cultural whole that, however paradoxically, displays unique elements and still is capable of representing some important general features. Precisely because some of the specific phenomena that have been analyzed and described in detail in Taiwan are ostensibly different in the People's Republic—things such as religious organization and belief, community organization, economic structure, sexual relations and, of course, family organization—the recording and analysis of these things will interest social scientists who lack specialist concern with China itself.

Valuable as this work is for those presently engaged in the attempt to understand sociocultural processes, it is also a reposi-

tory for those who are yet to come, and thereby fulfills one of
the most important, yet least overtly honored, responsibilities of
social science. When scholars of the future make their attempt
to better understand their own times by comprehending ours,
they will find their task is made easier because of works like
this. They would also be wise, as would we, to heed the admo-
nition of an old, obscure Chinese song—

Mountains green, lovely vales, a prospect fair to see;
Fields which now the fathers hold, their children's soon will be.
Let them not with smugness be too elate in mind,
They too have their posterity, who follow close behind.

October 1975   MORTON H. FRIED

Preface

I BEGAN to ask the questions to which this book is addressed only after settling in Yen-liao, a village in south Taiwan I originally selected as a fieldwork site simply because it seemed suitable for a general study of Chinese community life in a rural setting still largely traditional. But Yen-liao was different in at least one major respect from my preconception of a traditional Chinese settlement; I soon discovered that the so-called "large," "extended," or "joint" form of the family was commonplace, to the extent that more than half of the village's population were members of such units. In one sense, this meant that Yen-liao was more conservative than I had thought possible in Taiwan during the 1960s, for scholars have commonly seen the breakdown of the "large" family system as an early and important result of westernization and industrialization in twentieth-century China. But all reports, including those provided by anthropologists who had studied other Chinese villages, agree that the "large" family was uncommon even in the premodern context, so that in another sense Yen-liao deviates even from the traditional pattern. I was unprepared for Yen-liao's families; that they existed was a puzzle, and I spent much of my time in the field trying to solve it. Yet in this book I express my conclusion that Yen-liao's large and complex families developed owing to a particular combination of the factors having a bearing on family organization in a Chinese context.

Chapters 1, 2, and 3 provide necessary background for consideration of family organization in Yen-liao. In order to describe the circumstances under which the traditional arrangement of family life continues to flourish in the village, I have had to show in the first two chapters how the traditional pattern of local community organization has perdured and continues to encompass the entire area of Mei-nung Township, wherein Yen-liao is situated. Chapter 3 introduces principles of Chinese family organization; it therefore draws upon descriptions of family life in different areas of China as well as upon my own field data.

Yen-liao's families are the main subject of this book. I was fortunate to find myself in a village where the "large" family was comparatively common, for I was in a position to observe details of social and economic life within this kind of family framework, and to distinguish idiosyncratic elements from those falling into a characteristic pattern; and I was also able to compare the organization of families "large" and "small." (Preliminary reports on some of my findings in Yen-liao are in Cohen 1967, 1968, 1969a.)

Circumstances at this juncture of history are such that I am unable to state with confidence that my findings stand to be verified and hopefully expanded by the future field studies of other anthropologists. On the China mainland the "large" family can no longer be a viable institution if the transformation of society in the People's Republic has been as thorough as desired by the country's leadership. Even in Hong Kong, including the still largely rural New Territories, industrialization and urbanization have been along lines that discourage the maintenance of traditional "large" families. Taiwan has been industrializing at a rapid pace; while so far the major impact on rural society has been to attract people to the cities, it seems safe to say that continued industrialization will bring the factories, and with them new social and economic patterns, to the countryside. Although it is possible that life throughout Taiwan may change significantly under the impact of new political forces emerging from within or imposed from without, I would nevertheless hope that more studies of the traditional Chinese family system will be forthcoming. Such studies record a way of life doomed to extinction, and at the same time sharpen the baseline we must have if we are to understand the extent and direction of social change in modern times.

Although I must assume full responsibility for the data and my interpretation of them, I owe debts of gratitude to many individuals and institutions for advice and assistance at all stages of research and writing. A Social Science Research Council Fellowship supported the field study in Yen-liao and before that ten months' language training and documentary research in Taipei. Additional assistance was provided during the final months of the field study by Columbia University's East Asian Institute through a Contemporary China Studies Fellowship. Subsequent data analysis and writeup were supported by National Science Foundation grant no. GS–799–Task I, and by two more awards from the East Asian Institute. Many people in Taiwan made my stay a pleasant and rewarding experience, but I must record my gratitude especially for the kindness and cooperation of Yen-liao's residents and the many other persons in Mei-nung who greeted my inquisitiveness with good humor and hospitality. Mr. G. C. Lin was kind enough to interrupt his activities in Taipei and escort me to his native Mei-nung, where he provided introductions, guidance, and lodging while I was searching for a fieldwork site. In Yen-liao I was fortunate to be assisted and enlightened by Mr. R. Chung and Mr. H. J. Lin; they made the field study far more rewarding and enjoyable than it otherwise would have been. In the United States I wish to thank Mr. Abraham Shen for his help at many stages of data organization and analysis. And I thank Professor Morton H. Fried, teacher, colleague, and friend, for help and encouragement before and during the fieldwork, and for his critical reading of several versions of the manuscript. Finally, I must thank Professors Ernest Bueding, Elliot Skinner, and Marietta Voge for having helped me find a title for this book.

I use the Wade-Giles system for the romanization of words given in their Mandarin pronunciation, that of Rey (as found in Man, et al. 1958) for words in their Hakka form, but I omit the tonal marks used by both systems. Hakka words are italicized and set off by quotation marks; unless otherwise indicated, words italicized but lacking quotation marks are Mandarin. To facilitate comparison with other studies of Chinese society I generally use the Mandarin pronunciation for words common to both languages, the names of persons, and for terms mainly occurring in written form; Hakka words not used in spoken Mandarin are romanized according to their true pronunciation. The names of Chinese provinces and better-known cities are given in their usual post-office spellings. I have had to change the personal names and surnames of all Yen-liao residents, and Yen-liao itself is a fictitious place-name; but I give the true names of all other places in and out of Mei-nung.

The field study in Yen-liao extended from February 1964, to June 1965, and unless otherwise noted all events that I describe occurred during this period. Through correspondence and brief revisits to Yen-liao in June 1966 and June 1967, I was able to obtain additional information. I was back in Mei-nung for another round of fieldwork between August 1971 and July 1972; I was interested then in another set of problems, and while I visited Yen-liao frequently I lived in Mei-nung Town. Except for a few minor bits of information, I have not included in this book any of the materials most recently brought back from Mei-nung.

The New Taiwan Dollar (NT$) is the unit of currency in Taiwan. The official rate of exchange was NT$40 for US$1 during my Yen-liao field work; the New Taiwan Dollar's value in the free market fluctuated, but usually varied from the official rate only within a narrow range.

The Chinese word for "family" in its Mandarin pronunciation is *chia*. This term frequently appears in the text, but the reader will also encounter another word with the same spelling in Mandarin transliteration, the *chia*, which is Taiwan's traditional unit of land measurement (equal to 2.40 acres or .97 hectares); the Chinese ideographs are of course different (see character list).

M<small>YRON</small> L. C<small>OHEN</small>

October 1975

House United, House Divided

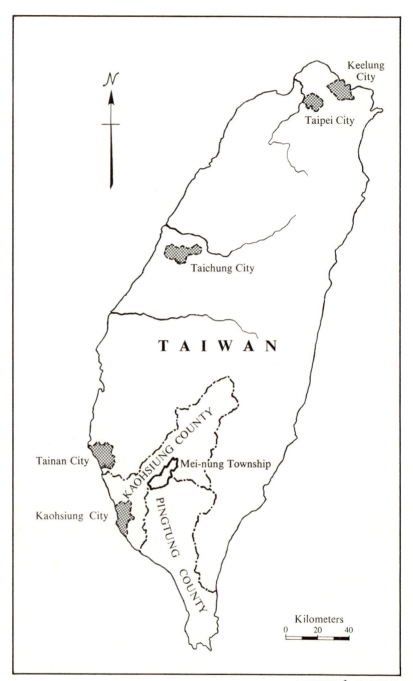

FIGURE 1 TAIWAN

CHAPTER 1

Introduction

YEN-LIAO is one of the many small villages in the predominantly agrarian southwestern Taiwanese township (*chen*) of Mei-nung, where there are also several larger villages, one town, and numerous scattered compounds or isolated homesteads. An administrative subdivision of Kaohsiung County (*hsien*), Mei-nung borders Ch'i-shan Township to the west, and the rural districts (*hsiang*) of Shan-lin and Liu-kuei to the north and east respectively; to the south, the Lao-nung River separates Mei-nung from Li-kang Rural District in Pingtung County. With a total area of about 120 square kilometers, the township forms the northeast extension of the Pingtung Plain; flatlands, suitable for wet rice cultivation, extend from Pingtung County and form a wedge bounded by mountain ranges lying on northeast–southwest and north–south axes. The administrative boundaries of the Township extend somewhat into the mountainous regions, and there are hilly districts in the northern part of the plain.

Hakka-speaking Chinese are the vast majority of Mei-nung Township's population, while in adjacent areas most people speak Hokkien; both Hakka and Hokkien, though mutually unintelligible, are Chinese languages. According to the 1956 census of Taiwan, Mei-nung Township's population of 42,736

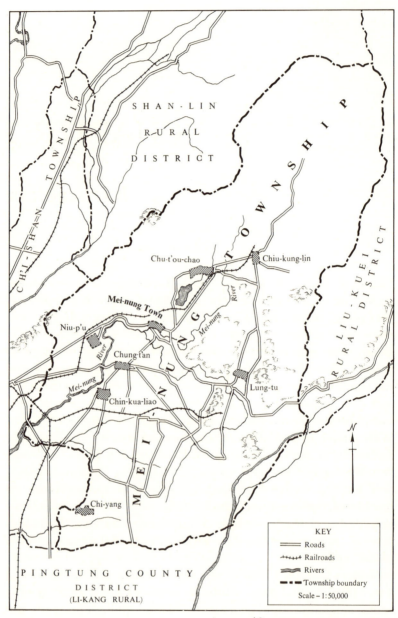

FIGURE 2 MEI-NUNG TOWNSHIP

included 41,496 Taiwan-born Hakka, or 97 percent of the total.[1] By the end of October 1964, Mei-nung's population stood at 52,222, according to official household registration compilations.

HISTORICAL BACKGROUND

When the Japanese occupied Taiwan in 1895, following the Sino-Japanese War, they assumed control of a people living according to traditions brought from mainland China (the "aborigines" by now were a small minority of the population). In many respects these traditions remained important throughout the Japanese period, although the Japanese introduced many elements of modern technology and education. Since Japan's surrender in 1945 Taiwan has been ruled by the Chinese Nationalist Government, for which the island was a refuge when the Communists took control of mainland China in 1949–50. Under the Nationalists, Taiwan's modernization and industrialization has accelerated, but society, especially in the rural areas, remains organized largely along traditional lines.

Mei-nung, first settled by the Hakka in 1736, figures late in the history of Chinese migration to Taiwan. Beginning a process that eventually eliminated the aboriginal population from all but the most inaccessible and mountainous areas of the island, small numbers of Chinese began to arrive as early as the twelfth century from the coastal regions of the nearest mainland provinces, especially Fukien. Persons speaking various dialects of "Southern Fukienese" (*Min-nan* or *Hokkien*) have always constituted the majority of Taiwan's Chinese population. Speakers of Hakka (*K'e-chia*) became an important minority only after immigrants from Kwangtung Province's northern counties (especially Mei Hsien and Chiao-ling Hsien) began coming to Taiwan in the seventeenth century.

In spite of Chinese immigration, the Chinese government,

1. Derived from Chen and Fried (1968:768), whose figures represent a 25 percent sample I have multiplied by four. The 1956 census does not include in the enumeration of Taiwan's population approximately 600,000 military personnel.

unlike those of several European countries, had little interest in Taiwan before the seventeenth century. There was first a short-lived Portuguese presence in 1590, which did little more than introduce the island to the western world as "Formosa." The establishment in 1624 of a Dutch colony in southwest Taiwan was followed by a Spanish landing at the northern end of the island two years later. While the two European powers struggled for control, Chinese immigration to Taiwan increased; it assumed even larger proportions during the two decades (1642–61) of Dutch rule, after the Spanish were expelled. Taiwan's attractiveness as a refuge was enhanced in 1644, when the Manchus invaded China and replaced the Ming dynasty; the warfare was especially severe and prolonged in the southern part of the country, where coastal regions also suffered pirate raids. In 1662 the Ming loyalist and military leader Cheng Ch'eng-kung (Koxinga) arrived in Taiwan with many supporters; helped by the earlier immigrants, Cheng's forces defeated the Dutch and established a government that remained independent until Cheng's grandson peacefully surrendered to the Manchu or Ch'ing dynasty in 1683, when Taiwan was incorporated into the Chinese Empire for the first time.[2]

During more than two centuries of Ch'ing rule, the steady arrival of new immigrants was augmented by the natural growth of Taiwan's Chinese population. The Ch'ing period was characterized by frequent violence between different local groups or against the government. Nevertheless, during this time the island's nonmountainous districts were transformed to support an extension of Chinese society. Commercial centers developed on a base of intensive agriculture, and there was likewise an expansion of the administrative system through the marking out of new county and subcounty districts.[3]

In southwestern Taiwan, Hokkien people very early occupied the fertile plains nearest the coast; large-scale Hakka immigra-

2. For a survey of early Taiwan history see Hsieh (1964).

3. See Ch'en (1964) for a general treatment of the demographic and sociopolitical expansion of the Chinese presence on Taiwan during Ch'ing.

tion did not occur until 1688, shortly after the Ch'ing gained control of the island (Chung 1970). The Hakka immigrants settled at various points on the right bank of the Hsia-tan-shui (now the Kao-p'ing River); to the west they faced and often fought with Hokkien settlers, and to the east they confronted frequently hostile aboriginal groups living in the foothills and mountains of Taiwan's central north–south range. For about fifty years the Hakka gradually expanded northward, as new flatlands between the river and the mountains were brought under cultivation (Chung: 1970), and the settlement of the Mei-nung region in 1736 marked the northernmost limit of the Hakka advance.

In Ch'ing times Mei-nung was under the jurisdiction of a magistrate in charge of Fengshan County (which included the area now divided between Kaohsiung and Pingtung Counties). The magistrate could do little to prevent the frequent violent encounters between the Hakka and their Hokkien neighbors; there were occasions when men from throughout Mei-nung were mobilized for combat, and some of the larger battles with the Hokkien were fought by men mustered from throughout the region of Hakka settlement in southern Taiwan. Involving most importantly struggles over land, water for irrigation, and access to marketing facilities, the Hakka–Hokkien conflicts had erupted on a large scale by the second decade of Hakka migration from the mainland; the response of the Hakka settlements to the continuing hostility was the establishment of a military organization known as the Six Units (*Liu-tui*), which remained active throughout the Ch'ing period (for further details on the Six Units see Chung 1970; Pasternak 1972:142ff.).

The Mei-nung villages, in the Right Unit, made up the organization's northernmost extension; while to the south, in present-day Pingtung County, were the five units designated Vanguard, Front, Middle, Rear, and Left. Hokkien settlements separated the Mei-nung Right Unit, at certain points only very narrowly, from the other Hakka settlements to the south; but the other five units constituted an almost solid block of Hakka territory, with only a few small Hokkien enclaves. In addition to its military functions, the Six Units provided the south Taiwan Hakka a framework for community organization. The Mei-nung villages were deeply involved in Six Unit activities; but the Mei-nung Right Unit, surrounded by Hokkien villages, was probably more self-contained in terms of the daily run of social life than any of the individual units to the south. For example, it is doubtful if in any of the five southern units endogamy was as pronounced as we shall see it to have been in Mei-nung. Because of Mei-nung's relative isolation from the Hakka living to the south, the two areas have come to be distinguished in popular speech as the "upper villages" and "lower villages" ("*chong tsong*" and "*ha tsong*").

After the onset of Japanese colonial administration in 1895, peace was imposed and government offices were set up in Mei-nung, and both have been maintained throughout the period of Chinese Nationalist rule. Although there has been no armed conflict in the area for many decades, it seems likely that the situation before 1895 must have helped to provide the strong sense of solidarity still displayed by Mei-nung's people in their dealings with the outside world.

COMMUNITY ORGANIZATION

Community life in Mei-nung to a large extent still follows a pattern traditional to rural China. Chinese local communities were characteristically arranged as a hierarchy of territorial units; the lowest-level community unit was a small hamlet or a neighborhood of a larger village or town; the village, sometimes together with a few neighboring hamlets, was the second level of community organization; several village units—and frequently the market town serving the villages (see Skinner 1964–65)—together formed the largest "face-to-face" community for the peasants. Several multivillage peasant communities might likewise be linked to form an even larger local unit, whose social and economic life centered upon a larger town, but at this "scale of local organization" unity was expressed mainly through the activities of the regional elite or "gentry." [4]

Before the Japanese occupation, each unit of the Six Unit organization constituted a multivillage community, while the highest level of community organization for the south Taiwan Hakka was the Six Unit organization as a whole. Nei-p'u, a town in present-day Pingtung County, was the site of the Six Units' military headquarters, and it was more generally a center for the south Taiwan Hakka elite; they managed and frequented Nei-p'u's temples and schools, which were founded and supported by contributions from Hakka settlements throughout south Taiwan. When the Japanese arrived in 1895 they dissolved the Six Units as a military organization, and through their monopolization of government at all levels they undermined the importance of Nei-p'u as a Hakka regional center; at present, an annual athletic competition among the south Taiwan Hakka communities and a fellowship fund for Hakka students are the only vestiges of the old Six Units.

The Mei-nung settlements that made up the Right Unit before 1895, however, remain linked to each other within a common community framework. Because this larger Mei-nung community includes the traditionally aligned settlements it extends beyond the western and eastern boundaries of modern Mei-nung Township, which as an administrative unit was first demarcated by the Japanese. Within the Mei-nung local community there remain intermediate units of community organization; each of these units comprises several villages and hamlets. The village of Yen-liao is at the lowest level of community organization; it is part of the higher-level Lung-tu community, together with several other hamlets and the three neighborhoods of Lung-tu proper; and the Lung-tu area as a whole is one of the nine major divisions of the total Mei-nung community. These nine units took form during the early decades of Hakka settlement; within each unit there has been an increase

4. Kuhn (1970:64) describes in terms of "scales of local organization" aspects of community life in China during Ch'ing (also see Cohen 1970b).

in population and in the number of smaller villages, such as Yen-liao.

The Lung-tu community entirely covers and extends slightly beyond three administrative wards (*li*), which had a total population of 9,435 at the end of October 1964 (according to the official monthly report based upon the household register). The three wards, demarcated by the government as administrative units below the Township level, do not coincide with any subdivisions of the Lung-tu community; in fact, the boundaries of the community and the institutions that are centers of community life were formed before the arrival of the Japanese. Its three major temples, which are the centers for Lung-tu's religious celebrations as well as many of its secular activities, proclaim it a community.

Among the people of Lung-tu there is a face-to-face familiarity not now duplicated at the level of the entire Mei-nung community, with its more than 50,000 people. Such familiarity extended throughout Mei-nung during the Ch'ing period, when the population could never have been much greater than 10,000, and even today persons with higher social standing in Mei-nung's various subdivisions do form a socially intimate group and provide the local leadership of the entire Mei-nung community. As far as the population at large is concerned, the strong tendency for marriage to be endogamous at the level of the larger Mei-nung community means, as we shall see, that in the absence of instant mutual recognition most people in Mei-nung can readily create a social relationship on the basis of more-or-less direct kinship links.

The activities of Mei-nung's leadership are concentrated in Mei-nung Town which, while central to the life of the community as a whole, is also one of its subdivisions. Like the other subdivisions, Mei-nung Town annually worships its own tutelary earth god (*"pac-koung"*) and holds feasts for members of the Town community. However, in Mei-nung Town there is also a separate shrine for the earth god of all of Mei-nung. This earth god is worshipped when the Town sponsors the annual "Second Month Festival"; there is traditional opera, and most

Town families hold open house for relatives and friends who come in large numbers from the other subdivisions. Thus the "Second Month Festival" mobilizes the larger Mei-nung community while it also dramatizes the centrality within the community of Mei-nung Town.

Other religious festivals involving the Mei-nung community also focus on the Town, which has always been the center of the community's secular life. The Right Unit headquarters was there before 1895, as were the meeting places of other organizations concerned with the community as a whole. Located in the modern Town are all government agencies operating within the Township, including most importantly the Township government office and Mei-nung police headquarters; also in the Town are the main or only offices of marketing and credit organizations such as the Farmer's Association, as well as most of the Mei-nung area's merchandise and service outlets.

In traditional China community stability was maintained by the combined force of custom and contract, and in Mei-nung modern developments have not yet provided or imposed alternatives to the traditional pattern. A person has a series of statuses as a member of the Mei-nung community and its subdivisions, the most important of which is "person from Mei-nung" (*"Mi-nung-ngin"*). "Person from Mei-nung" implies a dependency upon Mei-nung society expressed through adherence to customary usages such as those regarding marriage, residence, family organization, property and inheritance rights, and many other aspects of life. This acceptance of controlling customs confirms the other aspect of the status, which is reliability as party to a contract. "Person from Mei-nung" is not the only status involved in contracts, but within the Mei-nung community it is one of the most important. Linked to the various kinship statuses, for example, are the customary obligations between kinsmen, such as those for mourning relatives, but kinsmen may contract additional responsibilities.

Arranged through contracts are a large variety of economic activities, many crucial to management of the family farms which are the basic units of agriculture. Dyadic contracts involve such activities as land sale, borrowing and lending, labor hire, labor exchange, and marriage and adoption. For special purposes, larger groups can also be formed through contractual agreements. Very important to the region's economic life are "credit associations," whose members pool funds and by turn take them as a loan, and cooperative farming teams, who work as a group from the farm of one participating family to the farm of another. A form of contract we shall later examine in some detail (chapter 7) is the agreement between brothers or between a father and his sons to partition their family. Contractual agreements are not always written out, but if the stipulations of the contract are complex and the stakes are high, a written document does usually result.

As in the past, the protection of contracts does not depend significantly on government courts or law-enforcement agencies. Within the Mei-nung community ostracism remains the most effective sanction: contract violations can threaten a man's future participation in both the contractual and the community activities vital for individual or family security. Thus, while every level of community life in Mei-nung is organized in many ways by custom, there is also present at every level an equally important and interpenetrating network of contractual relationships (for a general discussion of contract in Chinese society see Cohen 1969b).

TRADITION AND MODERNIZATION IN TAIWAN

Rural society in Taiwan has remained largely traditional after fifty years of Japanese colonial rule and during the following period of Nationalist administration. Yet industry has come to assume increasing importance and now dominates the island's economy; at the same time, industrial technology has penetrated agriculture, now largely commercialized. It is important to consider, at least briefly, some of the factors behind the survival of traditional society in the countryside in the face of massive technological change, for we must know why the traditional Chinese family can be studied in modern Taiwan. But before turning to the nature of the Japanese and Chinese Nationalist impact, I must first note relevant aspects of the pre-Japanese situation.

Chinese society during Ch'ing was characterized by a "fluid" stratification system, for with very few exceptions social and economic alignments were not based upon hereditary classes or status groups. Hereditary discriminations were imposed upon the so-called *chien-min* ("mean people") who held "despised" occupations and could not freely participate in the imperial examinations; there was also a nobility, in part hereditary, which included the imperial clan. Both groups accounted for only a minuscule proportion of the population, while the vast majority owed their social and economic status to their achievements and failures, and to the particular economic circumstances of the families and regions into which they were born. This included the peasantry, the commercial and landlord classes, and the elite composed of degree-holders and higher-ranking bureaucrats (see Cohen 1970b, Elvin 1970, Ho 1962). But if there were no hereditary status barriers keeping a person down, neither were there any that might prevent him from sinking further; a family's ability to manage its affairs well was therefore its only real insurance against disaster.

There were several important institutional supports for this fluid social structure. Land and other property, overwhelmingly in the public domain, was bought, sold, and tenanted in the absence of "feudal" liens. Power and prestige, both local and national, were based upon wealth (especially if expressed in large holdings of land) and upon examination performance for scholarly degrees and positions in the government. The wealthy could sometimes directly purchase academic degrees and bureaucratic posts; this was especially true when the government was strapped for funds during the initial and final phases of the Ch'ing dynasty (Chang 1955). Upward social and economic movement was associated with closer adherence to an elite style of life (known as *li*, "ceremony," "propriety") similarly constituted throughout China. With upward mobility, the area of one's influence and interests, and the range of one's contacts, would shift to ever larger territorial units, and the highest-ranking degree-holders and officials can be said to have been members of an interacting group of persons drawn from throughout the nation (Cohen 1970b, Skinner 1964–65, Part 1).

Elements of Chinese social structure were expressed in the organization of agriculture. The crucial unit was the family; land, owned or tenanted, was cultivated as a family farm enterprise under family management. But this did not mean that the family was a completely self-contained unit of production. In the first place, such a situation was discouraged by the very nature of farming. For example, a characteristic feature of Chinese agriculture is an alternation between busy and slack periods; to maintain a full-time labor force would have caused a nonproductive drain on household resources during slack months (see Buck 1937:289–319). There were also fluctuations linked to variations in cropping cycles and factors such as field location, changing weather conditions, irrigation possibilities, and the like, while the relationship between family and farm was also conditioned by frequent changes in the amount of land under a family's control and in the size of the family labor force.

Nevertheless, it was through family management that the rural labor force was organized to undertake the varied tasks of cultivation. Family labor could be directly assigned to the farm, and the recruitment of outside labor could be accomplished through hire or through cooperative agreements with other families; the family was also the locus of decisions regarding matters of crop selection, disposal, and the like. If there was a labor surplus, the family might try to obtain outside work for some family members, or develop additional family enterprises. Just as the family was not the sole source of labor for the farm, neither was the farm necessarily the sole focus of family labor.

In traditional China, including Taiwan, the immediate context within which the fortunes of individual families advanced or declined was provided by their local communities, as was much of the regulation of social life. The rights and obligations of family members only rarely were directly enforced by the state bureaucracy, but generally were upheld by the sanctions diffused through the fabric of social and economic relationships, and by local persons who could be called upon to mediate disputes or apply punishment if necessary. The local community also afforded protection of the property rights of family units and of the contractual agreements that frequently linked families together for varying purposes and lengths of time.

In Taiwan, like the mainland, the role of the peasant family in the organization of farming meant that in many respects agriculture was self-regulating from the point of view of the Ch'ing bureaucracy. Initiatives on a much larger scale were required for major irrigation projects or land reclamation. While such activities might be undertaken by local groups or by the government itself, they had the effect only of modifying the infrastructure of agriculture, which largely took care of itself in terms of work in the fields. The government presence also taxed a portion of the island's agricultural output, and served as the final recourse (sometimes not very successfully) for protection of the contracts and property rights through which rent was also extracted from many family farms.

When the Japanese arrived in Taiwan in 1895 the stage was set for a process of mutual adaptation between conqueror and conquered that was to characterize the entire period of their rule. Although many aspects of life in Taiwan changed in response to the industrial technology introduced by the Japanese, the island itself was not significantly industrialized. Indeed, Japanese colonial policy did not contemplate the emergence of Taiwan as an industrial region:

> While the Japanese were leading their own economy toward self-sufficiency in manufactured commodities, economic change in Taiwan was being contrived with a still surer hand to move in an opposite direction toward complementarity with Japan. The output of the island was gradually shaped so as to furnish a net contribution of agricultural and semi-processed food and related commodities every year to Japan. (Barclay 1954:42)

Island-wide peace and security was the only radical social and political innovation the Japanese introduced; but the aim of the new rulers was to control rural society rather than remake it, for the Japanese had discovered that the social status quo, with due modifications, was in their favor:

> as [rural society] stood it gave [the Japanese] best access to regulation of the agricultural population and farming practices. It was in some respects a ready-made instrument for exerting the necessary control with the least disturbance of customary affairs. (Barclay 1954:52)

In fact traditional society gave the Japanese "best access to regulation" precisely because their goal was the increased commercialization of an agriculture organized in terms of family-managed farm enterprises; although some large plantation-like farms were established by Japanese corporations, the plantation system as such was not imposed upon the peasant population, and the "agricultural involution" that crippled Java did not develop (see Geertz 1963).

I have noted that the operation of family farms was in a context where a family's economic destiny was under its members' own management, with few if any hereditary strings attached. Although something resembling a caste barrier was introduced with the arrival of the Japanese, it did not change the social makeup of the Taiwanese although it did cut them off from many of the new opportunities opening up. But their own tradition probably did make it easier for the Taiwanese to adopt many of the innovations introduced by the Japanese, who in turn were made all the more willing to deal with rural society as it was. When the Chinese Nationalists took over they were impressed with the high productivity of Taiwan's agrarian sector. The strategic significance of Taiwan's agriculture became all the more apparent after the Nationalists were cut off from the mainland provinces. Thus, while the Nationalists undertook to industrialize Taiwan, they also continued the Japanese policy of actively encouraging the technological modernization of farming while leaving its management at the field level basically untouched. The Nationalist-sponsored 1949–53 Rent Reduction and Land Reform programs largely eliminated tenancy and the landlord class, but if anything these programs increased the importance of the small-scale family farm.

Agriculture in contemporary Taiwan thus reflects a process whereby technological change has been adapted to the preexisting organization of production. In spite of numerous improvements and innovations, farming is still small-scale and intensive. According to a 1955 survey of farm equipment used in Taiwan, only six out of a total of 160 implements were powered by motors, and only three were relevant to the operation of a family farm: the power sprayer (for insecticides), the centrifugal pump and the power tiller (Ma, et al. 1958:14, 327–33). As far as I have observed, the situation in 1965 (or in 1972) did not differ appreciably from that reported in the survey.

The most radical technological innovation has been the power tiller, yet even this device conforms to the old pattern of farming. It is a source of traction functionally the exact equivalent of the water buffaloes it is rapidly replacing; a plow may be attached to the tiller, or a cart for transport, and another accessory allows the tiller to serve as a pump. An earlier example of adaptation to preexisting organization would be the pedal rice thresher introduced by the Japanese (Ma, et al.:174). The operator places against the machine's cylinder a handful of newly harvested rice stalks; at the same time he presses a foot pedal to rotate the cylinder, which is covered by metal projections that remove the grains. This pedal-driven apparatus has almost completely replaced the older device, a simple arrangement consisting of a wooden tub, a ladderlike wooden frame and cover screens (*ibid.*:173). A man beats a handful of rice stalks against the frame, so that the dislodged grain falls into the tub below.

The new equipment is more efficient in terms of human energy requirements and the proportion of grain beaten from the stalks. However the new device fits into the harvest operation in exactly the same way as did the one it replaced; it is brought to the field and operated by the same crew that is harvesting rice with hand-sickles. (By 1972 many pedal rice threshers were motor-driven.)

Although mechanized in some respects, agriculture is still characterized by the intensive application of human energy at all stages of cultivation: plowing, transplant, weeding and harvest are small-scale and labor-intensive. Tractor farming is practical only in limited areas of Taiwan where the large holdings of government-owned corporations (confiscated from private Japanese companies) are used for sugar or pineapple mono-crop cultivation. Some of the agricultural innovations have actually led to a heightening of its labor-intensive quality. Encouraged by irrigation improvements and the introduction of new strains, the spread of multiple-cropping and intercropping has created greater labor demands, as has the introduction of new procedures such as insecticide spraying. Yields and sales have increased, but the new equipment and techniques are added costs, so that agriculture is far more commercialized than during traditional times (see Shen 1964).

When the Japanese assumed control of Taiwan, they took over the administrative system and greatly increased its efficiency. The marketing system of course underwent significant changes under the impact of improved communications and general economic development. However, the Japanese left the local communities essentially intact; they continued to provide a framework for an agriculture based upon small-scale family-managed farms; and under the Chinese Nationalists local communities have continued to flourish. These local communities have mediated the effects of technological innovation, economic development, school system expansion, land reform, and other such new "inputs," so that many of the social responses evoked by the innovations have been traditional. This is the general situation to be kept in mind when reading the chapters that follow; it will become apparent, I hope, that in Taiwan it is possible to gain additional perspectives on modernization precisely because the island still can teach us so much about traditional Chinese society.

CHAPTER 2

The Village

YEN-LIAO, with a resident population of 705 (May 31, 1965), is in the larger Lung-tu subdivision of the Mei-nung community. There is an intimacy borne of daily interaction in Yen-liao, which is set apart from its neighbors by various forms of cooperation restricted to Yen-liao families and through common religious activities usually focusing on Yen-liao's own earth god, the shrine guards the northern end of village road. From north to south the road first descends from a slight elevation, forks into two branches, and then comes together again. Buildings are along both sides of the road, starting from a point above the slope; the structures follow the fork of the road, with wet rice fields separating the two lines of settlement. Beyond a cluster of buildings where the two branches of the road merge are fields separating Yen-liao from the next village. Also in Yen-liao are several residences between the road and a hill to the west.

RESIDENCE

Most of Yen-liao's inhabitants trace their descent from persons who settled in the village during the nineteenth century. Linked to subsequent population growth has been the development of groups of agnatic (patrilineal) kinsmen. It is convenient

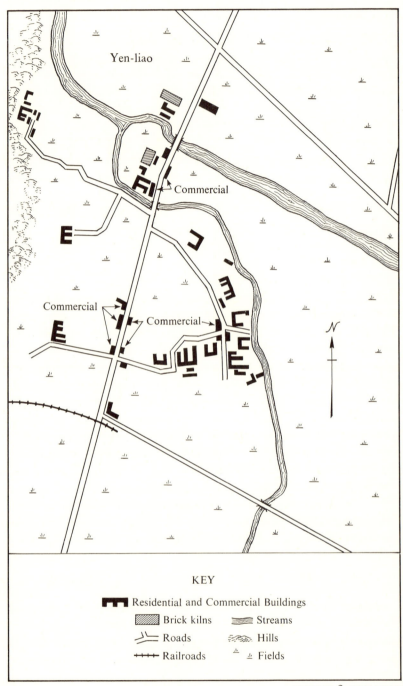

Yen-liao

Commercial

Commercial

Commercial

N

KEY

▮ Residential and Commercial Buildings

▨ Brick kilns   ≈ Streams

⋀ Roads   ⁂ Hills

+++ Railroads   ⊥ Fields

FIGURE 3 YEN-LIAO

to introduce these groups here, to discuss residence and population; later we shall see the importance of the agnatic groups in Yen-liao's social organization. Included in the agnatic groups are the male descendants (true or adopted) of earlier settlers, women who have married in, and daughters who have yet to marry out; there are also three men who married into the village uxorilocally (the husband enters his wife's natal family).

In Table 1 I set out the generations of settlement and present family composition of Yen-liao's agnatic groups, of which the Huang A and the Yeh A were the first established in the village; the founders moved in during the late eighteenth or early nineteenth century from their natal homes in nearby Lung-tu. The earliest dates in the household register [1] are for third and fourth generation Huang A and Yeh A born in Yen-liao during the late 1860s and early 1870s. Seven other agnatic groups have been

1. All demographic data specifically concerning Yen-liao are adapted, with my own corrections, from the household register maintained in the Mei-nung Township office. With reference to Yen-liao in particular, I am not able to use statistical compilations prepared by government offices on the basis of administrative divisions, since none of these demarcate the distribution of Yen-liao's population. The household register is an invaluable resource for the anthropological fieldworker in Taiwan; its format has not changed significantly since compulsory registration was initiated by the Japanese in 1905–6. Consistently employed has been a means of classification whereby every person in Taiwan (unless he or she is in violation of the law) is listed as residing at a specific address and as belonging to a specific household with a designated household head. The registry provides what amounts to an encapsulated life history of everyone covered, including among other items date of birth, sex, parents, adoptive parents (if any), changes in residence, spouse(s), and date of death. The register can be used not only as a source of data for the description of entire populations, but also to trace out specific ties between different individuals or families, and for the reconstruction of the membership of any family at any time during the period covered by the registration system. I have found the register most reliable with respect to data concerning adoption, marriage, birth, and mortality. Although the register may not be completely accurate about infant mortality (see Barclay 1954:22–28), major trends are certainly revealed in this respect also. The register is least reliable about residence. While address and household are legal units for purposes of registration and administration, they do not necessarily reflect actual "on the ground" circumstances of residence and family organization. But such matters may be easily corrected with fieldwork. (See A. Wolf: 1975 for additional details of Taiwan household register format and for another example of the anthropological use to which the register may be put.)

resident in Yen-liao for four or five generations; the founders of four groups, like the earlier arrivals, moved to Yen-liao from Lung-tu; two moved from other parts of the Mei-nung region, while one was born in a Hakka district of Pingtung County. The nine agnatic groups in Yen-liao for four or more generations represent continuity of settlement from Ch'ing times to the present; data concerning these groups can be used to document historical trends in population growth and in aspects of kinship.

Table 1
Yen-liao Agnatic Groups:
Generational Depth and Family Composition,
May 1965

Agnatic Group	Generational Depth (from first to youngest)	Number of Families
Huang A	8	15
Yeh A	7	10
Yeh B	5	8
Kuo	5	5
Lin A	5	6
Fu	5	6
Yeh C	5	2
Yeh D	5	7
Huang B	4 [a]	1
Huang C	2 [a]	1
Yeh E	2 [a]	1
Liu A	2 [a]	1
Liu B	3 [a]	1
Lin B	2 [a]	1
Yeh F	3 [a]	1
Chung	3 [a]	1
Wu	3 [a]	1
		Total: 68

[a] Surviving family members found in all generations.

I call them the "major agnatic groups" and for certain purposes I deal with them separately from the rest of Yen-liao's population. Excluded from the major agnatic groups are eight families, which arrived in Yen-liao only after World War II. While all major agnatic groups except Huang B comprise two

or more families, none of the immigrants belong to a multifamily group. The recent influx is largely linked to the development of the many small-scale commercial and manufacturing
enterprises now in the village.

Most members of Yen-liao's local agnatic groups reside in U-
shaped compounds (see Figure 4), as do similar groups elsewhere in Mei-nung and much of rural Taiwan; in the wings and
base of each compound are bedrooms, kitchens, rooms where
the family takes its meals and usually receives guests, and
rooms for storage. The central room at the compound's base
serves as an ancestral hall (*cheng-t'ing*, *"t'ang-ha"*) if it has an
ancestral tablet on a platform at the side of the room facing the
entrance; offerings are placed on a table in front of the tablet
during rituals of ancestor worship. Most of the time, however,
the ancestral hall is used by the compound's residents for
storage and different kinds of work. The central room in some
compounds has no ancestral tablet and is used only for secular
purposes. A compound is commonly the major building on a
plot of land set aside for residential use. Pig and water-buffalo
pens, compost storage rooms, outhouses, and the like are
usually at the edge of the residential site; they are built away
from the compound and next to rice paddies, streams, or roads.
Near the main compound there may be more residences or
storage rooms, but a variety of structures are built close to the
compound if its residential plot is small, or if crowding develops with population increase; the "filling up" of a site reflects a situation where land is only very reluctantly transferred
from agricultural to residential use.

When a new settler in Yen-liao began a compound he would
first form the base of the U by building a central room with one
or two rooms on each side; as his family expanded, new rooms
would be added, providing the compound's wings. Now at
some point the family would divide into smaller units, but there
might be no change in the compound's residential arrangements other than the construction of additional kitchens. Except
for the central room, all rooms in the compound are distributed
among the new families during division, together with other

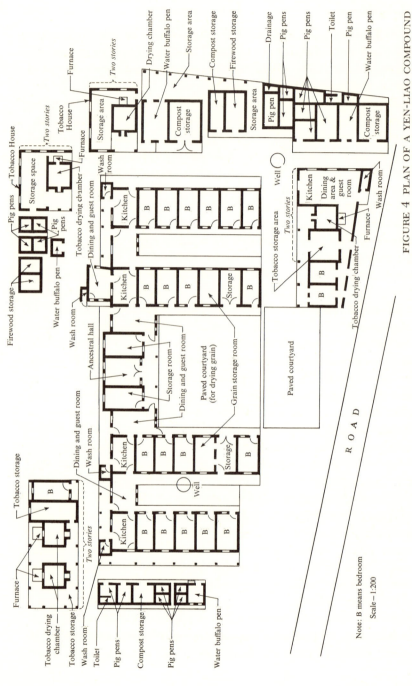

FIGURE 4 PLAN OF A YEN-LIAO COMPOUND
YEH A COMPOUND I

Note: B means bedroom

Scale — 1:200

such family property as land, farming equipment, or shops. Because the central room is not involved, the first family partition creates two or more families owning in common this room if nothing else. Thus in most compounds there eventually is a multifamily agnatic group, which continues to increase in its individual membership and in the number of constituent families. At any given time in Yen-liao there are compounds (and agnatic groups) at different stages of development; only the base of the U is completed in some compounds, others may already have one wing, while some may have the full U shape and even two or more sets of wings.

The arrangement of residences and other facilities in compounds, or on a site shared with a compound, is an adaptation to a situation where plots under cultivation are important economic assets; when a plot is developed for nonagricultural purposes, its removal from cultivation becomes a substantial portion of the development cost. The gradual expansion of compounds is a kind of economizing, for attaching new rooms to ones already built takes up less land than does the preparation of new sites. Economizing is also involved in the layout of the compound's "courtyard," a flat area (now often paved) very important for much farm work, especially the sunning of grain. A compound's courtyard is built at the very outset, together with the rooms forming the compound's base. Expansion from the base by extending wings along the sides of the courtyard is thus a further economy in land use. The courtyard, like the central hall, remains the common possession of the agnatic group as it increases in individual and family membership.

Because the Mei-nung region is one of Taiwan's most important districts for growing tobacco, a crop whose production is under strict government control, the area is notable for its many two-storied "tobacco houses" (a translation of the local Hakka term *"yan-leou"*). Like Yen-liao's other buildings, most of the village's 28 tobacco houses are built into compounds or share residential sites with them, while only six tobacco houses are on isolated plots. A tobacco house can be identified by the air vents protruding like small dormers from its roof. Each tobacco house has rooms for storing tobacco leaves and a drying chamber, the tobacco house's most important piece of equipment; a chamber's capacity is limited, so that a farmer's tobacco-growing permit stipulates both the area of land he may give to the crop, and the number of drying chambers he may have (the official Mandarin term for tobacco house is *yen-yeh kan-tsao-shih*, "tobacco drying chamber"). Farmers permitted several drying chambers usually build them together in one larger structure, and in Yen-liao's 28 tobacco houses there are 38 chambers. Many tobacco houses have been expanded for other purposes; some include a residence with bedrooms, kitchens, and storage space.

Table 2 outlines current residential arrangements in Yen-liao. Of the village's 68 families, 58 live in compounds or in structures adjacent to compounds; Huang A, the oldest and largest agnatic group, has four compounds; Yeh A takes up two, and all groups dating back to the nineteenth century are in compounds with the full U shape. Of the earliest post-World War II immigrant families, the Huang C and Liu A built quarters that later could be developed into U-shaped compounds. Yeh F rents rooms in the Fu compound, but the other families that arrived after 1950 live in buildings not designed to form the base of a U. The recent proliferation of such nontraditional structures is not simply a matter of changing architectural tastes since the end of World War II, for if the Huang C and Liu A families are the only postwar arrivals who built their houses according to the compound pattern, they are also the only ones with no major holdings other than their farms. The other new families (except for Yeh F) set up nonagricultural businesses when they came to Yen-liao, where they live in or near their shops. Three families from the older agnatic groups also live in shops some distance from the residential areas of their original compounds, and three others live in isolated tobacco houses. The new dwellings do not follow compound architecture, although sociologically the inhabitants are fully participating members of their agnatic groups. Such structures are able to compete with agriculture for land; because land is costly, including living quarters in a tobacco house or another enterprise is a relatively

Table 2
Yen-liao, Residential Arrangements, May 1965

1. Residence in Compounds

Agnatic Group	Compounds	Number of Families
Huang A	Compound I	6
	Compound II	5
	Compound III	2
	Compound IV (base and one wing only)	1 [a]
Yeh A	Compound I	7
	Compound II	3
Yeh B	One compound	8
Kuo	One compound	5
Lin A	One compound	5
Fu	One compound	6
Yeh C	One compound	2
Yeh D	One compound	5
Huang B	One compound	1
Huang C	One compound (base only)	1
Liu A	One compound (base and one wing only)	1

2. Other Residences

Agnatic group	Residence	Number of Families
Huang A	"Tobacco house" with living quarters	1
Lin A	Grocery store with living quarters	1
Yeh D	"Tobacco house" with living quarters	1
Yeh D	Ditto	1
Yeh E	Chinese medicine shop with living quarters	1
Liu B	Western-style drug store with living quarters	1
Lin B	Men's barber shop with living quarters	1
Yeh F	Rooms rented in the Fu compound	1
Chung	House with living quarters and business office (of nearby brick factory)	1
Wu	House with living quarters and business office (of nearby brick factory and lumber mill)	1

[a] Some members of this family still reside in Compound I

inexpensive way to provide more residential space. Thus the establishment of nonagricultural enterprises and departures from the compound pattern of residence are related developments even if the families involved should remain in Yen-liao; trends present in 1964–65 did not indicate that compound residence in Yen-liao was weakening, for such arrangements were encouraged by the dominant position of farming in Yen-liao's economy.

Considering its small population, there are a fairly large number of commercial structures in the village; its 18 shops include three grocery stores, two brick kilns, a lumber mill, a carpenter shop, two shops selling Chinese medicine, a western-style drugstore, a bicycle sale and repair shop, three shops selling candy, fruit, and ices, a beauty shop equipped with electric drying machines for permanents, two rice mills, and a men's barber shop. Most of these shops are roadside enterprises and therefore attract transients. Four shops have living quarters, and all but one are built on their own plots, away from compounds.

POPULATION

Population change in Yen-liao reflects sociological and biological factors; from the standpoint of individual families, birth is but one means of recruiting new family members, and family size may be reduced both through deaths and through the transfer of individuals to other family units. In the household registration records, 1906 is the first full year of population description. Unfortunately, 1920 is the first year with complete coverage of Yen-liao's major agnatic groups, for the earlier registration forms are not all available. The older records provide complete coverage, for 1907–19, of households that held 52 people out of a total population of 104 in 1920. The 1907–19 records do provide a few bits of information worth noting here. In the beginning of 1907, 41 persons were listed; from 1907 to 1919, the major factors involved in population change were births, deaths, and virilocal postmarital residence (upon marriage the man stays home, where he is joined by his bride). The 1907–19 records show that infant and child mortality took a heavy toll: all five male deaths were of infants and children under three years of age, equal to one-third of all male births; while infants accounted for three female deaths, equal to one-fourth of all female births.

The major factors of population change for all of Yen-liao during 1920–64 were births, deaths, virilocal residence, and migration (39 persons moved out during the latter portion of the period, and 68 moved in). The importance of male and female adoption declined throughout this period; between 1920 and 1939 there were 16 cases of adoption into Yen-liao families and 12 of adoption out; during 1940–64 adoptions in numbered six and adoptions out five. There was a decrease in the absolute number of adoptions, and the decline in their importance relative to other factors of population change was even more pronounced. Uxorilocal marriage, the reverse of the virilocal pattern, was only a minor factor of population change during 1920–64; of the three cases where men married into Yen-liao, two involved the same woman, who had been divorced by her first husband and then remarried. The lessening importance of adoption and the rarity of uxorilocal marriage was in the context of a drastic reduction in the infant and child mortality, reflecting the modern medical and public health practices introduced by the Japanese. During 1920–24, 40 percent of all males and 28 percent of all females whose births were registered did not survive beyond their second year; by 1960–64, infant mortality was reduced to two percent for males and six percent for females (Table 3 shows the overall trend of population growth in Yen-liao since 1920.)

While virilocal residence is a well-known feature of traditional Chinese society, it is but one expression of a patrilineal emphasis geared to the preservation of male lines of descent. In a traditional Chinese context, male lines of descent are highly individualized, for it is a man's major responsibility to insure to the greatest extent possible that he will have male posterity; should he have several sons it is crucial that at least one marries and has male offspring. One male in each generation is suf-

Table 3
Population Increase, Yen-liao, 1920–1965 [a]

	1920	1920 –24	1925 –29	1930 –34	1935 –39	1940 –44	1945 –49	1950 –54	1955 –59	1960 –64	1965, May 31
By period		34	39	54	71	44	63	108	138	135	11
Cumulative	104	138	177	231	302	346	409	517	655	790	801
Percentage increase		32.7	28.3	30.5	30.7	14.6	18.2	26.4	26.7	20.6	

[a] The figures include nonresident members of Yen-liao families.

ficient for the continuity of a descent line; for a man with many sons it is only of secondary concern, although quite desirable, that each provide him with grandsons. Likewise, if a man has no sons, it is only of secondary importance that he has patrilineal cousins or nephews who provide continuity for the descent lines of his father and paternal grandfather. The individualization of descent lines in the traditional Chinese context was reinforced by important economic considerations. In the final analysis, a man had to look to his own male offspring for security; while they might at first work with their father in the fields, in a family enterprise, or provide wages through outside employment, they would eventually become the only source of sustenance and protection for their parents' old age.

Since every man was the focus of a new descent line, the crucial task was to get and raise a boy to maturity, at which point the responsibility would fall upon his shoulders. Therefore, to highlight changing demographic conditions it is important to consider how families went about recruiting those men who survived to marry. During the more recent decades of this century there have been born to Yen-liao families numerous male infants who have survived, married virilocally, and had sons of their own; in traditional times, however, high infant mortality rates rendered problematic the survival to maturity of males and females alike and meant that certain descent lines might be terminated unless they could be continued through means other than biological reproduction. By combining household registry data with informant interviews I have determined how all spouses in all marriages that occurred in Yen-liao through May 1965 were recruited in the first instance. In order to specifically illustrate the means employed to assure continuity across generations, I discuss only the recruitment of husbands to the nine major agnatic groups; for obvious reasons I do not include the first generation (the founders of each agnatic group). Out of a total of 166 men, 164 married virilocally, and two who remained with their natal families adopted sons without marrying. Of the 166 men, 14 were adopted in the first instance, and three men married in. Thus only about 10.2 percent of the men were initially recruited through means other than birth. A somewhat different picture emerges if marriages before 1940 are compared with those which occurred later. During the pre-1940 period, 73 out of 87 men were recruited through birth and 14, or about 16.1 percent, in other ways. The latter percentage actually is a reflection of the pre-1920 demographic situation if we assume the average age at marriage to be about 20 for men. But between 1940 and 1964, 93 of 96 men married in their natal homes while men born elsewhere accounted for only three marriages, about 3.1 percent of the total.

Eleven of the 14 adopted males who survived through marriage in Yen-liao served to carry on lines of descent that otherwise would have terminated; there were nine instances where a man was survived only by an adopted son, while one man left two adopted sons as his sole posterity. These eleven adoptions were completed before 1926. Of the three men who were not sole survivors, two were adopted (1929 and 1931) in anticipation that they would be. Before the latter two adoptions, demographic patterns that must have been quite disturbing to the two men seeking sons had developed; these men married in 1916 and 1922 respectively, but all their sons born before the adoptions had perished. But then a son was born into the first family in 1931, and one into the second in 1933; and in each family these boys were only the first of many surviving sons. The child-bearing spans of the three women in the two families (one of the men had two wives) extended over much of the period of major demographic transition in Yen-liao. The two adoptions were customary responses to a situation that must have been common in traditional times; but the adoptions occurred when such traditional strategies were being rendered obsolete by the decreasing hazards of infancy.

ADOPTION

There were four procedures for male adoption in the Mei-nung area. Kidnapping was resorted to on occasion, and during Ch'ing two Yen-liao families abducted Hokkien boys. Now this was a risky business; sentiments aside, there were good reasons why a man would not be inclined to kidnap boys within Mei-nung. Since the aggrieved family and the offender would be members of the same community, there would always be the opportunity for the victimized family to bring the matter to the attention of local authorities or to directly seek revenge. Kidnapping was feasible, though dangerous, under the circumstances of more-or-less endemic feuding between the Mei-nung Hakka and their Hokkien neighbors; if kidnapping occurred during large-scale forays into hostile territory, a retaliatory move would likewise have to take the form of a major military action.

A more common form of adoption was straightforward purchase, usually arranged through a middleman. This procedure rarely if ever led to the establishment of social ties between the families providing and receiving the boy; indeed, both parties to the transaction usually had nothing in common except desperation—one for money and the other for a son. The context in which boys were marketed is highlighted by one case described by a friend of mine (from Mei-nung, but not Yen-liao); he relates how his grandfather was purchased from a soldier in the Ch'ing army who needed cash to support his opium-smoking habit. Expressed in kidnapping—obviously—and in purchase were relationships of antagonism and exploitation closely connected with broader patterns of regional hostility or economic stratification.

The other two forms of adoption are quite different, for they imply that the donor and recipient parties are linked through ongoing social relationships and obligations. Agnatic or *kuo-fang* ("*kouo-fong*") adoption has been noted in many areas of mainland China and Taiwan, and is one expression of the obligations between close agnatic kin.[2] The term *fang* simply refers to any genealogical subdivision of a patrilineal group, while *kuo-fang* means "to pass from one *fang* to another." In Yen-liao, the most closely related persons party to agnatic adoptions were brothers, while the most distant kinsmen were men with a common paternal grandfather. Affinal adoption ("*fan-ngoe-ka*") is the other form of male adoption based upon kinship ties. This involves a child's adoption into his mother's premarital home; in practice, the recipients can be the mother's brother and his wife, or the mother's parents; when the latter receive their daughter's son, it is often because they require a male to continue the patrilineal line. As far as a girl's parents are concerned, affinal adoption can be the culmination of a somewhat roundabout way of assuring male posterity; a girl is married out with the understanding that her new family will permit one of her sons to be given in adoption to the girl's parents, who thus obtain a male successor only by skipping a generation. Whether or not affinal adoption results from a marriage agreement, it is similar to agnatic adoption in that both are transacted on the basis of prior kinship links.[3]

The means employed to recruit the 14 men adopted into Yen-liao families can be summarized as follows: two kidnappings, four purchases, four agnatic adoptions, and four affinal adoptions.[4]

2. For Taiwan see Gallin (1966:167) and for mainland China Van der Sprenkel (1962:16). Note, however, that *kuo-fang* in Yen-liao is a form of *adoption*, and is not to be confused with another use of the term, which describes the *inheritance* by close agnates, who may be adults, of an estate which is heirless.

3. There is reference to affinal-type adoption in a monograph dealing with central mainland China (Fei 1939:71); in an area of north China, adoptions based upon affinal links are said to be specifically excluded (M. Yang 1945:84).

4. There have been at least two additional male adoptions; an infant was obtained in 1928 through agnatic adoption and died after one year, and in 1937 a man brought to his family a son from a liaison with an outside woman.

Adoption has been of minimal significance as a means of recruiting females on a permanent basis. I have recorded a total of
24 female adoptions into Yen-liao families (nine before 1920),
and it is likely that few, if any, escaped my attention. One of the
24 girls died, another married uxorilocally, while the others
eventually departed. Why, then, do families adopt girls? There
is, first of all, the common notion that a childless couple finds it
easier to have offspring of their own if a girl is first adopted. Of
the 24 girls 12 were indeed received by childless parents, and
subsequent developments took a variety of forms: six adoptions
were followed by the birth of male and female offspring and
five of those six adopted girls later married out while one died
before marriage; the parents by adoption of three girls did not
have surviving children of their own, a situation that in one case
led to the adoption of a son and the marriage out of the girl, in
another to the uxorilocal marriage of the adopted daughter, and
in the third to the virilocal marriage of the girl, who later supplied her parents with a son through affinal adoption. Three of
the twelve girls are still young children; a 1962 adoption [5] was
followed by the birth of a daughter, while developments since
the two 1964 adoptions remain to be determined.

The other 12 girls were adopted by parents who already had
children of their own; when eight of these 12 girls entered their
new families boys and girls were already present, in three cases
there were only sons, and in one case only a daughter. Of the 12
girls, what might be called guardianship was involved in the
adoption of five; in each case they were taken in by close kinsmen after the death of their father and their mother's remarriage; two of these five girls later were adopted to other families, two married, and one remains to be married out of her
family of adoption. All of the parents involved in guardianship
adoptions had sons and daughters of their own; guardianship
adoptions are not positive acts of recruitment, but rather reflect
kinship responsibilities.

5. This adoption bears special mention; it was of the affinal type, but based
upon links established through uxorilocal marriage. A Yen-liao man obtained
the daughter of his brother, who had married out.

The circumstances behind another four of these 12 adoptions are unclear; the girls were taken into families where children were already present and three of the adopted girls later married out while the fourth was adopted out once more. The possibility arises that "little daughter-in-law" adoption may have been involved in three cases (in the fourth, there was no unmarried son present at the time of adoption), if only because the remaining three of the 12 instances of female adoption we are discussing were definitely of the "little daughter-in-law" type. A "little-daughter-in-law" adoption occurs when a young girl is taken in by parents who raise her together with their son, with the intention that they will eventually marry. But whether there have been three or six such adoptions into Yen-liao families, none has led to permanent marriage. All of the girls later left for other families, except one who married the boy who had been her intended husband but divorced and departed after less than a year. It can be added that, as far as I know, there have been only two cases of the "little daughter-in-law" type of out-adoption. This form of adoption appears to have been only infrequently practiced in the Mei-nung area even during pre-Japanese times, a situation unlike that found in certain Hokkien-speaking areas of north Taiwan, and in parts of mainland China, where it appears to have been quite common (see A. Wolf 1966, 1968).

Guardianship aside, female adoption in Yen-liao has been through purchase or affinal adoption, but only three girls have been acquired through the latter means. The role played by kinship ties is thus of much less importance than male adoption: girls are of less significance in terms of family continuity or their future economic contributions, so that parents offer them for adoption far more readily. The greater importance of adopted sons to the families receiving them has its obverse the special context in which Yen-liao families have allowed a total of only eight sons to be adopted out (four prior to 1920); all the boys were adopted to kinsmen through affinal adoption (three cases) and agnatic adoption (five), and five of the recipient families (including one affine family) were also residents of Yen-liao. All the boys adopted out were the siblings of surviving brothers, who remained with their natal families. While the sons were released in a framework of social relationships and kin obligations, the same hardly applies to daughters. I have records of twenty out-adoptions of daughters by birth throughout Yen-liao's history (six prior to 1920), and my data may very well be incomplete. Nevertheless, the trend is clear: three out-adoptions were to affines, the rest involved purchase.

UXORILOCAL MARRIAGE

Three men have entered Yen-liao families through uxorilocal marriage (in 1916, 1928, and 1955) and one Yen-liao man has married out in this fashion (1950). These arrangements have a role similar to adoption in that the recipient families are provided with males in lieu of sons raised to maturity. Unlike male adoption, uxorilocal marriages have special implications for family life more appropriately discussed later (chapter 5); I note now, however, that a man married uxorilocally is frequently an object of community ridicule, as is the family he has joined. Because of the various undesirable features of this form of marriage, it is entered into only under special circumstances. The three men who married into Yen-liao had been from very poor families, as was the Yen-liao man who married out; two of the men who married into village families had first lived with them as long-term hired workers.

At the time of the uxorilocal marriages, all three families lacked sons, true or adopted, and in one family a son had recently died. The parents in the three families were at an age when any male taken into the household would have to be an able-bodied adult or very nearly so (the fathers ranged in age from 45 to 53). For one family, this predicament was due to the death of their son, but I do not know the circumstances of the other two families. In any event, the matter of male continuity now was linked to certain immediate economic considerations. The fathers in the three families were near or already into the time of life when they should begin to retire from farm work; men usually withdraw from heavier field labor as soon as possible after their fiftieth year, and by the age of 60 hope to be essentially free from farming. Thus, a male successor in the economic sense could be provided by uxorilocal marriage but not by adopting a young boy. On the other hand, the son who married out of a Yen-liao family left behind three brothers.

In contemporary Yen-liao, the only marked departure from the traditional pattern of family life has been the diminishing quantitative importance of secondary means of assuring male posterity, obviously because the introduction of modern medical and public health practices has resulted in a drastic decline in infant and child mortality. Traditionally, the family's organization as a unit of reproduction was reinforced by the major demands of a patrilineally oriented agrarian society: bear sons and find them wives. A desire to continue unbroken the male line of descent was encouraged in many ways; the linking of ancestor veneration or worship with the notion of filial piety provided strong ideological support, and on a more mundane level, the importance of sons (and daughters-in-law) was quite real. While traditional responses to the demographic imponderables have not been forgotten, they now need to be invoked only infrequently. The tradition of virilocal marriage persists, and it is clear that the birth of sons is still preferred.

KINSHIP ORGANIZATION

Yen-liao is fitted into Mei-nung society not only as a unit within a hierarchy of local communities, but also within a kinship framework. Kinship ties are created in the first instance through descent (by birth or adoption) and marriage; agnates, who have the same surname, assert their kinship by focusing on a near or distant common ancestor and through strict observance of surname exogamy. The two families party to a marriage become relatives, of course, but they also bring into the new relationship their earlier kinsmen. I shall first discuss agnatic relationships, then the ties created through marriage, and finally show how both dimensions of kinship provide in combination a total kinship framework for Mei-nung society.

Each of Yen-liao's local agnatic groups is a tightly knit community of kinsmen whose unity is manifested in a variety of ways, some of which we shall examine. But first I shall consider the process by which new groups are formed. A compound containing an agnatic group cannot be extended indefinitely. Eventually persons move out and set up their residences elsewhere, sometimes before family partition; some family members remain in the original compound and others occupy the new rooms. The new quarters may share the same residential site with the old compound, or else a new site may be established. After family partition some of the new families may find themselves with no rooms in the old compound, yet they share with their agnates the original ancestral hall.

Another compound can be built by including a central room in the new structure. But the new central room does not necessarily lead to the immediate establishment of an independent center for ancestor worship. This is illustrated by the Huang A, who now are distributed across three compounds with the full U-shape; and one Huang A family has built the base and left wing of a fourth compound (see Table 2). While there is a central room in each of the four Huang A compounds, only one serves as an ancestral hall. The date of the construction of the first ancestral hall of Compound I is unknown. It was rebuilt in 1900 and again in 1928. Construction of the central rooms of Compounds II, III, and IV began in 1928, 1946, and 1947 respectively.

Figuring back from 1965, there have been periods of 38, 20, or 19 years during which the various Huang A compounds have made no effort to establish separate sites for ancestor worship. But the architecture of each compound gives its resident agnates the option of declaring ritual independence, insofar as a hall for ancestral worship is concerned. This happened among the Yeh A, one of whose members in Yen-liao moved out of the original compound in the late 1800s and built another on a new site in the same village. Between the old and new Yeh A compounds (I and II; see Table 2) are fields, a road, and a compound belonging to another agnatic group. About thirty years after Yeh A Compound II was built, ancestral tablets were finally placed in what local residents would now agree was a full-fledged ancestral hall.

When a fully equipped ancestral hall is set up in a compound, the new tablets provide a genealogical charter for the resident families and in addition indicate the ancestral line shared with the "parent" compound. Thus there are different genealogical statements on the respective ancestral tablets in Yeh A Compounds I and II. In Compound I, a large framed document is attached to the wall of the ancestral hall, above the tablet itself. This document lists ancestors from the first to the sixteenth generations, while the tablet begins with the seventeenth. In Compound II, all generations have been listed on one tablet. The seventeenth generation is that of Yeh Tze-lang, the founder of the Yen-liao Yeh A; down through this generation the genealogies found in both ancestral halls are identical. In Figure 5, the differences between the two genealogies are indicated. The tablets in each Yeh A ancestral hall focus on an ancestor shared by all residents of the compound, and ignore collateral lines involving members of the other compound; they in fact describe compound residence in genealogical terms. The two Yeh A compounds show how with the expansion of an agnatic group beyond its original compound there is the possibility of fission, and how the dispersion of agnates among compounds can eventually be reflected in an identical dispersion of ancestral halls.

Elsewhere (Cohen 1969a) I have described in some detail what I would now characterize as levels of agnatic organization among the south Taiwan Hakka. Immediately above the family level are the compound-based local agnatic groups, while at what used to be the highest level there were large lineages, some of which drew their members from Hakka settlements in an area of south Taiwan much larger than Mei-nung. We have seen how during the traditional Ch'ing period this zone of Hakka settlement in south Taiwan was socially cohesive, in the

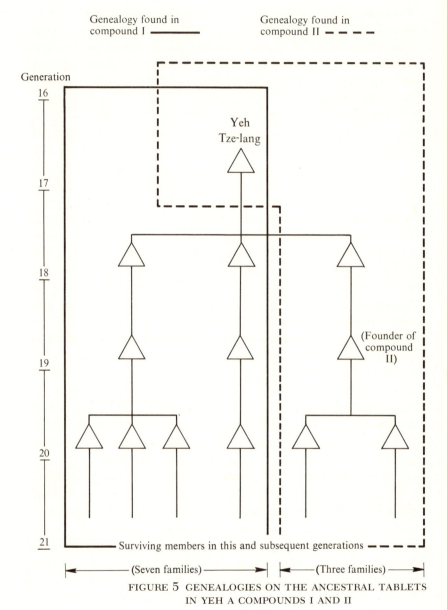

FIGURE 5 GENEALOGIES ON THE ANCESTRAL TABLETS
IN YEH A COMPOUNDS I AND II

framework of the Hakka Six Units military organization, within which the Mei-nung community was the northernmost unit. During the period of Japanese rule the political and military institutions that had united the south Taiwan Hakka were dismantled and the large lineages began to decline. These lineages had been landowning corporate groups whose members purchased shares when a lineage was organized or were the descendants of original shareholders. The membership of a lineage could include representatives of many local agnatic groups; while some of the constituent local groups in a lineage might have fissioned off from each other, others would be unrelated in terms of common descent from a recent Taiwanese ancestor. Thus the larger lineages often would take as their ritual focus an ancestor sufficiently remote in time to provide for the incorporation in one organization of an assemblage of local agnatic groups having in common little more than surname (for further details on lineage organization in Taiwan see Ahern 1973; Pasternak 1972; for mainland lineages see Baker 1968; Freedman 1958, 1966; Potter 1968).

There was no direct relationship between the formation of large lineages and the fission process which created new local agnatic groups. This fission process was behind the tendency for the size of local agnatic groups to be kept within limits. For its members, the local agnatic group defines an intimate sphere of kinship behavior, where families are closely linked by mutual obligations and frequently come to each other's assistance. An agnatic group centering upon a compound is a small and tightly knit community within a larger local settlement; such a community cannot expand indefinitely, and the balance between size and intimacy is often maintained or restored by the fissioning of compounds.

A compound-based agnatic group acts as a unit in many ceremonial contexts, such as weddings and funerals; when a member family is host for such occasions all other families in the agnatic group render assistance without being asked. The agnatic unit that can mobilize as a group is also a "social field" for member families; although economically independent, they are expected to grant each other "first rights of refusal" with respect to such matters as labor exchange transactions or employment. Again, agnates in the compound—especially those senior to the parties involved—are frequently called in to mediate family squabbles, and they are almost always asked to serve as members of the council assembled to oversee family partition, a service most men find quite disagreeable but are obliged to perform.

The notion of "social field" provides a bridge to the realm of kinship where ties between families are formed in the first instance through marriage and not by descent. Now in this context terms such as "matrilateral" and "affinal" tend to be frequently used, and in fact they are the key words in Bernard Gallin's paper (1960) dealing with nonagnatic forms of kinship in another area of Taiwan. It is true that affines do stand in a special position under certain circumstances. They tend to support their sisters' or daughters' husbands against their brothers when their families begin to prepare for partition; and after family division, there is usually a considerable weakening of the links between a woman's natal family and the new units formed by her husband's brothers, while the ties between her own new and smaller family and her natal home become more intimate. The importance of affines is thus linked to specific family developments, and the same is true of matrilateral ties. There is no abrupt change in the intensity of kin ties when upon the death of the senior generation in his wife's natal family a man may have as his affines his wife's several brothers, each of whom heads his own family. In the following generation, however, after the death of the man and his wife, kinship ties will be much weaker; the families now headed by each of his sons are in fact linked only by matrilateral ties to the families headed by the sons of their mother's brother, for the latter is also probably deceased.

In general, it appears that kinship behavior among families related through marriage does not retain its original intensity beyond the lifetimes of the married couple who initially provided the links. Thus new marriages not only create new kinsmen, they also maintain an active kinship circle as old relationships become less important. Yet the old relationships continue to be significant under certain circumstances, and in reference to all the kinship relationships created through marriage I use the term "cognatic." More remote kinship ties are commonly exploited to establish relationships in an otherwise unfamiliar situation, so that most people in Mei-nung carry in their heads fairly complicated genealogical charts; cognatic kinsmen in fact provide for a person a "social field" complementing the one his local agnatic group constitutes.

The pattern of marriage in Mei-nung reflects the continuing importance of kin ties that may have been established many years in the past. Surname exogamy conforms to the general Chinese practice, but there are cases (one in Yen-liao) where a man who bears the surname of his uxorilocally married father marries a woman with the same surname as his mother. Marriage is generally endogamous at the level of the Mei-nung community as a whole, but within the community individual families tend to develop a wide scattering of cognatic ties. By analyzing the household register and interviewing informants I have been able to determine the origin of all but seven spouses of Yen-liao residents since the village was first settled. Among Yen-liao's nine major agnatic groups, the characteristics of marriage have remained remarkably stable: the overwhelming majority of the 356 marriages have been with families resident within present-day Mei-nung Township; such marriages, including spouses marrying out, marrying in, and marrying within the village, account for about 88 percent of all 356 matches— about 94 percent if we include marriages with families in the Hakka settlements located outside the township boundaries but within the Mei-nung community. The aggregated data do not conceal great changes over time, for known marriages with families outside of the Mei-nung community have never exceeded ten percent of the total during any five-year period through May 1965.

People in Yen-liao voice their opposition to marriages between Hakka and non-Hakka; and they take the infrequent occurrence of such marriages as evidence that their sentiments determine marriage patterns. That marriages with Hakka not from the Mei-nung community are about as uncommon as those with non-Hakka indicates, however, that marriage patterns are not based exclusively on ethnic factors. Marriage links are for the most part confined within Mei-nung because local cognatic ties are most important to families committed to farming or other activities that fix them within the Mei-nung region and make them dependent on local social relationships.

From the standpoint of Yen-liao's residents, the village itself forms the innermost of three concentric spheres from which spouses are selected; beyond Yen-liao there is the wider Lung-tu area and finally the remainder of Mei-nung. Most matches have been within Lung-tu; but except during 1910–14 and 1915–19 the movement of spouses between Yen-liao and more distant sections of Mei-nung has never accounted for much less than a third of all marriages in any five-year period. Cognatic ties are especially important within the Lung-tu area, which for Yen-liao's inhabitants is a level of community intermediate between their own village and Mei-nung society as a whole; kinsmen are close by, and there are more contexts within which they come together. The location of kinsmen is not completely the expression of an emphasis on propinquity, however, for there is also a strong tendency precisely to achieve a degree of scatter in the distribution of cognatic relatives. Over time, then, the residents of Yen-liao have come to have kinsmen situated throughout the area covered by Mei-nung society as a whole, but kinsmen form an increasingly larger component of the general population the closer one comes to the village.

A desire to give considerable geographic spread to cognatic ties is one of the important considerations in what might be called a family's kinship strategy. We can get an idea of the results of this kind of planning by considering the distribution of cognatic ties formed as each member of a sibling set (brothers and sisters) marries. Since most individuals remain in their family of birth or adoption until marriage, married siblings together constitute the focus for the cognatic kinship network developed during their lifetimes by their family elders. This network includes the families from which brothers get their wives and those into which their sisters marry. Figure 6 illustrates the extent to which there is regional distribution of the cognatic ties established through the marriages of different siblings within one set. After eliminating marriages that are not primary,[6] those for which relevant information is not available, those involving less than two siblings, and those with persons outside the Mei-nung community, we have out of all Yen-liao marriages the marriages of 293 persons who are members of 65 sibling sets. Only the members of three sibling sets, none including more than three persons, have been matched with spouses who are all from one region; in all but nine of the 48 sibling sets consisting of five persons or less, scattering is emphasized to the extent that the number of different regions providing spouses is more than one-half the number of siblings in a set, while the same is true of nine out of 18 sibling sets with six or more members.

The sibling data also reflect Lung-tu's greater desirability as a source of spouses. Out of our total of 293 persons, 155 are involved in situations where two or more siblings are married to spouses from the same area; 78 of these spouses are from Lung-tu, and another 7 are from Yen-liao itself, amounting in all to about 55 percent of this group.

It might be said that in Mei-nung kinship is too important to be wasted on kinsmen, so that the importance of cognatic ties within the larger body of social relationships is indicated by the almost complete absence of multiple direct marriage ties between local agnatic groups. My research has found no such multiple ties between Yen-liao agnatic groups and those outside the village (but I cannot speak for the seven out of all Yen-liao marriages where the origin of the outside spouse is unknown to me). The situation is the same where both spouses are from Yen-liao, except as I shall note. Since the founding of the village, in 14 weddings both bride and groom have been members of the nine major agnatic groups, and only between the Huang

6. Primary marriages are those most important for the establishment of cognatic ties; they include all first marriages except for uxorilocal and "little daughter-in-law" marriages; they do not include widower remarriages and the taking of secondary wives (concubines).

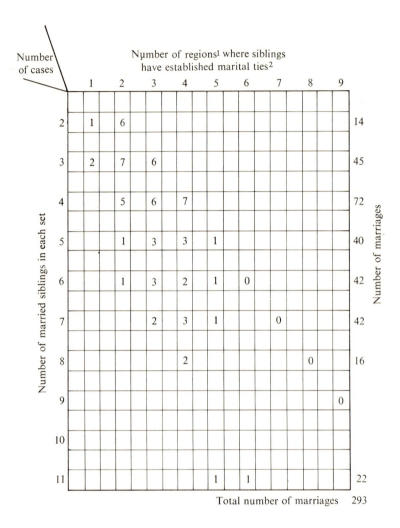

1. As among the following: Yen-liao, Lung-tu, (other than Yen-liao), Mei-nung, Chung-t'an, Chin-kua-liao, Chi-yang, Chu-t'ou-chiao, Hsin-wei, Hsin-liao (the last two settlements are beyond the boundaries of Mei-nung Township).

2. Primary marriages only (see footnote 6).

FIGURE 6 DISTRIBUTION OF COGNATIC TIES FORMED THROUGH MARRIAGE OF SIBLINGS, YEN-LIAO

A and Yeh B have there been two marriages; let me briefly describe the events which followed the first of these, for they show that this apparent exception to the practice of nonrepetition is in fact powerful evidence of its strength.

The bride was a Yeh B whose father had died without male offspring, after her marriage to the Huang A. Her mother had died some time ago, and her two younger sisters still in the Yeh B compound were promptly adopted out to other families. Following these events the woman's Huang A husband died, shortly after she had borne him a son. She was now completely isolated, and the situation was more than she could bear; she left her son to be cared for by his father's brothers and moved from the village to another district, where she eventually found herself a new husband. The woman's departure removed the last link between the Huang A and Yeh B; the ties created by marriage extend to entire local agnatic groups because they contain the families contracting the marriage and their descendants, and even though she left a son behind, there was no longer a descent line among the Yeh B with which he could claim affinity.

Similar events have not conspired to destroy the second Yeh B match or any of the others that have served to link Yen-liao families and agnatic groups, and the application of the principle of nonreplication to entire local agnatic groups expresses a crucial link between the agnatic and cognatic dimensions of the kinship system. There have been among Yen-liao's major agnatic groups 13 out of a potential maximum of 29 marriages, given surname exogamy and allowing for only one marriage between two groups. Owing to the practice of nonreplication, each marriage already entered into has contributed significantly to the ramification of Yen-liao's kinship network, so that all the major agnatic groups are now directly or indirectly linked. The very logic of the nonreplication strategy would imply that beyond a certain point marriages within the village would provide diminishing payoff in the form of new kin ties, and since 1953 there has been only one new marriage among the major agnatic groups; the most recent match in 1959 was especially significant, for it restored the link between the Huang A and Yeh B, and also provided the Yeh B with their only connection with another agnatic group in Yen-liao.

In Yen-liao and at all levels of society in Mei-nung, a total kinship framework is provided through the combination of agnatic and cognatic relationships. A common surname forms a basis for agnatic affiliation, but at the same time surname exogamy enforces the development of crosscutting cognatic ties. Agnatic kinship is generalizing: it groups people into larger aggregates on the basis of presumed or actual descent from a common progenitor; cognatic kinship is particularizing, for it supplies social connections for persons who can trace out their positions in an interconnected sequence of marriages and births or adoptions.

Agnatic kinship can serve as a framework for groups organized at different social and territorial scales; in the past, lineages could expand beyond the confines of Mei-nung and draw their memberships from throughout Hakka society in southern Taiwan. Even at the most intimate levels of social life agnatic kinship differentiates aggregates, but the local agnatic group in fact forms the minimal multifamily community in Mei-nung society. The particularistic qualities of cognatic kinship tend to confine within smaller regions the marriages that create new relationships, for the ties are established so that the new kinsmen will be accessible to each other. Cognatic bonds thus are primarily concentrated within the Mei-nung community, and over time an increasingly dense matrix of kin ties has developed. Cognatic relationships are therefore now significant at the level of Mei-nung society as a whole; Mei-nung itself is by now a social field within which many if not most persons can establish ties with each other on the basis of near or remote cognatic links.

THE ECONOMY

Agriculture continues to dominate Mei-nung's economy and the region produces the two annual crops of rice characteristic of much of rural Taiwan. But Mei-nung Township differs from the rest of the Taiwanese countryside, including immediately adjacent regions, in the disproportionate attention given to-bacco cultivation. In 1961, 1531 Mei-nung households planted 1001.87 hectares of tobacco (Ag. Cen. Kaohsiung 1963:137), amounting to 14.2 percent of all agricultural households grow-ing tobacco in Taiwan and 15.6 percent of all land given to its cultivation (Ag. Cen. Taiwan 1963:74).

In Yen-liao, as in Mei-nung generally, most persons are members of families that both own and cultivate land; in this category are 60 of the village's 68 families. Yen-liao also follows the general pattern of crop cultivation in Mei-nung. Rice takes pride of place, for the two rice crops harvested annually define the overall cycle of agricultural activity, dividing the agricul-tural year into three periods. The first, figured from transplant to harvest, extends from middle and late February to late May or early June. The first harvest is immediately followed by trans-plant of the second crop, which in turn is harvested during a period extending from early to late October. There follows a stretch of about four months, often called the "winter period," during which other crops are planted. The cycle of agricultural activity is also conditioned by the availability of water. The dry season, extending from October to April, overlaps with the greater portion of the first rice-growing period and during this time rice is grown only in those fields which may be dependa-bly irrigated. Starting about May, rainfall is sufficient to permit rice cultivation over a much wider area. During the dry season sweet potato is the main crop on single-crop rice fields. During the winter season, sweet potatoes as well as soy beans are grown on both double-crop and single-crop fields. At this time, however, they are up against a very formidable competitor, to-bacco, which is grown exclusively during the winter period and on both single- and double-crop fields; the extension of the winter period into the following rainy season makes this pos-sible.

Yen-liao is fully representative of Mei-nung Township's em-phasis on tobacco production; families there began growing the crop in 1938, the year it was first introduced in Mei-nung, and during the 1964–65 season it was grown by 37 of the 60 land-owning families. In comparison with other major crops grown in Yen-liao, tobacco production requires by far the heaviest labor input; the average labor requirements of different crops in Taiwan are given in Table 4, but the intensity of the tobacco-related labor input is even greater than indicated by these statistics, since tobacco is grown only during one of the three annual crop seasons. The greatest labor demand would be in an agricultural year including two crops of rice and one of tobacco; or one crop of rice, one of sweet potato, and one of tobacco. And these are precisely the cropping cycles employed by tobacco farmers.

Table 4
Average Labor Requirements per Hectare
for Major Crops in Taiwan, 1961

Crop	*Workdays*
Tobacco (one crop)	789.0
Ponlai Rice (1st and 2nd crop combined)	204.3
Chailai Rice (1st and 2nd crop combined)	193.4
Sweet Potato (one crop)	119.4
Sugar Cane (one crop)	231.9
Peanut (one crop)	190.2
Soybean (one crop)	140.3
Banana (one crop)	142.8

SOURCE: Lu 1962:487–91

Tobacco is competitive with other crops because it generally provides high cash returns and is protected from market fluctuations by the Taiwan Tobacco and Wine Monopoly Bureau, a government agency in total control of tobacco production; although a cultivator cannot predict his final gross receipts, he knows that his entire crop will be purchased by the Bureau according to a fixed price schedule, based upon leaf quality, announced before the onset of the cultivation season. Table 5 gives some indication of tobacco's competitive position against other major crops in terms of 1961 Taiwan-wide averages. A cultivation cycle including two crops of rice and one of tobacco yields harvests having a greater value than any other mono- or multiple-cropping cycle. Gross income, however, is indicated as higher for sweet potato, another possible winter crop, than for tobacco. But tobacco far exceeds sweet potato, and all other crops, with respect to field costs and the percentage of field costs that comprises human labor. If labor is not included as a field cost, the average per hectare gross income is NT$27,092 for tobacco, again higher than all other crops. Of course, while

Table 5
Average per Hectare Costs and Income
of Major Crops in Taiwan, 1961 (NT$)

Crop	Field cost	Value of main product	Gross income	Labor portion of field cost	Labor as percentage of field cost
Tobacco	32,975	39,600	6,625	20,467	62.1
Ponlai rice (first crop)	8,430	15,882	7,452	4,450	52.8
Ponlai rice (second crop)	7,792	15,984	8,192	4,156	53.3
Chailai rice (first crop)	7,788	16,895	9,107	4,324	55.5
Chailai rice (second crop)	6,787	14,130	7,343	3,792	55.9
Sweet potato	8,099	15,908	7,809	3,894	48.1
Peanut	8,197	11,158	2,961	4,789	58.4
Soybean	7,533	10,569	3,036	4,174	55.4
Sugar cane (one year)	11,348	19,420	8,072	5,369	47.3
Banana (one year)	16,767	25,545	8,780	7,376	44.0

SOURCE: Lu 1962, part II

labor cannot be eliminated as a field cost, neither can it be considered as equivalent to manufactured commodities such as chemical fertilizer.

When assigning cash value to *all* labor, it must be kept in mind that only a portion of the labor is hired; the remainder is supplied by family members, either directly or through labor exchange agreements with other families. Thus, the cash returns for crops comparatively high in value but more demanding in labor will largely be a function of the degree to which the work force is composed of family members. In other words, the cultivation of tobacco results in a very substantial increase in the economic value of those family members who work the family farm.

For most crops, labor requirements are not constant during the cultivation period. There is usually an alternation between busy and slack periods, and in Taiwan this alternation is most pronounced for rice cultivation, with labor demand greatest during harvest and substantial during transplanting and weeding. But families growing tobacco do not experience such fluctuations; the labor demands of tobacco are not only high, but at certain phases of the tobacco production sequence they are in competition with those of rice. Tobacco-growing eliminates the winter period as a slack season; work begins shortly before the second rice harvest, extends through the winter period, and terminates only in middle or late May of the following year. For tobacco-growing families, the slack season is a three-month period beginning after the second rice crop's transplant in early June.

Tobacco production, which includes tobacco plant cultivation and tobacco leaf curing, can be divided into six phases: seedbed preparation and sowing; first transplant; final transplant; field cultivation; harvest and curing; sorting, packing, and sale. The Taiwan Tobacco and Wine Monopoly Bureau assigns farmers yearly quotas for the area of land they can plant to tobacco, the number of plants that may be grown, and the total weight of the final product. In general, the only option the tobacco-grower has is to comply with Bureau regulations or cease growing tobacco altogether. Farmers may decline when the Bureau offers them the opportunity to increase their quota; however they must reduce the area they grow when ordered to do so, and may not make such reductions unless ordered. If a farmer stops growing tobacco for a year, his permit is revoked.

As a result of such strict control, tobacco cultivators remain committed to the crop year after year. Although individual quotas may be increased or reduced, tobacco farmers cease production only with the greatest reluctance; none of the tobacco-growing permits issued to Yen-liao farmers has been given up since 1945. In 1965, 27 permits enabled 37 Yen-liao families to grow the crop; 21 permits were held by individual families, while six permits were shared by 17 other families. (One of the 17 families sharing a permit had moved from Yen-liao to a neighboring hamlet about 20 years before.) Permit-sharing is legal only in cases where a tobacco-growing family divides, and all shared permits in Yen-liao are a result of family partition.

Through various forms of cooperation farming families increase the economic value of family labor and minimize the amount of wages paid outsiders. But the degree to which a family can cooperate with others depends on the number of such family workers available, and even under the most favorable conditions most families must hire additional workers during the busiest periods.

The most common form of cooperation is known as "labor exchange" ("*kao-koung*")—simply an agreement between families to swap a certain number of "*koung*," a term I translate as "workday," but which means more precisely "an able-bodied adult performing a full day's work at a given task." Tasks which require that several people work together for one or more full days are usually calculated in workdays. These include the major phases of rice production, such as transplant, initial weeding, and harvesting; also the two tobacco transplants, cultivation, harvest, and sorting. Labor exchange is reckoned within the context of the same agricultural operation; workdays may be exchanged during rice harvest, for example, but rice harvest workdays are not supplied in exchange for tobacco-sorting workdays. The reciprocity labor exchange requires is strictly defined. Workdays, if not repaid with family labor, must be compensated for by its equivalent; usually the debtor family tries to hire someone to work in their stead. Failing this, they present the equivalent in wages.

All work figured in workdays can involve labor exchange, but those tasks which absorb more labor and allow little flexibility in timing are most prone to be involved. For tobacco farming, labor exchange is most important during harvest and sorting and is also used during cultivation, and first and final transplant. In general, families living close by exchange more labor than those separated by any distance; labor exchange among families belonging to the same compound-based agnatic group is quite common; an agnate's request to swap labor usually takes priority over a similar request from someone who is not a relative, but the strict reciprocity is no different from that between non-kinsmen. Labor exchange within the local agnatic group is most important for tobacco-growers during harvest, and accounts for the major portion of nonfamily labor. Labor exchange during tobacco sorting is restricted by the fact that neighboring families must sell their crops at about the same time; but these are the very circumstances which encourage tobacco farmers to swap labor with cognatic kinsmen living in other parts of Mei-nung. Thus, different dimensions of Mei-nung's kinship system are highlighted during different phases of tobacco production.

A smaller portion of the labor that families supply each other is called "help" (*"t'en-chou"*) and is distinguished from labor exchange. Relationships through marriage largely provide the network through which "help" flows. Here there is an ongoing obligation between families to provide assistance whenever requested and whenever available. "Help" is not strictly figured in workdays, nor is it restricted to particular tasks, agricultural or otherwise. Rather, it is an enduring relationship that can involve many forms of mutual assistance. "Help" figures prominently in many different kinds of long-term and short-term work during the agricultural slack season. The reciprocity aspect of "help" is seen in two ways. On the one hand, there are "exchanges" of labor. For instance, Yeh Wang-ch'uan, the head of one Yen-liao family, sent his son, a carpenter, to Lung-tu to "help" his sister's husband build a new ancestral hall. The following summer, the Lung-tu relatives sent the Yen-liao family a man to assist in the rebuilding of their kitchen.

There is also reciprocity in that "gifts" are often exchanged between families having "help" relationships. Thus, two Huang families, headed by brothers, often "help" Yeh Ta-jen and vice versa. Yeh's wife is the sister of the two Huangs' father (now dead). Yeh says the families have only a rough idea of how many workdays they have supplied each other. When one family thinks that workdays received have begun to exceed those contributed, it looks for an opportunity to provide "help." The Yeh and Huang families often give each other gifts of farm produce.

Tasks associated with labor exchange sometimes also involve "help," but when cognatic kin "help" during the busiest farming periods, reciprocity often takes another form. Poorer families work for their richer relatives; in return, the more fortunate kin give "gifts"—usually rice or pork. For example, Yeh Wang-lai's son-in-law, who lives in another part of Mei-nung, does not grow enough rice to feed his family. He often comes to Yen-liao during rice harvest and "helps" Wang-lai, while the latter gives his son-in-law some grain each year.

Agriculture dominates but by no means monopolizes Yen-liao's economy. Table 6 shows that about 70 percent of the men and 93 percent of the women in Yen-liao's working population are involved in farming. Note, however, that 22 men who farm are concurrently engaged in long-term nonfarming endeavors; they, together with 43 men who do not farm at all, constitute about 46 percent of the male working force. There are another 25 men, about 18 percent of all male workers, who are available for short-term wage labor, but only a minor proportion of this work would appear to be nonagricultural. Taken as a whole, however, it seems clear that the nonagricultural activities of the male working force amount to a sizable proportion of their total working time. While Yen-liao's total labor force is about evenly

Table 6
Disposition of Resident Labor Force by Sex,
Yen-liao, May 1965

Farming	M	F
Farmers on family farms	37	71
Farming concurrent with long-term non-farming occupations	22	6
Farmers on family farms also available for short-term farming and non-farming wage labor	20	37
Semi-retired farmers, lighter tasks only	8	3
Persons who do some farming, but mainly supervise labor hired for family farm	7	2
Short-term wage laborers from landless families (farming and non-farming)	5	7
Nonfarming occupations	43	10
Total labor force	142	136

divided between the two sexes, only about 12 percent of the women are involved in long-term nonagricultural occupations. Women, in fact, provide most of the farming "manpower," as full-time workers on family farms and as short-term wage laborers. Even though most domestic work also is undertaken by women, they are predominant in agriculture; in this respect the Yen-liao situation appears to confirm the comparatively greater productive role of women that many observers of mainland China and Taiwan consider characteristic of the Hakka.

Several points can be made about the pattern of nonagricultural employment in Yen-liao. Among the nonfarming occupations, listed in Table 7, none would necessarily suggest movement away from an agrarian context; only a minority are full-time salaried positions, and none of these involve factory employment. However, of a total of 81 occupations listed, 57 involve shops, plants, or other capitalized enterprises owned by Yen-liao families, and only six enterprises, supporting merely ten jobs, belong to landless families. Thus, most of the enterprises are undertaken by farming families, and the 47 persons in the village's labor force these enterprises support are

Table 7
Nonfarming Occupations in Yen-liao, May 1965

	Resident labor force			
	Concurrent with farming		Nonfarming	
	M	F	M	F
Shops, plants, and other capitalized enterprises in Yen-liao	13	6	23	9
Shops and plants owned by Yen-liao families but located outside of the village	2	0	4	0
Service occupations	7	0	5	0
Salaried occupations	0	0	11	1
Totals	22	6	43	10

members of such families. In Yen-liao, then, nonagricultural economic activities for the most part are linked to agriculture within the framework provided by family organization. In fact, to appreciate economic conditions in Yen-liao, and in the rest of Mei-nung, the type of enterprise that must be considered is the family, rather than one of the several activities individual family members may engage in. This phenomenon of economic diversification within a family context is one manifestation in Yen-liao of the still traditional organization of family life—a subject to which we must now turn.

CHAPTER 3

Aspects of
Chinese Family Organization

MANY OF the forces impinging on family life in Yen-liao are
unique to the Mei-nung region or to the present period of Taiwanese history. However, the family is still organized along
lines characteristic of traditional China during Ch'ing. Since it
is sometimes easy to see change where there has been none, in
this chapter I shall discuss and relate to the Yen-liao situation
certain traditional characteristics of the Chinese family.

For such purposes the important unit is the *chia*, and let us
first note that while the *chia* has generally been identified as
the "family," Chinese terminology in fact designates the *fang*
together with the *chia* as the smallest units within the Chinese
kinship system. Though the term *fang* is relative, and may be
used in reference to agnatic subdivisions of varying size and
genealogical depth within the lineage, it is also used for the
conjugal unit consisting of husband, wife, and children (see Hu
1948:18; Fried 1953:31). As for the *chia*, it has been defined as
"the economic family, i.e., the unit consisting of members re-

A portion of this chapter is adapted from my "Developmental Process in the
Chinese Domestic Group," which originally appeared in *Family and Kinship in
Chinese Society*, ed. Maurice Freedman (1970). I thank the publisher, Stanford
University Press, for permission to use this material here.

lated to each other by blood, marriage, or adoption and having a common budget and common property" (Lang 1946:13). Of course, a *chia* may vary in size, in number of generations, and in the number of *fang* in each generation.

However, like *fang, chia* is a relative term of many uses. In the Mei-nung area I often heard agnates who shared a common ancestor many generations removed refer to each other as "people of the same *chia*" ("*t'oung-ka ngin*"). Even people with identical surnames who were in no position to trace their actual genealogical ties (if such existed) would use the same phrase. Needless to say, closer agnates would not hesitate to count themselves as members of the same *chia*. I do not know the extent to which this wide range of usage was found in China. Certainly it has been most common to think of the *chia* as a family arrangement of some sort, although there has been some confusion over the term, as was noted in a summary of work on the subject: "At the base of our hierarchy is the family or *chia*. Exactly what the term means has never been agreed upon and perhaps it is a variable which is subject to local variations" (Osgood 1963:355).

In its narrowest sense, the word *chia* does refer to a group which is the basic unit of domestic organization and whose members are united not only by kinship, but also by claims the men in the group have on property we may call the *chia* estate. This meaning of *chia* is quite precise in the phrase *fen-chia,* "to divide the *chia*," which applies to a specific, bounded kin group acting in terms of an equally well delineated body of holdings. There is nothing vague about *fen-chia:* division has or has not taken place. If it has, two or more *chia* exist where before there was only one, and the estate of the original *chia* is distributed accordingly. It is in reference to such domestic groups that I use interchangeably the terms *chia, chia* group, and family.

Some of the problems encountered in dealing with Chinese family units might be clarified if it is first understood that while the *chia* is a discrete kin group, it can display a great deal of variation in residential arrangements and in the economic ties among its members. For purposes of analysis, the *chia* estate, economy, and group can each be considered as three basic components in *chia* organization. I shall first discuss each component separately, and then show how they could connect with each other in a variety of ways. The *chia* estate is that body of holdings to which the process of family division (*fen-chia*) is applicable. The *chia* group is made up of those persons who have rights of one sort or another to the *chia* estate at the time of family division. The *chia* economy refers to the exploitation of the *chia* estate (and the benefits derived therefrom) as well as to other income-producing activities linked to its exploitation through remittances and a common budgetary arrangement.

Fei Hsiao-t'ung remarks that the *chia* is the "basis of the collective aspect of ownership" (1939:59); the *chia* estate, the economic foundation of the *chia* group, can include land, usually the most significant property for all but the poorest families, and other items such as residences, household effects, farm structures and tools, livestock, and also perhaps shops or other commercial holdings. In general, brothers held equal rights to the estate, and ultimately it would be divided among them; in some areas, the oldest brother might receive a slightly larger share (van der Sprenkel 1962:16). We shall see in later chapters that the *chia* estate is not the total aggregate of property owned by *chia* group members as individuals or as smaller units within the group; but it seems clear that for the members of the vast majority of Chinese families the *chia* estate was much more valuable, and more important to survival, than all other forms of property combined.

That the *chia* economy is largely organized along collective lines has been noted by McAleavy:

> The general rule was that the fruit of the labor of all family members, whether they worked at home on the family land, or earned money from jobs outside the home, had to be put in the common fund from which the family supported itself and which, on partition, was divided among those entitled (1955:546).

Because the *chia* is organized to advance the interests of the group as a whole, the collectivism in the economy is most prominent with respect to distribution and consumption, as all persons in the group are provided for by pooled income. In production the collective economy is less apparent; while some members of the group keep the estate productive, the contributions of others may very well be from outside earnings obtained in a variety of ways. Production could be individualized because it was arranged to promote the family's welfare by taking advantage of whatever opportunities the outside world might offer.

The arrangement of economic roles is an important element in *chia* organization. There is an obvious contrast between those helping to supply the family's income and dependents (the aged, the ill or disabled, children, students). The former category includes managers and workers; often enough a person can switch from one role to the other or hold both concurrently, but usually the roles are most clearly differentiated in larger and wealthier families undertaking several lines of activity. By far the most important managerial role is held by the person controlling family fiscal affairs; he is the family accountant and is usually in charge of distributing family funds and other resources.

The person managing the family economy is not necessarily the *chia-chang* ("family head"), an ascriptive status held by the oldest male in the senior generation—the father or the eldest of several brothers—who is considered the *chia*'s representative to the outside world. Lang and McAleavy agree that financial management is a specialized role, but one that need not be held by the formal family head. According to Lang, the person in charge of family funds is known by a special term if he is not the *chia-chang;* money earned by family members is supposed to be contributed "to the family treasury administered by the family head or his assistant, the family manager (*tang chia*), who could be a man or a woman" (1946:17). McAleavy, on the other hand, says that the *chia-chang* and the *tang-chia* are identical (1955:540), but that the *chia-chang* as effective family head need not be the senior male (*ibid.*:543). He summarizes the findings of Japanese field studies that the family head, as the

person who controlled finances, was not necessarily the senior
family member:

> The Japanese investigators in North China found cases where a
> widowed mother exercised the powers of family head in prefer-
> ence to her adult son, and still oftener cases where a junior
> member was recognized as head of the family over his seniors on
> account of his greater industry or ability (McAleavy:542).

Despite their different interpretations of Chinese family terms,
both Lang and McAleavy agree that the role of financial manager involved special expertise and responsibility; this remains
true in Yen-liao, where the man who is family head in terms of
overall authority and management may not be in charge of family finances.

As we turn to the *chia* group, we shall first consider its structure and size. The significant differences in *chia* structure have
long been recognized, and scholars now commonly refer to
"conjugal," "stem," and "joint" families. The terms were first
adapted to the study of Chinese family organization by Olga
Lang (1946:15), who defines them as follows: the "conjugal family . . . consists of man, wife or wives, and children"; the "stem
family," includes "parents, their unmarried children, and one
married son with wife and children"; and the "joint family"
comprises "parents, their unmarried children, their married
sons (more than one) and sons' wives and children." Families of
each type are either "complete" or "broken." By "broken"
Lang means the absence of some but not all individuals defining the type: a stem family lacking a mother is broken; if the father also is absent, it is a conjugal family. Although according to
Lang a conjugal family may be reduced to one person and still
preserve its typological credentials, it is often important for the
sake of analysis that isolated individuals be identified as such.
Lang notes that in one form of the joint family the parents are
dead and the oldest generation consists of several married
brothers, an arrangement commonly called a "fraternal joint
family." We shall later see that stem and joint families share
certain features that set them apart from families of the conjugal

type; therefore sometimes I place stem and joint forms in the category "complex family."

It has long been known that the majority of Chinese families were small during traditional times (as is undoubtedly still the case today) and to confirm and discuss this pattern we need only to refer to a recent treatment of data collected during the early twentieth century. Taeuber (1970) has analyzed a hitherto unpublished 1929 survey of 38,256 farm families in 22 provinces of mainland China; units of six people or less make up 76 percent of all families and account for 59.1 percent of the total surveyed population; those with seven to nine persons make up 17.6 percent of all families and account for 25 percent of the population (1970:81). The overall average family size is 5.2 persons (*ibid.:*71), which tallies well with earlier findings which show that "the average Chinese family ranges in membership from four persons to six persons" (C. K. Yang 1959a:6).

Unsurprisingly, Taeuber's data demonstrate that the largest families—those which have ten or more members—make up 6.5 percent of all families, but account for 15 percent of the total population. The farther apart families are in size, the greater the chance they will have different structures; while the very large families, which must include many joint families, are greatly outnumbered by smaller families—most of which we would expect to be stem or conjugal—the disparities decrease when viewed in terms of the proportion of the population participating in different family structures. The data Professor Taeuber must work with do not let her tell us the actual relationship between family size and structure; she can report only that the survey classified 62.8 percent of all families as "nuclear," taken as including only fathers, mothers, and children (1970:81).

We have so far been treating separately each component of the *chia;* we shall now consider how the connections between the estate, the economy, and the group could vary. This can be illustrated by assigning each component only two possible alternative characteristics. The *chia* group is either concentrated or dispersed; if concentrated, all members live in one household, and if dispersed, they live in more than one. Similarly, the *chia* estate can be either concentrated or dispersed; if concentrated, the members of the *chia* group exploiting it are from one household only; if dispersed, exploitation is by members of the *chia* group residing in two or more households. The *chia* economy is either inclusive or noninclusive. An inclusive economy is one in which all members of the *chia* group participate. Participation need not necessarily be productive; dependents may also be involved. If some members of the *chia* group do not participate in the *chia* economy, it is noninclusive. The significance of variations in the connections between *chia* components has not been given its due in the literature; by and large the Chinese family has been described in terms involving or assuming the existence of a *chia* in which the estate is concentrated, the group is concentrated, and the economy is inclusive. It can be shown, however, that this is not always the case.

First of all, an inclusive economy can be found in association with a dispersed estate and, of necessity, a dispersed group. In *The Golden Wing* (1948), Lin Yueh-hwa describes at one point in the story how Dunglin entered into a partnership with his sister's husband and established a shop in a town near his home village. Dunglin's share of the shop actually belonged to his *chia* as a whole, as did some land in the village. Though Dunglin lived and worked in the shop (frequently coming home), his wife lived in the village with his mother and the *fang* composed of Dunglin's brother, his brother's wife, and their children (Lin 1948:11ff.). The economy certainly was inclusive: "As the family had not been officially divided, the capital and money income of the store, as well as family lands and their produce, were still common property, belonging to both brothers. Thus the two men took an interest in each other's work and planned together for the good of the whole family" (*ibid.*:13).

Dispersion on a somewhat greater scale was found in a family distributed between the village of Nanching and the nearby city of Canton:

> Wong Han was a wealthy landlord with considerable landholdings in the village and an import and export firm in the city of Canton. A man in his early sixties, he lived with his wife, two concubines,

two married sons and their wives, one unmarried son and two unmarried daughters, and three grandchildren, all as one household
with common property. Although the married sons and their wives
spent most of the time in their common city residence, family
unity was effectively maintained among the fourteen members.
(C. K. Yang 1959b:17)

An inclusive economy and a dispersed group can also be
found together with a concentrated estate. In such a case only
family members in one of the households exploit the estate;
other members of the group receive remittances from or send
them to the estate. Most of those receiving money from the estate were, in traditional times, dependents such as students
studying for the examinations or a small minority of apprentices
who might pay their masters some sort of "tuition" or who
might continue to get additional spending money from home.
Remittances to the estate by officials, merchants, craftsmen, salaried workers, etc. were much more common. In his description
of the rise and fall of gentry families, Ho gives many examples
of the remittance system among the gentry and wealthy merchants (Ho 1962:292, 312).

Though this discussion has not covered the entire range of
variations possible within the inclusive economy, the main patterns have been set forth, and we now turn to the noninclusive
economy. It is, of course, always associated with a dispersed
group; one or more members of the group are economically
independent and residentially separated from the rest. The remaining members can exhibit varied residential and economic
connections with the estate identical to those found in the context of an inclusive economy.

I have been considering the residential distribution of *chia*
group members instead of dealing with the household as such.
Now the household is a kind of domestic unit; Fei (1939:96)
calls it "the basic territorial group," comprising all who live and
eat together, including boarders, servants, and apprentices. But
the situation in Yen-liao accords with earlier descriptions which
indicate that the household as such is not a very viable group-
ing. Within their own household, members of a *chia* are es-

tablished far more securely than other residents, and changes in a household's non-*chia* component display little regularity. The affective bonds between family members and others in the household vary from case to case, as does the nature of their economic relationship; the nonfamily residents may be paying rent, receiving wages, or simply guests. They are never fully absorbed into the family's economic life and have no rights to the *chia* estate of their host (see Fried 1953:83ff).

Yet there is an important relationship between household and *chia* in that certain characteristics of family organization appear only when the *chia* group is located primarily within one household, and for most dispersed *chia* groups it is possible to identify what I call a "primary household," containing the majority of *chia* members; if other members of the group form their own households, these are "secondary households." In order to illustrate the full range of significant domestic forms, terms that describe the composition of the *chia* group can also be employed with reference to the distribution of the members of a dispersed group among households. Thus, while a dispersed group may be "joint," the group's primary household can be "stem," and so on. Table 8 shows how the elements of *chia* organization can combine in different ways to produce a variety of domestic forms. Of course, several of these may coexist in one household; but it is safe to say that in traditional China, especially in the rural areas, the overwhelming majority of households contained concentrated *chia* groups or were primary households of groups that were dispersed.

Families undergo changes in structure, and in any discussion of such changes the anthropological notion of "developmental cycle," explicitly formulated first by Meyer Fortes (1949:63ff.; 1958), deserves close attention. Fortes was correctly critical of the fact that with the typological treatment of family structure, little or no attention was given to developmental process; he pointed out how it must be "recognized that these so-called types are in fact phases in the developmental cycle of a single general form for each society" (1958:3). Within any developmental cycle, the individual goes through four phases, the last

Table 8
Summary of Variations in Family Form

Residential distribution of chia group	Chia *group composition*			
	isolated individual	*conjugal*	*stem*	*joint*
concentrated	x	x	x	x
dispersed		x	x	x

Residential status of household	*Composition of* chia *group members within household only*			
	isolated individual	*conjugal*	*stem*	*joint*
Residence of concentrated *chia* group; estate concentrated, economy inclusive	x	x	x	x
Primary household of dispersed *chia* group; estate concentrated or dispersed		x	x	x
Secondary household of dispersed group	x	x	x	x
a. participates in *chia* economy, exploits part of dispersed *chia* estate	x	x	x	x
b. participates in economy only	x	x	x	x
c. does not participate in economy	x	x	x	x

of which is "marriage and the actual or incipient fission of the natal domestic group" (*ibid.:*9).

Now three assumptions lie behind Fortes's critique. One is that the rate of development or change among the families in a given society is constant; the other is that all families change; the third is that the "life-cycle" of the individual is *necessarily* tied in with developmental changes in the family. If such assumptions are correct, it might still be said that typologies (but certainly not archetypes) are useful for dealing with a developmental situation in that they provide needed labels for sorting out families on the basis of specified variations in complexity. In fact, however, the developmental cycle concept requires modification when applied to the Chinese case, and under such circumstances a typology becomes useful indeed.

When viewed in developmental terms, changes in Chinese family structure can be kept distinct from changes in family personnel. New families form by splitting off from old ones; families increase in size through births, adoptions, and marriages; they get smaller due to deaths, marriages out, adoptions out, and because some members may fission off and form new families. It is possible for a family to continually replenish its membership without undergoing changes in structure, varying only in that there might be alternation, to use Lang's terms, between the complete and broken forms.

Both Lang (1946:10) and Levy (1949:55ff.) have noted that in traditional China it may have been quite common for stem families to maintain themselves for many years. Poverty and poor health care may have left many families with only one son surviving to maturity in each generation, but for a joint family to be maintained without some members forming new families is improbable enough to be a limiting case; to maintain a joint family without expanding indefinitely, many men would have to die or otherwise be eliminated each generation, together with their wives and children. It is nevertheless possible for at least some types of families to endure consistently in the absence of division; using the developmental cycle approach for such cases would be feasible only if developmental cycle meant nothing more than life cycle.

On the other hand, one of the new families created through division may retain the original form, or all the new families may be at a more simple level. Levy claims that in traditional China new families were most commonly formed through the *famille souche* pattern of division, which creates conjugal families and maintains stem families (1949:55–56); for a joint form of family to endure would appear to require at some point the creation of additional conjugal, stem, or joint families.

Freedman (1961–62; 1966:44ff.) has suggested that in traditional China there may have been two basic developmental cycles. One, found among wealthier families, was characterized by the emergence of new joint families through the partition of old ones of the same type, with conjugal and stem families often resulting at the same time. The other cycle was prevalent among less well-to-do families, which were prevented from development beyond the stem level of complexity first by high mortality rates (which in many cases meant only one son would survive to maturity) and second by the propensity, in those families where more than one son survived, for the sons to separate after a comparatively short period.

Given the existence of "rich" and "poor" cycles, it follows that there must be intermediate ones, and that families changing their economic status likewise change their developmental pattern. Freedman's approach in fact removes from the developmental cycle idea much of its original meaning; there is no uniform cycle in Chinese society as a whole, and even within each of the two suggested cycles there is no consistent pattern of change demonstrating that family form is a clearcut indication of developmental phase.

These points are elaborated simply to show that the developmental cycle cannot be used for Fortes's purpose, which is to account for the variations in family structure. When applied diachronically, the developmental concept can be a useful tool not to account for variations but rather to gauge changes. For the purposes of this study the three types of family structure encompass all variations. Arranged from the simplest to the most complex, they define the limits within which changes in either direction may occur. At the same time they describe the maximal developmental sequence, which goes from conjugal family to stem to joint to fraternal joint and back to conjugal.

However, many other sequences are possible. In Table 9 I have set out for Yen-liao's major agnatic groups all sequences of development that have terminated in family division between 1900 and 1965. Families may attain joint form before division, which results in the establishment of families that may be conjugal, stem, and joint in varying combinations, and the division of other families while they are still stem leads to the appearance of conjugal units only. The crucial point is that none of these sequences can be explained purely in terms of a general pattern of family development, but only in conjunction with additional variable factors impinging on such development.

Table 9

Sequences of Family Development Terminating in Family Division During 1900–1965, Major Agnatic Groups, Yen-liao

Form at beginning of sequence	Intermediate forms (if any)	Form prior to separation	Form(s) resulting from separation	Cases	Number of families resulting
Conjugal	Stem	Joint	Conjugal	10	23
Conjugal	Stem	Joint	Conjugal and stem	7	17
Conjugal	Stem	Joint	Conjugal and joint	3	6
Conjugal	Stem	Joint	Stem and Joint	2	5
Conjugal	Stem	Joint	Joint	1	3
Conjugal		Stem	Conjugal	5	10
Conjugal		Stem	Conjugal	2	2 [a]
Conjugal		Joint	Conjugal	4	8 [b]
Stem		Joint	Conjugal	2	6
Stem		Stem	Conjugal	1	2
Joint		Joint	Conjugal and stem	4	14
Joint		Joint	Stem	1	2
Joint		Joint	Conjugal and joint	2	5

[a] Changes in form through death of parents.

[b] Conjugal families which turn fraternal joint through the marriage of the family head's brother, whereupon family division results in the creation of new conjugal families.

Such variable factors are not what Fortes has in mind when he makes a distinction between domestic and external realms:

> Marriage, inheritance, succession, and so forth, are events in the internal system, or, to be more specific, domain of the domestic group; but they are simultaneously events in the external domain, where the domestic group is integrated into the total social structure in its political, jural, and ritual aspects (Fortes 1958:6).

Fortes is referring to sanctions, norms, and other factors behind what is uniform in the process of family development. While such factors lend support in the Chinese context to patterns of marriage, residence, property relationships, etc., they act to define, once again, the dimensions of the maximal development sequence; they do not tell us why the specific developmental histories of different families may be unidentical and produce in differing sequences family structures that may endure for unlike lengths of time.

Given the fact that both of the domains in Fortes's analysis shape family development, we may proceed to deal with those important processes which concern the distribution of authority within the family, and changes in the jural status of family members. At all stages of family development, there is a family head with overall authority in the management of family affairs. In most cases, the family head would be the father (see C. K. Yang 1959a:10), and two important phases in his direction of family affairs can be distinguished. The family head had first to supervise the careers of his sons if he hoped to launch his family on a course in which the unit would be preserved intact and hopefully enriched. With the maturation of sons, their marriage, and their entrance into economic life, the managerial responsibilities of the family head shifted to the coordination of his sons' activities for benefit of the family as a whole, and to the preservation and supervision of the practices that made the family an economic entity.

The nature of the family head's management during the second phase was linked to the full emergence of his sons as jural adults. We have noted that sons held basically equal rights to the *chia* estate. According to Freedman such rights mean that "every male born or fully adopted into the family is, from the moment of his existence as a son, a coparcener" (Freedman, 1966:49). Actually, while the coparcenary rights of males provided reinforcement and sanction for the collective exploitation of the estate, these rights were a bit less immutable than the quote from Freedman indicates, for just as males could be "fully adopted into the family," they could equally be fully adopted out. In chapter 2 I described sale and the agnatic and affinal forms of adoption as traditional to the Mei-nung area; as I noted, boys were usually sold outright only by parents desperate for money, and in the written contract confirming the adoption there was often a clause that specifically eliminated the young boy as coparcener to the estate of his natal father. But the very circumstances of the sale suggest that there was not much to the estate from which the boy was dispossessed. Agnatic and affinal adoption are very different factors, for we have seen that in such cases the parents often adopt out their sons because of certain obligations to kinsmen, or even as a result of specific agreements with them; sons adopted by kinsmen might become coparceners of estates poorer than the ones from which they had been cut off. Now adoption along kinship lines was widespread in China, which suffices to indicate that circumstances of birth did not alone define a man's coparcenary status.[1]

I digress to the subject of adoption because it highlights the fact that males are not born coparceners but grow into that position, and this raises the subject of the general relationship between jural status and rights to the estate. I would first note that in the Mei-nung area men can give up their share of the natal estate as late as the time of their marriage, should it be of the uxorilocal variety, but it is true that men who marry in this fashion come from poor families and thus have little to lose; on the other hand, it probably is also true in the majority of cases that should partition occur when some of the eligible parties are still very young children, they will be counted as having rights to equal shares in the estate. In most cases they cannot assume independent control over their shares until after they have married, however, and it is safe to say that the status of a son or brother as coparcener is not fully secure until his marriage confirms him as jurally adult; it is then that he exercises his first

1. An example from Shantung during late Ch'ing may be cited; in a document drawn up in conjunction with an instance of family partition there is the following clause: "the second [of the sons] has no share in or right to any portion of this property, as he cannot carry the family property away with him when he is 'adopted out' " (quoted in Johnston 1910:152).

major claim on *chia* wealth, expressed as the *chia*'s endowment of the wedding ceremonies. These establish for him and his bride precisely the domestic semiautonomy which has in it the potential for partition at some future time.

My fieldwork in Yen-liao leads me to propose that there are two jural statuses, "dependent" and then "expectant," before "adult." A jural dependent has no rights within his family. His parents have complete jural authority, including the right to dispose of him through adoption or sale, in which case jural authority is likewise transferred. In the family he is completely under his parents' control and, in theory at least, must obey them at all times. The "expectant" status relates to the family's obligations to members not yet jurally adult, the most important of which is to endow their weddings. Such obligations obviously can be voided when a person controlling a jural dependent disposes of him, but as a dependent grows older, such rights of disposal appear to weaken, while his status as dependent is maintained to the extent that he is still under his father's authority. With the dependent's growing physical maturity, his relationship with his father or another authority-holder is articulated less in terms of sanctions and more as a series of balanced claims and counterclaims. The son's claims are the endowment of his wedding and ultimately his portion of the *chia* estate; and the father claims from his son obedience, devotion to family welfare, and contributions to the family economy. During this period, then, the son's jural status is "expectant" in that it is largely defined by his family's responsibility for the arrangements that will make him jurally adult.

I am less convinced about the relevance of "expectant" status to women—at least in traditional China; with respect to authority and rights of disposal, the woman's status as a jural dependent seems to have extended throughout the period preceding marriage, although marriage nevertheless was a claim a woman held against her natal *chia*. In contemporary Mei-nung, however, the "expectant" status seems equally well defined for men and women. Jural adulthood is signified by marriage, which fully confirms a man as coparcener and redefines his position within the domestic unit. A woman commences her jural adulthood as a wife in a new household; together with her new duties are certain rights and privileges (see chapter 6).

We can now see that Lang, by designating conjugal, stem, and joint families, in fact classifies Chinese families according to the distribution of coparceners who have had their rights to the estate firmly established through marriage. These different arrangements of coparceners are but some of the elements that result in each form of family being qualitatively different in certain respects from the others. If the relationship between the distribution of coparceners and family forms gives added meaning to the terms used for the latter, however, it also questions the appropriateness of the terms. Freedman (1966:48–49; 1970a:9) quite correctly points out that incorporated into the long-standing usage of the term "joint" family there is a confusion between Chinese (and Indian) families constituted as "joint" property-owning units and the morphology of such families. While I have indicated that not all males in a *chia* need necessarily be regarded as coparceners, I certainly agree that in the property-owning sense "a stem family is also joint" (Freedman 1966:49), and that a new morphological term is needed. But habit and a conservative commitment to standardization limit me to the old usage.

With the jural adulthood of sons, the Chinese family came under a constant tension produced by the conflict between unifying forces on the one hand and those making for fragmentation on the other. The major divisive force was generated precisely by the equal rights to the *chia* estate held by the brothers; they now had the choice of staying together or fragmenting into smaller family units. It seems clear that the continuation of family unity was encouraged by situations where the advantages, especially economic, derived from such unity outweighed those forthcoming for the parties concerned in the event of partition. The nature of the Chinese family's sensitivity to economic factors has been summarized by C. K. Yang:

> The Chinese family . . . was like a balloon, ever ready to expand when there was wealth to inflate it. As soon as there was enough land or other forms of production to employ the married sons, they would remain in their father's household, with property and in-

come managed in common under the leadership and authority of the parents, and the process of expansion of the small household into a "big family" began. Should wealth increase, the membership of the family would expand further by adding concubines and their children. The longer life span of the well-to-do also augmented the size of the expanding family. Sufficient economic means being a necessary ingredient, the "big family" was more common among large landowners and well-to-do merchants than average peasants and workers. (C. K. Yang 1959a:9)

Whether it was hastened or delayed by a family's particular set of economic activities, the implications of division were the same for each family. Family division was a jural act; together with partition of property there was termination of many kinds of obligations. In the final analysis, the responsibilities of kinship in a post-division situation were quite contingent; the separate families headed by brothers could suffer or enjoy very different fates. The implications of division were well understood by Smith, who was

struck with the undoubted fact that the mere act of dividing a property seems to extinguish all sense of responsibility whatever for the nearest of kin. It is often replied when we ask why a Chinese does not help his son or his brother who has a large family and nothing in the house to eat, "We have divided some time ago." (Smith 1970:251)

For some, the result of family division was the acquisition of one of the more ambivalent statuses involved in Chinese family organization. Often enough, partition occurred when one or both parents were still alive but well advanced in years; under such circumstances elderly parents might find that their family had been divided out from under them, with the new families headed by their sons undertaking to support the parents collectively. A common arrangement was for the parents to eat in rotation among the new families, while living in quarters their sons had agreed to set aside (Fei 1939:74; Johnston 1910:150; Smith 1970:251). In one sense, parents involved in such an arrangement can be said to be members of more than one family and household; in another sense, however, they are somewhat less than full members of any family, because this kind of collective arrangement for the father's support following division means that he is no longer coparcener to any portion of the old family estate. There are several cases of this sort in Yen-liao, where the father gave up his rights most readily under pressures generated by a combination of advanced age and a meager estate; the father was too old to directly retain and cultivate a share of the land, while his sons were unwilling to set aside and work a plot specifically for their parent's support, a procedure frequently followed when land and other holdings are sufficient. Since parents who are supported jointly by their sons in a post-division context have in fact been deprived of their family membership, I call them "collective dependents."

A man becomes a collective dependent because of the nature and timing of family division. His age is not a direct factor, and more generally there is in Yen-liao far from a one-to-one relationship between a person's age and the family statuses he holds; the transfer of financial management from father to son, the attainment of jural adulthood and other status changes are not simply linked to a person's "life cycle," but are involved with family organization. If division produces collective dependents, decisions within the family often determine whether a student is to go on with school or enter the family work force.

Different patterns of family development involve not only changes in *chia* group composition but also changes in the interconnections of the group with the other two components of *chia* organization. As I have noted, scholars have usually discussed the *chia* only as it takes the form of a concentrated group, a concentrated estate, and an inclusive economy. To illustrate development under such circumstances, I shall choose—somewhat arbitrarily—to view a *chia*, newly formed through division, which consists of a man, his wife, and some unmarried children. They derive their income from land they own or rent. All live together in one household, and if there are secondary sources of income, these are combined with that derived from working the land. Let it be further assumed that the estate remains sufficient to provide for the rearing and livelihood of the younger generation. These children, all still at home, enter their adulthood; the daughters may marry out and the elder of the sons—there are two of them—obtains a wife.

Shortly thereafter, the second son also marries. The sons' wives contribute to the family economy and they have children of their own. The group is now complex, consisting of two *fang* in the second generation. The parents die, but the two *fang* continue to live together for a period of time. Finally, each demands complete control over its share of the estate, and the *chia* divides.

The above sketch of Chinese family development has been frequently described. (See Freedman 1961–62:347.) A conjugal family develops into a stem family (Lang's definition does not necessarily imply the existence of the *famille souche* pattern described by Levy [1949:55–56]), and after the marriage of the second son the family becomes joint and then, with the death of the parents, fraternal-joint. Although the three components have remained in unchanging relationship with each other throughout the history of this *chia*, with alternative patterns of development the connections between the components could change. In a situation in which the estate and group are concentrated and the economy is inclusive, there were many possibilities. Simon's account of the history of Ouang-Ming-Tse's family illustrates some of these (Simon 1887:209ff.; cited by Freedman 1958:23ff.). Simon records Ming-Tse's description of the development of the *chia* headed by his paternal grandfather:

> At that time my grandfather was far from rich. . . . When the number of children was found to be on the increase, it was decided that the boys should learn trades, and go to town to add to the common weal. My father was the one to begin. He had six brothers and sisters younger than himself, and chose the trade of carpenter. His apprentice fees were paid for three years, and his wants provided for until he was able to maintain himself. He was soon, however, able to save something to bring home to the fortnightly meetings. Three other sons followed his example, and my father increased the size of his field with their savings, pushing back the boundaries, and as soon as he could give employment to one of them, he recalled him. Only one, the youngest, remained at Fou-Cheou [Foochow] and became one of the first merchants in the town. (Simon 1887:226–27.)

Of his father's two older brothers, one was already established as a government official and the other had remained on the farm throughout (Simon 1887:226). How the official achieved his success is not made clear, nor is it indicated why the youngest brother never returned. During many of the years that it existed, then, this group was dispersed. While they were apprentices, the boys remained *chia* dependents. Next came a period of self-support, which meant exclusion, followed by a re-entry, into the economy, first through remittances sent home and then through participation once more in the exploitation of the estate. No information is provided about the presence or absence of economic ties between the estate on the one hand, and the official and the merchant on the other. If there were no such ties, these two remained members of the group only insofar as they demanded their shares at time of division (*ibid.*:230).

Though this is a success story not duplicated by the majority of *chia* in China, it does illustrate some of the more important junctures that must have characterized the development of many of them. The first of these is the initial dispersion of the group, most often on the basis of decisions made by the family head regarding junior members of the group. In situations where there was only one son—we have noted that this may have been quite common—dispersion might occur only in the face of extreme poverty (see Fei and Chang 1949:272), natural calamities, or war; for in ordinary circumstances, the primary concern was the continued exploitation of the estate. For the poor with more than one son, dispersion was often a grim necessity forced upon them by the inability of their land to support many people. Nevertheless, dispersion was tied in with the notion that diversification of the economy into nonagricultural activities was one means of achieving success, and there are good indications that the advantages in such an arrangement were recognized by poor and rich alike. The poor often made the attempt, or wished they could, and the rich frequently owed their favorable position to successful implementation of diversification schemes. While entry into officialdom was perhaps the single most important route to success in traditional times, the family support required for this might be only one aspect of a tendency to invest in many directions. The following passage from Chow Yung-teh's study of Kunyang County, in Yunnan

Province, is suggestive: "In large families, the members were distributed among different occupations. Some took up agriculture, some became scholars, and some became merchants. This diversity was one of the reasons the gentry family was powerful" (1966:113).

Chow's analysis is based upon material gathered in the 1940s, but his findings indicate the maintenance of a pattern well established during the preceding imperial epoch. Ho (1962:291) has called the traditional inclination to diversify "the policy of family division of labor" and he notes that it was "fairly common in Ming-Ch'ing times." For example, Ho describes the way one man managed his sons' careers after making a fortune in the Yang-chou salt trade: "He apprenticed his eldest son to the salt trade, . . . entrusted his second son with managing the family property . . . and gave fullest opportunity to serious studies to his brilliant youngest son" (*ibid*:290).

I would suggest that the tendency to diversify was also found among the peasantry, but was less obvious. Peasants were prone to marry at a later age and have fewer children survive to maturity, so that in many cases available labor must have been absorbed in the cultivation of family lands. Among the very poor, with little or no land, the effort was to obtain minimal subsistence by any means available. But given a land base of some sort, the hope of economic advancement through diversification might enable the poor to rationalize their desire for many sons. This was noted by Martin Yang in his study of a village in Shantung:

> When a son is born to a poor family, he is not looked upon as someone who will further divide the family's land but as someone who will add to it. . . . The parents begin to hope that when their sons are grown up, one will be a hired laborer, another a mason, and they will earn not only their living but add another fifty dollars or so to the family every year. (M. Yang 1945:84)

As an example of the successful realization of this desire to diversify, Yang describes a joint family consisting of a father, four married sons, and their wives and children. The *chia* group was dispersed, but the economy was inclusive and the estate concentrated: two brothers worked outside and sent remittances home, while the other two continued to till the family lands. After the father died, the family continued to live together for "almost a decade" (M. Yang:238). Yang indicates why this was so:

> the economic reason was especially emphasized. The brothers believed that none of them could have a secure livelihood if the common property were to be divided into four parts, because each would be too small to support a family of six or seven persons. Besides, the two remaining brothers would find it hard to work the fields without each other's help. (*ibid.*)

It was quite possible for diversification to develop while the *chia* group continued to be concentrated. However, an effort to diversify in a rural setting often, if not usually, meant leaving one's parents and home community for a length of time (Fei and Chang 1949:271ff.; Chow 1966:117). The physical mobility associated with such attempts to diversify the *chia* economy must be kept distinct from that possibly resulting from family division. In Yen-liao there were several cases of brothers converting their portions of the estate into cash at the time of division, and leaving the village to seek their fortunes elsewhere. R. F. Johnston describes a similar situation in Shantung during the last years of Ch'ing:

> If as a result of repeated divisions the family property has become . . . small . . . or the family is so large that an equal division would leave each with too little for his support, the usual arrangement is for the entire property to be mortgaged or sold to the nearest relatives who are willing to buy. The cash proceeds are then divided equally among the brothers, who separate to seek their fortunes, each according to his bent. (Johnston 1910:153)

These men had participated in the dismemberment of the *chia;* those who leave while still belonging to the original *chia* group might very well be concerned with promoting the *chia's* survival and advancement.

Following the dispersion of the group, the issue then became one of success or failure. Here, of course, the rich had advantages over the poor, for unless he was supported by a lineage or

some other source of non-*chia* funds, a youth leaving the farm
was unlikely to get a chance to compete in the examinations.
For the very rich, even if a career outside officialdom were intended, the influence that could be brought to bear by powerful
members of a group would probably ensure success in most
cases. Apprenticeship was a common means of effecting the
dispersion of the group. Within this category some positions
were more desirable than others, so here prior ties and influence also played a part (see Fried 1953:185ff.).

In terms of the *chia* economy, success meant the onset of
remittances, and there are good reasons to believe that most
persons did send home a portion of their earnings. Yang has
spoken of this in general terms:

> Most of the villagers who seek work in the city . . . sent their
> earnings back to their homes to be used to buy land and build
> houses for the family. If they are married, the wives and children
> remain in the family home. If they were single when they left the
> village, they usually return to marry a girl chosen by the family.
> (M. Yang 1945:228)

Though this passage perhaps overstates the case, it does provide some clues about why this tendency could be so prevalent.
Through partition a son often established economic independence from his parents as well as his brothers. This was observed in Shantung, by Arthur H. Smith: "It not infrequently
happens that one of the sons becomes disenchanted and com-
missions one of the neighbors to tell the father that it is time to
effect a division" (Smith 1970:251; see also Johnston 1910:149;
Fei 1939:66ff. provides examples from central China). However, this rarely, if ever, occurred before his marriage (Fei
1939:66ff.). In all probability, most sons who went out to work
did so at an early age, so that paternal authority might in itself
be sufficient to ensure that they faithfully sent home a portion
of their earnings. And there were compelling reasons for the father to see that a youth living outside would send home as
much of his income as possible. Matters of support aside, if his
son had married brothers working the estate, there was already
the possibility of family division. The sons remaining at home
also were quite anxious for remittances from their younger

brother, which could enable them to expand the estate or at least reduce the burden of rents or other expenses. After marriage, the person working outside was now cooperating with his equals, for if he was earning money for the estate, his brothers were exploiting it for all. Thus both before and after his marriage, the additional source of income, contributing to the maintenance of the estate as a whole, served to counter divisive tendencies that might develop between the *fang*.

If remittances were sufficient to provide for the expansion of the estate, this might provide the outside worker with a job back home; or a dispersed group might be formed (or maintained) by the expansion of the estate to different locales, and the setting up of new households. Ouang-Ming-Tse noted that his younger brother living in Foochow had bought some land in the village, "which is cultivated by his eldest son." He added that "when he gives up his business to two of his sons, as he soon will do, he will return here" (Simon 1887:227). It cannot be determined from the text if this simply meant a shift from one to the other of the two households containing the *chia* group, or if family division is implied. Similar dispersed estates and their associated households were observed in Taiwan, where mobility was pronounced.

It is probable that many, if not most, of those who went out looking for work were failures. Failure did not necessarily mean an inability to survive, for the critical standard was whether survival was accompanied by remittances. In fact, failure, like success, might sometimes result in a return to the original *chia* household, and such a return could also occur during times of war or other disturbances. In Nanching, before 1933, for instance, there were about one hundred families with "long-term" emigrants. By 1948–51, war and economic depression had forced many of the emigrants to return, so the number of such families had been reduced to forty or fifty (C. K. Yang 1959b:71).

The *chia* group, then, was distinguished by the potential of its membership to rejoin the *chia* economy and household, as well as by the possession of an estate. The possibility arises that a good deal of the movement of persons in Chinese society, movement connected with "horizontal" or "vertical" social and economic mobility (Ho 1962), or with efforts to achieve such mobility, in fact occurred within a *chia* framework.

The *chia* is still the basic domestic unit in present-day Yen-liao, and I have suggested that in Taiwan the retention of much of the traditional structure of rural society was a direct expression of policies adopted by the Japanese and maintained under the Chinese Nationalists. It must be said, however, that the Chinese administration, operating in terms of its own historical tradition, has been somewhat less consistent in applying this policy precisely with regard to matters of the family. When Japan surrendered, the Chinese legal system as it had developed up to 1945 was applied to Taiwan. The new laws were very much unlike those decreed for the island by the Japanese, who codified but maintained many earlier practices. The Nationalist code, among other things, gave sons and daughters the right to inherit their father's property equally. If this right of inheritance had been widely exercised, the *chia* as a framework of family life would probably have been destroyed or modified beyond recognition. But while the law may have some applicability to urban areas, in rural society it has not (so far at least) been used to implement changes that would undermine traditional family organization.

In Yen-liao the *chia* is the major property-owning unit, even though it has no legal existence as such in terms of the contemporary national legal system. Most Yen-liao plots are registered at the local Land Office in the names of single individuals, though some are registered jointly—especially those used for residences. The way land is registered is relevant to *chia* composition and ownership, but in no way do the records indicate that it is the *chia* which as a unit owns land, and that the transmission of land across generations is associated with family partition.

One of the connections between the local system of property relationships and land registration is that *chia* land is indeed registered in the names of different members; a father, his sons, and sometimes grandsons. The father's death is followed, sometimes several years later, by the reregistration of his land in the name of one or more of his sons. Since such local practices are in conflict with contemporary inheritance laws, the legal problem is resolved by having women sign away all claims when they marry or upon their father's death. Both the distribution of land registration among male *chia* members, and the surrender by women of their rights to land, by now are quite standardized procedures. In a sense, they have become customary responses to the threat to traditional practices posed by a legal system that stresses individualism and equality of the sexes with respect to property.

I do not imply that the state-supported legal code in Taiwan is ineffectual, although this appears to have been the case over much of mainland China during the Nationalist period (see McAleavy 1955). Quite the contrary, its present effectiveness is demonstrated by the implementation of the Land Reform laws (see Gallin 1966:93–98), which were used to support policy, and by the fact that many practices survive only insofar as they are rendered legal. There have been several instances where inheritance claims that violated local procedures were nevertheless pressed, and resulted in court decisions favorable to the plaintiff. These cases occurred shortly after Taiwan was restored to Chinese rule, and involved mainlander men married to local women; the latter were encouraged by their husbands to demand their share of the land registered in their deceased fathers' names. The defendants, of course, were the women's brothers, who were forced to make cash settlements. It was precisely disputes of this sort in Mei-nung which popularized the practice of demanding, as a condition of marriage to a mainlander, that the woman's inheritance rights be waived before the wedding. That this is now done points to the continuing authority of the *chia*. The threat to customary practices originated in marriages contracted with men who at least initially were not involved in social and economic relationships organized within the same local context that lends *chia* organization support.

We can now provide an overview of the domestic arrangements that currently characterize Yen-liao's entire population. I have outlined in Tables 10, 11, and 12 the situation as of May 31, 1965; the tables show, first of all, that family affairs were by no means localized within the village; while one family has a secondary household in Yen-liao, about 13 percent of *chia* group members are absent from the village's primary households (Table 10). Given almost the entire body of evidence from mainland China and Taiwan, the distribution of family forms within Yen-liao's households is quite remarkable; joint units, though outnumbered by simpler types, are found in nearly one-third of all households, which in fact contain 54.7 percent of Yen-liao's population. Joint household size averages 17.1 persons, with the smallest household containing 9 people and the largest 30. Table 12 shows that, with regard to family form, there is in fact very little difference between primary households and entire *chia* groups; only two *chia* groups, one joint and one stem, are so dispersed as to be represented in Yen-liao by stem and conjugal households. The large number of joint families and households means that we can more readily generalized as to how they are organized; also, a situation where many joint families are maintained within a small village must surely offer important clues as to the general principles behind joint family formation and continuity.

Table 10
Primary Household—*Chia* Group Relationships,
Yen-liao, May 31, 1965

Primary households	No. of households	Resident chia members	Non-resident chia members with economic ties to primary household [a]	Non-resident members without economic ties	Total chia group membership	Percentage of chia group members resident in Yen-liao
conjugal	32	185	16	1	202	91.6
stem	14	127	13	10	150	84.7
joint	22	377	34	30	441	85.5
Totals	68	689	63	41	793	86.9

[a] Including students away from home and men drafted for military duty.

Table 11

Resident Population According to Household Relationships,
Yen-liao, May 31, 1965

| | *Households of concentrated* chia *groups or primary households of dispersed groups* | | | | *Secondary household* | *Collective dependents* [a] |
	conjugal	*stem*	*joint*	*total*		
Number	32	14	22	68	1 [b]	
Percentage of total	47.0	20.6	32.4	100.0		
Total membership	185	127	377	689	8	8
Percentage of total household membership	26.9	18.4	54.7	100.0		
	Total resident population:			705		

[a] Parents jointly supported by sons who have already separated into several *chia*.

[b] This household is one of several maintained by a *chia* with 42 members; the economy of the *chia* is inclusive and their primary household is in a hamlet not far from Yen-liao.

Table 12

Structure of Yen-Liao *Chia* Groups
and Their Primary Households

| | | *Primary household in Yen-liao* | | |
Chia *group*		*joint*	*stem*	*conjugal*
joint	23	22	1	
stem	14		13	1
conjugal	31			31
Totals	68	22	14	32

CHAPTER 4

The Conjugal Family

WE HAVE seen that there can be changes in household residence as a family grows more complex. In Yen-liao, the members of conjugal families are most likely to be concentrated within one household, for constraints on dispersion are much greater if family membership is limited to father, mother, and dependent children. Family organization is at its simplest under such circumstances, which I shall refer to as Stage 1 of conjugal family development. In Stage 2, the children begin to contribute to the family economy; the alternative is for the children to live away from the primary household as economically autonomous *chia* group members, an arrangement I also include within Stage 2.

In Yen-liao's 20 Stage 1 conjugal families husband and wife reside in one household and constitute the entire work force; while the husband may have a job off the farm, the important roles of family manager and family worker are less clearly defined in these units than in more complex families, and in the management of family funds there is likewise not a sharp distinction between husband and wife. In all of these families the husband's dominance and the wife's domestic responsibilities are obvious constants. From the point of view of family development, however, it is more useful to consider how the economic relationship between the spouses can vary from family to family and be influenced by different economic activities.

Occupational specialization at Stage 1 in part manifests a sexual differentiation of work roles which remains constant throughout the course of family development. Only men undertake most traditional lines of nonagricultural work, such as carpentry, metal-working, Chinese medicine, and the like, which require specialized training. Cooking, washing and mending clothes, and caring for small children are primarily women's work. Pig-rearing is an important agricultural sideline for most Yen-liao families, and daily fodder preparations and feeding also form part of the women's domestic routine.

Work role differentiation between husband and wife is less emphasized in the management and cultivation of the family farm. Such differentiation is also less prominent in poorer families with small holdings; both spouses frequently work as short-term wage laborers in the Yen-liao area, and for some landless families this employment may be the only source of income. Other forms of employment for wives are closely linked to their domestic work, as is the case with one woman (family C13) [1] who tends a grocery store which also serves as her family's residence, and with another who helps run a refreshment stand adjacent to her home (family C16). These women must care for young children; by helping to run a household-based family shop they can give more time to earning income than those women who must try to combine farming or wage labor with similar domestic responsibilities.

I have suggested that in China diversification of family undertakings was traditionally regarded as economically advantageous. Although I emphasized diversification in the complex family, in Yen-liao the tendency to diversify is in fact present even among Stage 1 conjugal families. (I do not include situations where farming or any other single line of work is combined with short-term wage labor, for the latter is resorted to only when inadequate income cannot be supplemented by

1. The family identification code is used for all Yen-liao families, listed in Appendix A.

other means.) At one extreme, diversification is an effort to sat-
isfy the subsistence needs of families with little land and surplus labor; at the other it can be an arrangement profitable in
terms of total family earnings, even though the diversion of family labor may lead to a decrease in farm income through higher
labor costs or reduced productivity. While the resources and en-
trepreneurial skills that can be applied to an attempt at diversification differ from family to family, the ability to diversify is
also conditioned by the small size of the work force and the re-
striction of the wife to household-based activities.

Yet seven of the 20 Stage 1 conjugal families have in fact
diversified their activities. Out of five families where only the
husband has developed nonagricultural specialties there are
four (C2, C4, C9 and C19) where the husbands are "self-
employed" and able to arrange their time in order to join their
wives in working the family farm when they are most needed,
and one (C12) where the man holds a full-time salaried position
that keeps him in his office except during weekends and holi-
days. I have noted the arranging of diversification along somewhat different lines, directly involving the wife in nonagricultural work through the establishment of household-based
enterprises. Husband and wife jointly operate family C13's grocery store and family C8's equipment for grinding glutinous
rice, and agricultural work is likewise shared. The wife's participation in such nonagricultural enterprises becomes feasible by
locating them in the household, and is all the more desirable
when the family labor pool is limited to two persons. Family
C9's Lung-tu tailor shop is managed by a man whose wife only
does farming and domestic work; the tailor shop had to be located in a larger settlement, but its operator notes that if his
wife could have helped one of his three workers need not have
been hired.

When considering diversification, it should not be forgotten
that even within agriculture there can be a variety of undertakings and it is safe to say that a proliferation of agricultural lines
and the development of nonagricultural specialties are both expressions of the traditional strategy. To illustrate the consider-

able involvement of a Stage 1 conjugal family in economic activities on and off the farm we turn again to family C8, Yeh Po-pin's household.

Po-pin and his brothers divided their family in 1960. Their father, still alive, had moved to a temple 25 years earlier and severed economic ties with his family. The division settlement gave Po-pin .43 *chia* of paddy land, .27 *chia* of dry land, and a small amount of uncultivatable wasteland; he also received two rooms of the family's portion of the compound, some pigpens, and a water buffalo pen. The family had a tobacco house before division and a tobacco quota of .90 *chia* registered in Po-pin's name. Though the registration was not changed, each brother got one-third of the original quota and they continue to share the tobacco house; they also "share" their mother, who eats in rotation at each of the three households. Po-pin sold his rooms in the compound to his brothers a few years after the division and built a new house in a corner of one of his fields; he also built fishponds and an expanded complex of pigsties. Now his paddy land is reduced to .30 *chia*, enough for his share of the tobacco quota. After tobacco harvest he plants rice on .20 *chia* of paddy and leaves the remainder for sweet potatoes; he grows sugarcane on his dry fields, raises many pigs, and keeps his fishpond well stocked.

Po-pin graduated from a well-regarded agricultural school and many in the village say this accounts for the higher-than-average yields from his farm. His education prepared him for veterinary work in Yen-liao and surrounding areas, where he also sells livestock medicine. He recently invested in a motorized grinding machine, which he and his wife use mainly for pig food preparation but also to process glutinous rice brought by local women at the approach of festivals like the Lunar New Year. Such festivals used to be preceded by an afternoon of drudgery for the women, who had to spend hours at large stone grinders preparing flour for holiday sweetcakes; but now they are freed by a small payment to Po-pin (or to a Yen-liao rice mill which has installed a similar device).

The general management of family enterprises may be distinguished from fiscal management and control. The first involves the disposition of family workers and the operation of the family farm or other enterprises, while the second concerns family funds.

With respect to general management, the husband's supremacy in Stage 1 conjugal families reflects the prevalent pattern of male dominance. Yet managerial responsibilities are shared by husband and wife to varying degrees. Their authority is most nearly equal in the poorest families owning little or no land and dependent upon miscellaneous short-term wage labor, where management involves little more than looking for work, often on a day-to-day basis; and the almost desperate economic circumstances of such people provide ample motivation for both spouses to independently seek and accept whatever jobs may be available. Even under such circumstances the husband's dominant position is to a certain extent confirmed by his status as family head (*chia-chang*), for at the very least he is in a position to obtain most of the information about job opportunities. People looking for workers tend to come to him first for commitments on his wife's behalf as well as his own; he is also more readily able to directly seek work at the homes of prospective employers. The wife finds for herself only a minority of the jobs she holds during the year, and she provides her husband with an even smaller proportion of his year's work. During the busiest farming periods she usually is reluctant to make any commitments without first confirming that her husband has not already arranged for their work.

Management is largely monopolized by the husband in families exclusively dependent upon their farms (C1, C10, C11, and C18); he sets the time for major agricultural activities, arranges for the hire or exchange of labor, and assigns his wife her farming duties. But the woman is by no means a passive bystander; she is fully aware of the farm's situation and does not hesitate to discuss it, and she frequently assumes full responsibility when her husband is ill or attending to other matters. When she participates in harvest or other team labor it is generally understood by the other workers, especially if they are hired, that her aim is as much to check on their performance as it is to do her own work.

The two patterns of diversification into nonfarming activities have different implications for the arrangement of managerial responsibilities. The wife's role in farm management has broadened in the five families where the husband has monopolized nonagricultural work. Owing to the small amount of land cultivated by family C4 throughout the year and by family C19 between tobacco seasons, the women merely must tend to routine tasks such as minor weeding, and the "self-employed" men can readily adjust their schedules and be at work on the farm during the busier periods. Families C2 and C9 have larger holdings and cultivate tobacco. The women are more actively involved in management—sometimes they supervise the hired workers—but the two men are able to return when farming is most hectic; family C9's tailor shop in Lung-tu closes on tobacco harvest days and its workers are added to the harvest team.

In family C12 the woman plays a larger role than her husband (who has a full-time clerical job) in supervising daily farm activities. The woman has no one else to care for her small children and so cannot participate directly in most farm work. She gives directions to the workers, upon whom the family overwhelmingly depends, and sporadically oversees their activities. Her husband, however, hires most of them and supervises them on weekends.

Diversification through the establishment of household-based enterprises keeps the husband in close contact with the family farm but also involves the wife in nonagricultural management. This arrangement is most pronounced in family C13, which among Yen-liao's conjugal families has the largest land holdings. These are given to long-term crops only, including sugarcane, bananas, and fruit trees, and cultivated entirely by paid workers. Except at meals, the couple is rarely seen together; if the husband is in the store his wife is usually in the fields, but if the wife is tending the store the husband may very well be on one of his frequent business trips. He still has the dominant managerial position in the family and in most cases handles such matters as purchases from wholesalers and recruitment of field workers.

Male dominance also characterizes financial management in Stage 1 conjugal families, but again there are considerable differences in the extent to which this dominance is expressed. Such differences are all the more apparent because in Yen-liao it is commonly held that funds ought to be kept in the household and be accessible to husband and wife in common. Most families do adhere to this norm, but a minority keep no common store of cash, and in the others there is considerable variation with respect to the amount of money a man is willing to dispose of in this fashion; and those wives who can take cash directly from the till may nevertheless have varying degrees of managerial control over family funds in general.

Variations in the disposition of family funds are due in part to factors idiosyncratic from the point of view of the family economy, and in part to economic considerations. The idiosyncratic elements can be most pronounced in families dependent on farming or on a single nonagricultural, household-based enterprise, for such occupations pose no obstacle to a man inclined to keep all funds in his pocket. A case in point would be family C14, where the husband is a barber who enjoys gambling, drinking, and making love in the wine houses. He keeps money in a drawer while at work in the shop, and takes it all with him when he leaves. He gives his wife only what she needs at the moment for household expenditures.

Among the economic factors conditioning financial management are a family's wealth and occupational situation. Wealthier families keep money in banks, or with the Farmer's Association, more for security than investment; the husband controls the deposits and withdrawals of such funds. Their assets may include funds brought in by the wife's activities, but such a situation implies the presence of jointly managed enterprises where it is difficult or impossible for the husband to be sole manager of fiscal affairs. So, for example, the operation of family C13's grocery store requires that sizable sums of money be accessible to husband and wife. When the man is supervising the farm or away on business his wife must make decisions regarding purchases, credit, and payment as she deals with customers or wholesalers.

In family C8, headed by Yeh Po-pin, the wife's involvement in fiscal affairs is more limited. Yeh directly controls the bulk of family earnings through his veterinary work and by overseeing the sale of pigs, tobacco, and other crops. Either may supervise sales of fish and the processing of glutinous rice, but Yeh receives all funds that first come into his wife's hands. Yeh himself handles all investments or expenditures connected with the upkeep of family enterprises. The small amount of cash kept at home is used by his wife only for food and other daily necessities.

There is a very sharp distinction between general and financial management in family C12. Lin T'ung-hsing, his wife, and four children of preschool age are supported in part by Lin's job at the Farmer's Association, where he is a clerk, and also by the family farm of .63 *chia*. The family grows no tobacco but uses hired labor to harvest annually two rice crops and a "winter" crop of sweet potatoes, while pig-rearing is as usual the wife's responsibility. Financial control is completely in Lin's hands, though I noted earlier that his wife has the dominant role in farm management. Part of Lin's monthly salary is used to clear up some of the debts that accumulate from one payday to the next, while Lin keeps the remainder in his pocket. Lin controls other family income by disposing of field produce and hogs through agencies of the Farmer's Association. In the absence of a family till, Lin's wife must directly approach her husband when she needs money for household expenses or to pay workers.

As long as only husband and wife have productive roles, the family economy is at its simplest. The situation changes during a conjugal family's second stage of development, when one of the dependent children assumes a productive role. The parents remain the main actors during Stage 2, and there are similar variations in their own economic relationships; but their economic responsibilities are now clearly differentiated from those of their working children.

All children are still single in seven of Yen-liao's 12 Stage 2 conjugal families (C21–27), while in the remainder some sons have already separated from their fathers (C28–29) or daughters have married out (C30–32). The unmarried person who contributes to the family economy is involved in fiscal management only to a slight extent, if at all; he turns earnings over to his parents or works for the family. If a common fund is kept, he has no direct access to it; whatever money he gets comes either from his father or from both parents, depending on the extent to which they share access to family funds.

A man who heads a Stage 2 conjugal family is more sharply defined as the manager of his family's finances than is the husband in families at Stage 1. This is especially evident if there are single family members working outside, for all other things being equal the father expects to receive their earnings. My own inquiries reveal that wages of single workers living with their parents in Yen-liao are turned over to their fathers in every case (at least as far as the father knows). All of these resident workers are short-term wage laborers whose jobs are most frequently in or near Yen-liao; their fathers with little difficulty can find out exactly how much they earn. The employers are almost inevitably on familiar terms with their workers' parents; when looking for workers they often approach the fathers, and they sometimes directly pay the latter the son's wages. A father's control over his children's economic activities is thus strengthened by the context of local society. This is not uncommonly a bitter pill for the worker to swallow, but the taste is somewhat sweetened by the understanding that he may keep some pocket money for refreshments and entertainment, and I am told by several men responsible for their family's finances that this kind of allowance amounts to between 20 and 30 percent of total wages. Since short-term wage labor usually brings in no more than NT$25.00 daily, NT$7.50 would be the most retained; out of this most men spend NT$5.50 for a day's pack of "New Paradise Cigarettes," the most popular brand.

Paternal control is equally strong when single workers live away from home but remain in the village. A boy from family C31 and another from a joint family eat and sleep in the Yen-liao households where they are full-time servants; one works for relatives in his own compound, the other for a nonrelated neighbor. In each case, the employer household forwards the wages directly to the worker's father, after setting aside some pocket money for the worker.

In Stage 2 there is the first appearance of the redistributive system which remains important in the economic life of more complex families; the roles of redistributor and financial manager may be restricted to the father exclusively, or to varying degrees shared with his wife, but certainly not with their children. When the children receive money or other forms of support it is for particular purposes, while their contributions to the family may be disposed of by their parents in a variety of ways. Thus when such wage earners spend large sums they in fact are using redistributed family funds. A young man from family C21 was one of many Yen-liao workers who spent several weeks converting a wealthy family's stony and uneven fields to plots suitable for wet rice cultivation. His earnings paid for a second-hand bicycle far superior to the very battered and faulty vehicle he had ridden previously, but the purchase had been approved by his widowed mother, and was made only after the money had passed through her hands.

The redistributive role in Stage 2 conjugal families is added to the others monopolized within the husband–wife unit, and the range of variations increases accordingly. But a glance at the particular arrangements in one family (C29) should suffice to illustrate the interconnections among the elements of economic organization discussed so far. Although Kuo Hsun-lai's four eldest sons now head independent family units, his own still includes his wife, daughter, and three more sons. Kuo has one son in the air force and another in junior middle school; the other two children contribute to the family together with Kuo and his wife, who is concerned mainly with domestic work. Kuo is 63 and lets his children do the heavier work on the family's .60 *chia* farm, while their work outside also adds to the family income. Kuo and his wife both hold keys to a closet drawer which is one receptacle for family funds, the other being Kuo's shirt pocket. Cash in the drawer is replenished or withdrawn by Kuo as he sees fit, while his wife accounts to him for the money she removes for her own purposes or for their children, who can also ask Kuo for funds. Kuo receives the outside earnings of family members. His son often works as a banana packer for the local branch of the Fruit Grower's Cooperative; together with his wages he gives his father a slip of paper on which the Cooperative itemizes pay according to hours worked. Kuo knows the local farmers who employ his children, he says, and the wages they provide.

Three members of Stage 2 conjugal families are single persons living and earning incomes outside of Yen-liao (C22, C25, and C27); they cannot be controlled as strictly as workers in the village, but two of the nonresidents (one is female) regularly send remittances home (C22 and C25) and all three remain tied to their Yen-liao families by economic obligations within a redistributive framework. On the one hand they are requested to remit funds according to their earnings and in consideration of family needs, and on the other they receive the same support due other family members and can return to Yen-liao when they are ill, unemployed, or beset with other problems.

When a father launches his children onto their working careers, his authority is transformed into a claim for the family over their future earnings or labor; this claim is now reinforced by the children's powerful counterclaims to a proper marriage at the appropriate time. As conjugal families turn complex, redistributive relationships remain organized through clearly defined economic roles, which are characteristic of any family whose working members are not confined to a single husband–wife unit. But in the complex family the redistributive arrangements are supported by the new rights of adulthood conferred through marriage upon the boy who stays with his natal family and likewise upon the girl who enters her husband's household.

CHAPTER 5

Complex Family Organization

IN THE COMPLEX family, ties among adult males replace the dominance of adults over minors as the main support of family organization. The basis of the jural equality of married men in a family is that each is a coparcener to the estate and can demand its partition. Such men must be satisfied with each other's behavior. In this context we shall first consider some of the circumstances under which a *chia* group can develop a *chia* estate that is concentrated or dispersed, and a *chia* economy that is inclusive or noninclusive.

Decisions made by a father when his sons are still jural and economic dependents have a crucial bearing on the *chia* group's subsequent residential and economic arrangements. Many of these decisions concern the son's education, which in some cases can be terminated because of his family's poverty or need for labor; in others the education can be managed so that his future employment will be assured, while at the same time family expenditures will be minimized; and in yet others the son may be given full support and be encouraged to proceed as far as his capabilities allow.[1]

181190

1. In Taiwan, a six-year elementary school education is compulsory, while nursery schools and kindergartens are becoming increasingly popular; after elementary school a student may go on to junior (three-year) and senior (three-

Certain decisions regarding a boy's education can contribute to the development of economically noninclusive and residentially dispersed *chia* groups. Table 13 lists the 40 persons who are economically autonomous but belong to *chia* groups whose primary households in Yen-liao are stem in one case and joint in six. The parents of the 11 men holding jobs allowed their sons to continue in school so that after graduation they might qualify for better salaried employment. The career officer and the policeman in J18 are brothers; their family was able to support their studies at Mei-nung's junior middle school, but lack of funds made attendance at a better senior middle school impossible. Neither could they be absorbed into the family labor force, which was already large and supplementing farm income with wage labor. Both men were encouraged by their father and older brothers to take the entrance examinations of the provincial normal schools; these are tuition-free and guarantee future employment as an elementary school teacher, but for these very reasons the competition was (and still is) severe and the brothers failed. Their family nevertheless was determined to assure them independent livelihoods; they were sent to neighboring Ch'i-shan's senior middle school, admission to which is easy because the school is inadequate as a training ground for the college entrance examinations, and after graduation the options of both brothers were restricted. Pressure on the older brother, now with the police, was less severe; he took entrance tests at the provincial normal university, which produces senior middle school teachers, and at an officer's training school. He gained admission only to the latter, where attendance carries with it a commitment to many years of military service that most men find undesirable, but convinced his family to let him remain home and try for the police academy a year later. The younger brother was only given one opportunity to take entrance tests; he was told to enter any tuition-free school that might accept him.

A desire to reduce the number of persons living off family

---

year) middle school and then to a four-year college; or he may go to a variety of three- to six-year technical or professional schools, which accept graduates from junior or senior middle schools.

Table 13
Economically Autonomous Members of *Chia* Groups
with Complex Primary Households in Yen-liao

Chia Groups	Autonomous Units	Residence	Occupation	Dependents	
				Male	Female
S4	Husband, wife, 4 children	Kaohsiung City	*Husband:* Port Official *Wife:* Drugstore Operator	2	2
	Husband, wife, 1 child	Pingtung City	*Husband:* Railroad Administration official *Wife:* Housewife	1	
J4	Husband, wife, 1 child	Brazil	*Husband:* Grows flowers *Wife:* Helps husband	1	
J5	Husband, wife, 4 children	Kaohsiung City	*Husband:* Post Office clerk *Wife:* Housewife	2	2
	Unmarried son	Kaohsiung City	Oil refinery worker		
J7	Husband, wife, 3 children	Kaohsiung City	*Husband:* Policeman *Wife:* Housewife	2	1
	Husband, wife, 2 children	Kaohsiung City	*Husband:* Oil refinery worker *Wife:* Housewife	2	
J11	Husband, wife, 1 child	Taipei	*Husband:* Policeman *Wife:* Housewife	1	
J18	Unmarried son	Kaohsiung City	Policeman		
	Unmarried son	Tainan City	Career Army officer		
J19	Husband, wife, 5 children	Hsin-wei (Liu-kuei Rural District, Kaohsiung County)	*Husband:* Operates Chinese Drugstore *Wife:* Helps husband	2	3

holdings was also a factor influencing the career of the policeman in family J11, although his father allowed him to take the
entrance examinations of several senior middle schools and also
supported his study at "supplementary sessions." [2] But re-

2. "Supplementary sessions," or *pu-hsi-pan* are private tutorial classes which
students must attend if they hope to remain competitive with their peers. *Pu-*

peated failures led to attendance at the Ch'i-shan senior middle school, which was followed by conscription into the armed forces; upon release he was told to immediately attempt to gain admission to the police academy.

None of the other eight men now economically autonomous are college graduates. Five were admitted to five-year agricultural or technical schools following the completion of their studies at junior middle school, and in each case the decision not to attend a four-year senior middle school resulted from failure to gain entrance to those offering good preparation for college; two men educated during the Japanese period graduated from the two-year technical schools to which limited numbers of Taiwanese were admitted following completion of their primary level studies; and the man in family J19 was apprenticed to a practitioner of Chinese medicine after he failed to advance beyond junior middle school.

These eight men had their educations supported so that they might be provided with livelihoods and, hopefully, would advance family fortunes by improving and diversifying the family palette of skills; but planning in the family must confront external factors, such as the school system and the job market, which can have a decisive influence on family organization and form. Thus the man from *chia* group J4 who migrated to Brazil received permission to depart on the grounds that his technical training legally qualified him to accept a formal "job offer"; such "invitations" from "firms" in Brazil provide one of the few legal means to emigrate from Taiwan (as of 1964–65), and they are commonly available for a fee. All six men working for civilian government agencies obtained their positions after passing examinations to which they had been admitted on the basis of their school diplomas. Government jobs of the sort these men

---

hsi-pan are in session during the afternoons, evenings, and weekends of the school year, and for most of the summer "holiday." Students failing the entrance examinations for higher-level schooling prepare themselves for another try by a year's full-time attendance at *pu-hsi-pan*, if their families can afford the tuition. *Pu-hsi-pan* instruction commonly supplements the income of elementary and middle school teachers, who draw from their regular classes most of their tutorial students.

now hold are desirable because their location in big cities involves a variety of fringe benefits; free housing in particular is a direct benefit which encourages most men to bring along their wives and children, so that the latter may profit from the superior schooling available in urban centers.

For one example of the effect of differential examination performance on family development, we can cite events in 1946, one year after Japan's surrender; then the Taiwan Provincial Government for the first and only time conducted civil service examinations for purposes of direct recruitment (since then, there have only been tests to establish qualifications). Three men from Yen-liao, all technical school graduates, entered the competition; one of two who passed is from family S4 and now works for the Taiwan Railway Administration in Pingtung, where he lives with his wife and children; the other, from J7, is with the Kaohsiung port police and lives with his wife and children in that city. The man who failed works for the Mei-nung Township office; he still lives with his parents in Yen-liao, and his wife helps work the family farm. All three men receive approximately NT$1200 per month plus rice allowances and tuition grants for their children.

Among the economically autonomous men are three from *chia* groups J5 and J18 who are still unmarried; we saw in chapter 4 that other persons in this category do send a portion of their earnings back to Yen-liao, the amount reflecting the judgment of the primary household's head. A more complex quid pro quo governs the relationship between the primary households and the eight married men who are separated residentially and economically. These men live outside of Yen-liao together with their wives and children, that is, on a *fang* basis; just as the men do not send remittances to their primary households in Yen-liao, neither are their dependents within the *fang* supported by *chia* resources. Also, these men do not control enterprises or other resources that would provide additional funds; they live solely off their jobs. Only the man in *chia* group J19 has no salaried position; but *chia* funds were in fact used to purchase and stock the Chinese medicine store he operates, and

HARROWING: THE OLD WAY

PLOWING: THE NEW WAY

RICE HARVEST, YEN-LIAO
NOTE "TOBACCO HOUSES" AT REAR

TOBACCO HARVEST

SELLING TOBACCO

GATHERING SUNNED RICE IN COMPOUND

BETROTHAL
GROOM'S PARTY MAKES OFFERING BEFORE ANCESTOR TABLET
AT BRIDE'S SIDE

LOADING THE DOWRY
"TOBACCO HOUSE" TO THE LEFT

DOWRY EN ROUTE TO GROOM'S HOME

GUESTS ARRIVING FOR WEDDING FEAST

BRIDE WITH HER NEW FAMILY, MEI-NUNG, CA. 1935

BRIDE WITH HER NEW FAMILY, 1965

NIGHT-TIME PRAYER TO YEN-LIAO'S
TUTELARY EARTHGOD

ANNUAL FESTIVAL (SECOND-MONTH FESTIVAL),
MEI-NUNG TOWN

while this enterprise is part of the *chia* estate, other *chia* members seem satisfied that it does not generate a profit beyond what is sufficient to support the resident *fang*. A man in *chia* group S4 does have a wife who owns and operates a drugstore; but since she had the store when she married, her case falls into a special situation with respect to the *chia* economy, and we shall be concerned with this situation later (chapter 6).

The absence of other than job-related incomes among married men living away from home with their wives and children and not remitting funds reflects the fact that even such jobs are as much considered a result of *chia* investments as are income-yielding enterprises like the Chinese drugstore. Thus, a man who uses his earnings to support his own wife and children is considered by his equals in the family to be using *chia* funds in order to meet *chia* obligations. Should the man somehow find himself in a position to generate an income considered surplus relative to the immediate needs of other members of his *fang*, he will be expected to turn the excess money over to the primary household for redistribution; these are the circumstances under which autonomous secondary households are confined to those lacking an income in excess of agreed-upon subsistence requirements.

The total *chia* group remains highly visible even when it comprises more than one economically autonomous unit, for there are many forms of social interaction linking the constituent households. *Chia* group members constantly visit back and forth and eat at each other's homes, with the primary household the main center of activity. All members return to their primary household in Yen-liao for the lunar new year celebrations—with the obvious exceptions of some men in the military, persons who have left Taiwan, and those who must keep watch over outside holdings. Other *chia* members live and feast as a unit for several days, and indeed such homecomings may result in overcrowding. This was felt most severely in S4's primary household, which ordinarily has nine members; during the 1965 lunar new year period they shared room and board with another nine persons who otherwise make up two autonomous *fang* living outside in as many households.

Though *chia* members come together for other events, such as weddings, funerals, or local religious celebrations, additional kinsmen and friends show up as guests or play ceremonial roles; in a funeral, for example, the mourning rites distinguish categories of agnates irrespective of their distribution across *chia*. It is only during the lunar new year that the *chia* as a unit presents sacrifices to its ancestors, dines and lives together. Everyone is expected to be with his *chia* on the lunar new year's first day; eating elsewhere or entertaining a non-*chia* member verges on the socially unacceptable, and while isolated individuals such as bachelor mainlander friends may participate in the new year's day feast, their situation is considered rather unfortunate.

The annual assemblage of the *chia* gives ceremonial emphasis to a group which in fact is united by ongoing obligations between its members. I noted earlier that *chia* funds are used to pay for the weddings of members who return to Yen-liao from wherever they may reside; and among these people are those who have never remitted funds to their primary household. For certain purposes the economically autonomous *chia* group members sometimes assume a portion of the expenses that would otherwise be borne by the primary household in Yen-liao. In Yen-liao the joint primary household of family J7 consists of three *fang* headed by brothers in the second generation; two more brothers from the same generation hold jobs in Kaohsiung City and live with their wives and children in two households. Attending school in the same city is the son of one of the brothers still in Yen-liao and this student rooms and boards on a rotation basis with each of his uncles. Again, each of two sisters in *chia* group S4 has at different times lived in her brother's Pingtung household while studying in that city.

The *chia* group thus continues to possess a very real social and jural unity even under conditions of economic and residential fragmentation. But in the final analysis this unity has as its focus the *chia* estate; adult *chia* group members not directly linked to the estate share with those who are a deep interest in the joint holdings, for it is important to all of them that the maintenance of the common body of holdings be compatible with their own interests. In general, men know that they can always call upon *chia* resources or rejoin the primary household should circumstances warrant such actions. In most cases, men return to Yen-liao with their wives and children because of illness or economic failure, but the motive can also be a positive desire for economic advancement.

The importance of the estate for the family's unity is illustrated by the events connected with changes in residential and economic arrangements in J4 when I was in Yen-liao. This *chia* includes a father and his three married sons, the youngest being the man who went to Brazil; before 1964 two of the brothers lived in the Yen-liao household while the youngest had been working in Pingtung for several years and lived there with his wife and infant son. In early 1964 he returned with his wife and child to Yen-liao where they were fully absorbed into the family economy. In February of that year he migrated to Brazil, but his wife and child did not leave until June 1965; once more, the *chia* consisted of two autonomous households. The man now in Brazil was rebuffed by his father and brothers when he first told them of his plans; they did not think he would succeed in that country, and his father was especially opposed to financing the journey with family funds. The youngest son was adamant, however; he warned his father that if he got no family support he would obtain money by demanding partition of the estate and selling his share. At this point, the father and older brothers surrendered to the youngest son; the family borrowed some funds, and a small plot of mountain land was sold, but the family farm remained intact. The *chia* group also survived, and there was no question in anyone's mind that the son's wife and child would remain in the Yen-liao household until they were able to leave Taiwan. In fact, the emigrant was well within his rights when he made his demands; although these generated a great deal of bitterness, the result in reality was an investment of family funds. The *chia* group members remaining in Yen-liao are still far from convinced that their representative in Brazil will succeed, but they certainly wish him well, and they take very seriously the implications of his continuing membership in the *chia*. And my most recent information (1971) is that remittances have begun to arrive.

We are in a better position to appreciate the economic dimensions of *chia* organization once it is understood that the unity of a dispersed group is not dependent upon its members' participation in a common budgetary arrangement. The noninclusive economy can be fully considered along with other possibilities as an expression of the interplay between family arrangements and external factors. Viewed from this perspective, the noninclusive economy is in several respects geared to the economic advancement of the *chia*. Enlargement of the family labor force exploiting the estate may reach the point of diminishing returns, and if some workers find employment elsewhere this alone may increase their economic value to the extent that the estate's output can be used less for subsistence and more for reinvestment. With smaller estates dispersion can be beneficial, even if output only provides for the needs of those remaining in the primary household; people who move out and succeed to the extent that they can provide their own support have in their estate an investment which may at least provide for their survival in the event that their independent undertakings fail. Such a situation is more desirable than one where it may become mandatory to dispose of the holdings created through the partition of a small estate if they are too minuscule to support a family of any size.

There are positive benefits to dispersion: it can be employed as a strategy for advancement in the absence of pressures within the estate, and it can benefit a *chia* precisely because the economic efforts of its members are individualized while the unity of the group is maintained. The noninclusive economy is thus one expression of the diversification strategy; and like others it may be motivated by hardship, ambition, or a combination of both.

During my stay in Yen-liao there were four nonresident salaried workers sending remittances to a like number of complex
primary households. Table 14 shows that the circumstances associated with remittances are quite similar in each case; each
worker is a married man whose wife and children remain in the
Yen-liao primary household. We have seen that funds are not
forthcoming from a man who uses his wages to support his wife
and children in a separate household, and I have suggested that
by providing such support the man in fact satisfies obligations
to the *chia*; from this it follows that notions of rent or payment
for board are not involved in the requirement that a man who
leaves his wife and children behind must send money home.
Such funds are treated as is any income earned by *chia* members, and the wives of men living outside, no less than the other
women, participate in farming or household work.

Table 14
Residential Arrangements Associated with
the Remittance of Funds by Outside Salaried
Workers to Their Primary
Households in Yen-liao [a]

Chia group	Occupation	Location
S10	Salaried worker in Chinese drugstore	Chi-yang, Mei-nung Township
S12	Truck driver	Shan-lin Rural District, Kaohsiung County
S14	Truck driver	Chia-hsien Rural District, Kaohsiung County
J6	Career officer, Air Force	Taichung City

[a] In each instance the worker's status was that of married son,
who lived at the work site. His wife and children lived at the
primary household.

The air force officer in family J6 sent his wife back to Yen-liao in response to urgent requests from his older brother, who complained that there was a shortage of labor for the family farm. Yet with the departure of his wife and children the officer was further obliged to mail the Yen-liao household NT$600 out of his monthly salary of about NT$1000. This officer gets free housing from the government, but the rest of the men living alone were deterred from sending for their wives and children mainly by the costs of establishing a new household.

Five primary households in Yen-liao are linked to non-resident *chia* members who continue to directly exploit the *chia* estate; in Table 15 I summarize the conditions under which these persons work. In most cases the dispersion of residence parallels that of the estate; only in *chia* J14 are there two persons living outside but working together with members of the primary household. Yet these two farmers live outside of Yen-liao because of the expansion of *chia* enterprises, and their situation is thus identical to that of all others listed in Table 15 as "operators." But among the remaining ten it is much more obvious, for they are dispersed in conjunction with the distribution of expanded estates. All of the enterprises located outside of Yen-liao were established through the investment of *chia* funds and thus have a most intimate relationship with the primary households.

One aspect of this relationship is reflected in the absence of a consistent pattern of coresidence with respect to the operators of outside enterprises, their wives, and their children. A *chia* is a cohesive social and economic unit for the exploitation of holdings incorporated into the *chia* estate. If the estate should be dispersed, the distribution of *chia* members may take conjugal ties into account, but it will also reflect an arrangement geared primarily to the coordinated exploitation of the estate as a whole. We may refer once again to Table 15, which shows that in some cases only one person is an operator and lives apart from his or her spouse (S13, J14, J22), while in others both husband and wife are operators and live together (J2, J14, J19). That coresidence on a conjugal basis does not necessarily fol-

Table 15

Residential Arrangements Associated with Dispersed *Chia* Estates, Yen-liao, May 31, 1965

Chia group	*Status of enterprise operators (relationship to head of chia)*	*Enterprises*	*Location*	*Residence of spouses and children*	
				At site of enterprise	*At primary household*
S13	Married son	Truck	Kao-shu Rural District, Pingtung County	Operator	Wife and children
J2	Married son; married son's wife; their eldest son	Dormitory and farm	Pingtung City	Operators(3); operators' other children	
J14	Married son; his wife	Farm	Near Yen-liao	Operators(2); their children	
	Married son	Truck	Taipei	Operator	Wife and children
J19	Married son; his wife	Chinese drugstore	Liu-kuei Rural District, Kaohsiung County	Operators(2); their children	
J22	Unmarried daughter; married son; another married son's wife	Grocery store and farm	Chiu-kung-lin, Mei-nung Township	Operators(3)	Spouses of married operators and their children

low when more than one person cares for outside holdings is shown by *chia* J22, where in a secondary household linked to two enterprises there is a married man, his single sister, and his brother's wife.

Another illustration is provided if Yen-liao's one secondary household is viewed in the context of the overall distribution of its *chia* group. There are 42 persons, with Lin Shang-yung the family head. In the oldest generation only Lin himself survives. In the second generation the marriage of each of his three sons has led to the formation of as many *fang*. The first of these has 22 members; in addition to the father and mother it includes five sons and two daughters, the wife and seven children of the first son, and the wife and four children of the second. The second *fang*—12 persons in all—consists of a father, a mother, four sons, four daughters, and the wife and child of the first son. In the third *fang*, with the father and mother there are five young children. The Lin *chia* has established four households, each associated with a part of the estate. In a village next to Yen-liao there are the buildings and fields obtained (and later expanded) by Shang-yung when he separated from his brother. In Yen-liao the *chia* owns a rice mill, and in yet another nearby settlement it operates a shop selling fertilizers and animal feed. About 25 miles to the south, additional land and buildings have been purchased. In the management of all these holdings, a common budget is maintained, and funds and goods are transferred as needed. Shang-yung continues to live at the site of the original holdings. With him are some members of the first and second *fang:* the two daughters of the first *fang*, the oldest married son, and two of his children, the father and mother of the second *fang*, their seven unmarried children, and their married son's wife and child. The married son had lived there before his induction into the army. Part of the first *fang*—the second married son, his wife and four children, and the two youngest unmarried sons—reside at the rice mill. Living in the south is another unmarried son of the first *fang*, and the wife and remaining children of the first married son. The mother of the first *fang* also lives there, and the father divides his time between the south and the rice mill. The entire third *fang* is quartered at the shop.

Lin Shan-yung's *chia* also illustrates how in the context of a dispersed estate there can be considerable mobility between the different households where members of the *chia* group reside. In Yen-liao, for example, the rice mill's living quarters were occupied in sequence between 1949 and 1965 by four different conjugal units from the Lin *chia* for periods ranging from three to five years.

If dispersion is linked to the *chia* estate, it is a product of that estate's expansion, but if it is associated with salaried positions it can either reflect an early phase in a *chia*'s economic development, or it can be an adjustment in lieu of the expansion of the *chia*'s holdings. A dispersed estate comes about through the management of *chia* resources in a context no different from one where the allocation of funds maintains the estate in concentrated form, and we may now proceed to a more general discussion of the *chia* estate and its interconnections with complex family organization.

If diversification of the family economy is an apparent tendency among conjugal forms, it is the dominant characteristic of complex primary households. Among Yen-liao's stem and joint households there is an exclusive reliance upon the family farm only in one joint (J5) and two stem households (S2, S7). The salience of diversification is further indicated in that none of the remaining 33 households depend upon miscellaneous short-term wage labor as the sole alternative to agriculture. There are some important differences in the pattern of diversification between stem and joint households. Only five stem units (36 percent of the total) have developed a like number of capitalized nonagricultural enterprises, while 15 joint households (68 percent) boast a total of 27. With an average of 6.4 persons linked in a productive capacity to each joint household, it might appear that such units could operate additional businesses more readily than the stem households, where the average number is only 3.8. But Table 16 shows that the situation is more complex: among households in the stem category, proportionately fewer workers are full-time farmers and proportionately more are full-

Table 16
Disposition of Work Force Linked to
Yen-liao Stem and Joint Primary Households,
Tobacco-Growers and Others, Yen-liao

	Stem households						Joint households					
	Tobacco growers		Others		Total		Tobacco growers		Others		Total	
Disposition of work force	Number	Per cent	Number	Per cent	Number	Per cent	Number	Per cent	Number	Per cent	Number	Per cent
Full-time farming	19	73.1	4	14.8	23	43.4	67	59.8	3	10.7	70	50.0
Full-time non-farming												
Full-time operators of enterprises	1	3.8	3	11.1	4	7.5	11	9.8	11	39.3	22	15.7
Full-time salaried employment	5	19.2	2	7.4	7	13.2	7	6.3	0	0	7	5.0
Full-time service	0	0	3	11.1	3	5.7	0	0	0	0	0	0
Total full-time non-farming	6	23.1 [a]	8	29.6	14	26.4	18	16.1	11	39.3	29	20.7
Part-time farming												
With operation of enterprise	1	3.8	1	3.7	2	3.8	5	4.5	3	10.7	8	5.7
With service	0	0	1	3.7	1	1.9	1	.9	0	0	1	.7
With miscellaneous wage labor	0	0	8	29.6	8	15.1	21	18.7	11	39.3	32	22.9
Total part-time farming	1	3.8	10	37.0	11	20.8	27	24.1	14	50.0	41	29.3
Miscellaneous wage labor only	0	0	5	18.5	5	9.4	0	0	0	0	0	0
Total work force	26	100.0	27	99.9 [a]	53	100.0	112	100.0	28	100.0	140	100.0

[a] Total off due to rounding.

time nonfarmers; diversification away from farming is about
equally emphasized among both groups of households, but
among those of the joint variety, enterprises—as opposed to salaried occupations—take up a proportionately larger segment of
the family labor force.

Tobacco-growers are differentiated in Table 16 because the
arrangement of a tobacco-growing household's estate and economy are among the many facets of its domestic life over which
tobacco cultivation can exert an important influence. Tobacco
cultivation is a factor at the family level because of two features
I have already described: tobacco has higher monetary returns
than other crops yet incorporates labor-intensive cultivation and
processing techniques. Such methods require, during much of
the agricultural year, mobilization of labor on a scale the cultivation cycles of rice and other crops can match only during
brief "busy periods," if at all. These characteristics of tobacco
production mean, all other things being equal, that the family
farm worker who is a member of a tobacco-cultivating household has a greater economic value than one whose household
does not have a permit to grow the crop; this would be the case
if both households owned fields equal in area and quality,
which they worked with labor forces similarly matched in
numbers and performance. But such ideal comparisons cannot
be made precisely because the incorporation of tobacco production into the farming routine increases the importance of the agricultural component in a household's economy.

Table 16 shows that the smaller work force characteristic of
all stem households is arranged very differently among tobacco
growers than among others. About three-quarters of the workers
in tobacco-growing stem households are exclusively concerned
with farming, while all but two of the remaining workers work
full time at salaried positions. These proportions occur because
farming has a competitive advantage over most alternative
forms of employment for stem households that grow tobacco.
There is no indication of a similar major focus among other stem
households, but rather a situation where farm holdings and *chia*
enterprises are inadequate relative to the needs of family mem-

bers. Much of the work force is well scattered among different occupational categories, for they have taken whatever work opportunities are available, but there is underemployment to the extent that about half of the workers in this group turn to miscellaneous short-term wage labor.

Tobacco cultivation involves a greater emphasis on agriculture, which in stem households means a considerable increase in the proportion of the family labor force involved in the direct exploitation of the *chia* estate. The estate absorbs the efforts of most workers in all joint families, and the contrast is with respect to farming as opposed to operating other enterprises. About 60 percent of the labor force associated with tobacco-growing joint households consists of full-time farmers and close to 20 percent combines farming with miscellaneous wage labor.

In the other joint households about 80 percent of the workers fall into two categories, but they are about evenly divided between full-time operators of enterprises and workers who combine farming with miscellaneous wage labor. The emphasis on short-term wage labor is thus characteristic of both stem and joint households where tobacco is not grown, but in stem households not cultivating tobacco only about 30 percent of the labor force is exclusively concerned with the exploitation of the *chia* estate; this is in contrast to about 74 percent in stem households which do grow the crop, about 61 percent of the workers in joint households where tobacco is not grown, and about 81 percent of those in joint households where it is grown.

The greater significance of the *chia* estate relative to the distribution of the labor force is in fact a characteristic of all joint households, but this relationship is obscured because in stem and joint households alike the effect of tobacco production is to increase the value of family farm labor. In joint households the increased value of the tobacco worker can be seen in that tobacco is grown by every household of this form with a purely agrarian estate, while in those not cultivating tobacco the greatest emphasis is on nonagrarian enterprises. Thus, among joint households enterprises are owned by all five households not growing tobacco but by only 10 of the 17 that do. Among the stem households, there are only four with enterprises added to their farms, and two of these households grow tobacco. Enterprises are equally distributed across the stem households, each with one, but the greater variability with respect to the 27 enterprises owned by joint units can be diagrammed as follows:

	Number of non-farm enterprises in *chia* estates of joint primary households				
	4	3	2	1	0
Number of families					
Tobacco Growers	1	1	3	5	7
Others	1	0	1	3	0

With respect to non-tobacco growers among stem and joint households, deemphasis of agriculture in favor of a more diversified set of economic activities is indicated by Table 17, where per capita land holdings are consistently much smaller than among tobacco growers if figured relative to all persons linked to the primary household economy, to all members of the work force, or to full- and part-time farmers combined. These lower ratings are the combined expression of situations in which poverty-stricken households own little or no land, and those where resources have been invested in nonagricultural enterprises. It might therefore appear inconsistent that non-tobacco growers have the higher land–man ratio if calculated on the basis of full-time farmers. In fact, however, it is because of the relatively diminished importance of agriculture to the family economy that such positions are held by only seven persons from four households. In the absence of tobacco, less labor is needed per unit of land so that the value of a full-time farmer's contribution to his family increases, at least up to a certain point, together with the area of land under his care.

At the stem level, the intimate connection between family form and the condition of the *chia* estate that characterizes joint households (where the labor force is largely absorbed by the estate through tobacco cultivation, enterprise operation, or a combination of both) does not exist. In the final analysis it is the

Table 17

Per-Unit Landholdings (in *Chia*) by Categories of Households and Persons, Yen-liao

| | | | | Per capita landholdings | | |
Household category	Number of households	Average per household land holdings	All persons linked to primary household economy	All persons contributing to primary household economy	Full and part-time farmers	Full-time farmers only
All stem households	14	.99	.10	.26	.41	
Stem, farming only	12	1.15	.12	.32	.50	
tobacco growers	7	1.43	.14	.38	.27	
others	5	.76	.09	.14		
All joint households	22	2.18	.12	.34	.43	
tobacco growers	17	2.45	.13	.37	.44	
others	5	1.26	.07	.22	.37	
Households with full-time farmers						
stem, tobacco growers	7	1.43				.53
stem, others	3	.81				.61
joint, tobacco growers	14	2.69				.56
joint, others	1	2.30				.68

series of opportunities provided by the *chia* estate that provides
the framework and support for a stem household's transformation into one of joint form, and the continued development of
the family is most assured in situations where the *chia* estate
expands as the *chia* group grows more complex. For example,
Huang Yu-lai, who heads *chia* J2, owes his family's prosperous
condition to a lucrative job landed by his oldest son during the
Japanese period. This was in fact a stroke of luck, but remittances to the primary household were invested in land and enterprises to provide Yu-lai's other sons with niches in the family
economy. In other cases of expansion, capital has been provided through the manipulation of resources already available,
loans, or from the income generated by services or existent
holdings.

The operation of such factors is illustrated by the expansion
of the estate owned by Lin Hsin-chen's *chia* (J13). This involved the utilization of available holdings in that Lin built his
carpentry shop in 1955 on land already belonging to his *chia*.
But construction costs were met through loans and savings. According to Lin, the family had been able to accumulate a surplus only because of his earnings as a carpenter before he had
his own shop; at that time the family farm and short-term wage
labor were additional sources of income, but these could not do
more than meet subsistence requirements. The new enterprise
generated an even larger surplus, and Lin added additional
rooms to the shop in 1964 to provide space for a new business.
This most recent undertaking is a store that sells and services
batteries used in vehicles and also sells other electrical appli-
ances; it was established for Lin's younger brother, who had
just been released from the army and was to be married a few
months later.

Lin's family does not grow tobacco, and in general it appears
that farms not producing this crop provide little or no capital for
expansion. Tobacco-growing families, on the other hand, are
able to increase their holdings as a direct result of proceeds
from tobacco sales. One expansion of this sort, which occurred

in 1964, can be verified by examining family expenditures, tobacco receipts, and the utilization of surplus income.

We will take as our case the family headed by Yeh Hsia-chü (J19). There are six adults and seven children; Hsia-chü is 67, his wife 65. Though Hsia-chü controls family finances, he ceased years ago all but minimal participation in family work, which in Yen-liao is now the responsibility of Hsia-chü's oldest son, his third son, and his two daughters-in-law. Hsia-chü's second son lives with his wife and children in another town; there he runs a Chinese medicine shop, which has yet to yield a profit sufficient to warrant remittances to Yen-liao.

Farming is the major enterprise of Yeh Hsia-chü's household; supplemental income is derived from pig-rearing and a power tiller, which Hsia-chü's first son operates both at home and outside. The expansion of the *chia* estate has included several purchases of land; with the acquisition of .37 *chia* in 1964, total family holdings now include 3.09 *chia*. This as well as past expansion has been financed by tobacco grown on 1.70 *chia,* and this crop's role as the major source of family income is indicated in Tables 18 and 19. During the period covered by the tables, Yeh Hsia-chü's household spent a total of NT$175,363; NT$51,363 was for support and social purposes and also includes expenditures connected with the repair or replacement of agricultural equipment; the additional NT$124,000 was for the land purchase. Table 18 shows that family net income during the same year was NT$131,864; if all other expenditures are deducted, there remains only NT$80,501 for the land, but Hsia-chü's family had additional funds accumulated during previous years. In the year under consideration, tobacco provided 61 percent of total net income; and tobacco production has been the major source of income since Hsia-chü's family began to cultivate the crop.

The directions in which families expand their economic activities influence the degree of specialization that develops. Families building up agricultural holdings, as in the case of Yeh Hsia-chü, keep more members involved in farming tasks than

Table 18
Family of Yeh Hsia-Chü, Agricultural Income,
1963 Tobacco Season Through 1964 Second Rice Harvest

Crop	Rice Crop (first and second combined)	Bananas	Vegetables	Sweet Potato	Tobacco
Area Planted (*Chia*)	4.30	.08	.04	.80	1.70
Yield	29,560 catties (1 catty = 1.3 lbs.)	160 plants			3,700 catties
Disposal	tax: 1,180 catties; fertilizer exchange: 3,800 catties; compulsory sale: 4,350 catties; free sale: 12,570 catties; home consumption: 7,660 catties.	sale	home consumption	pig fodder	sale
Cash Receipts, NT$	41,908	7,500			110,000
Labor Input (work-days) family	329				556
hired	264	10		44	407
Labor Costs, NT$	6,600	200		880	8,585
Other Expenses, NT$	2,408	800		2,590	20,850
Net Income, NT$	32,900	6,500		−3,470	80,565

TOTAL INCOME: NT$116,495

do those families expanding in other ways. But in all complex families there is a greater degree of differentiation; they of course tend to be larger, but they are complex because they contain more adults. In conjugal families, a proliferation of tasks necessarily requires that these tasks all devolve upon a very few persons. Where there are more workers, however, the tendency toward increased specialization is apparent with respect to both work and management. This is true even in families that are primarily or exclusively agricultural. In Yeh Hsia-chü's household there is a clear division of responsibility. The third son operates the power tiller; he has the expertise because the tendency to specialize has restricted the machine to his use. The oldest son, however, has his own role as the manager of farming operations; he plans the daily work and decides when and how much additional help is required. This man's position illustrates the important distinction between labor and managerial roles. His own role combines both of these elements, for in addition to managing the farm he also labors in the fields with his wife and sister-in-law. Furthermore, his brother, when not plowing land elsewhere, joins him in working on the farm. With respect to farming, then, there are four worker roles, only one of which is managerial.

Table 19
Family of Yeh Hsia-chü,
Summary of Sources of Income 1963–1964

Sources of Income	Receipts	Expenditures	Net Income
Pigs	NT$29,200	NT$7,293	NT$21,907
Power Tiller	6,900	3,560	3,340
Wage Labor	150		150 [a]
Grain Associations	10,480	20,508	−10,028
Tobacco Cultivation			80,565
Other Crop Cultivation			35,930
TOTAL INCOME: NT$131,864			

[a] Compensation from other families for labor-exchange debts.

Role specialization of course becomes more pronounced with a greater diversification of the *chia* estate, and both specialization and estate diversification are provided with greater potential for expression by increasing family complexity. The way the three processes can be closely linked is illustrated by the development of Huang Yu-lai's family (J2). I have already noted that when his first son struck it rich the result was the *chia* estate's expansion and diversification. During the Japanese period Yu-lai decided to let his oldest son continue his education as far as possible while the second son helped his father in the fields. The first son was a good student and after graduating from primary school he was one of the few Taiwanese admitted to a two-year agricultural institute. After finishing the course, he managed to get the lucrative job in Pingtung and began to send money home. Since the third son also showed promise he was encouraged to continue his studies, and after graduation he worked hard to pass the examination for a higher-level school. He did not succeed, however, and became *"chou-k'ong"* ("book crazy"), a term used for people who suffer breakdowns after failing entrance examinations; his illness lasted several years, and his father desperately sought means to cure him. The third son finally did recover, and by this time money the first son was sending home had accumulated into a tidy sum; also by now wives of the first two sons had augmented the work force. With the third son available for work and with money to invest, the family built a brick factory, and made the third son manager.

After Japan's surrender the fourth son graduated from a higher-level agricultural school and completed two years of military service. Investment now proceeded in several directions. Most of the time the first son's job kept him in Pingtung, where he lived with his wife; their household was next to a large college, and family funds were used to buy adjacent land and erect a student dormitory. In the village, meanwhile, the family started a transport business with the purchase of two trucks, and the management of this operation was given over to the fourth son.

The many enterprises of Yu-lai's family have involved it in complex legal, economic, and social relationships with the outside world, and in Yen-liao these are handled primarily by the fourth son, who is also the main liaison between the primary household and the branch established by the first son in the south. The fourth son transfers family funds back and forth as needed, by motorcycle. Yu-lai, now aging, has left the management of family fields to the second son.

In stem households, insofar as family enterprises are concerned, both work and management roles are distributed fairly evenly between fathers and their married sons, but in joint households only four of 17 surviving fathers have managerial specializations in contrast to 32 out of their 41 married sons who live with them (another 4 sons who live outside also manage family enterprises). In stem and joint households alike, unmarried family workers are generally not given managerial positions, for these are associated with adult status; if they assume control over an aspect of the family economy, or if a new enterprise is established for them, this usually will be at about the time of their marriage or even later.

As a father grows older, he naturally participates less in family work in joint households; but differential complexity as such must be considered as a separate factor. In stem households a desire or need to diversify activities or the estate away from farming leads either father or married son to new specialties, and the father may be encouraged to continue his participation in family work if there are only two male adults in the household. Thus there is no regular retirement pattern among the heads of Yen-liao's stem households; the three men who no longer work were born in 1895, 1909, and 1917, but the three oldest household heads still active have as their years of birth 1893, 1907, and 1910, while the remaining six were born between 1913 and 1918. (Widows head two stem families.)

In a joint household there are fewer constraints placed upon withdrawal from family work at an advanced age. All five men born between 1896 and 1899 have retired, as have eight of the twelve whose dates of birth fall between 1901 and 1912. It is of some significance that of the four men (1901, 1904, 1910, 1911) still at work three manage enterprises (grocery store, Chinese medicine shop, tile factory) and one provides a special service (cement worker); all the retired household heads had been farmers, and if their families diversified it was through the activities of their sons. Retirement from the rigors of farming is a pleasant prospect for most men, and below we shall consider how this is linked to joint household development. But if it should happen that the father takes on his own specialty, it may be easier for him not to give it up; and if he keeps it after his sons have theirs, his contribution to the family economy may be such that it poses an obstacle to his own retirement.

It is commonly said in Mei-nung that fate is cruelest to the

oldest son, whose father will almost surely pass on to him before anyone else the hard life of farming. The Yen-liao evidence
suggests that there is considerable truth in this observation, at
least with respect to tobacco-growers. More generally, a father
usually attempts to arrange work and management specializations among his sons first in response to what he feels are immediate needs and only later in terms of the possible expansion
of the estate and economy. As the first son matures he is most
likely to be assigned work relating to the existing estate, should
the father feel that this is required, although we have seen that
scholastic ability and other circumstances may be taken into
consideration. In farming households there is also the father's
desire to gradually retire from work and turn toward the management of his younger sons' careers and family affairs in general. That the ultimate distribution of work and management
specialties within the joint family is influenced by a father's
plans is shown in Table 20, where I group as tobacco-growers
and others second-generation males belonging to *chia* groups
with joint primary households. Persons in both groups are classified according to birth sequence and in terms of work or management roles, and the high priority given agriculture by those
who cultivate tobacco is clearly reflected in the nearly complete
monopolization of farm management by eldest sons. We also
may detect in the distribution of occupational roles among tobacco growers as a whole the general strategy according to
which these roles are assigned. If oldest sons are given responsibilities that indicate an effort to consolidate the *chia* economy,
there is a steady increase in the percentage of nonagricultural
positions held by second and third sons, as emphasis is increasingly placed on expansion and diversification.

As conjugal households develop into complex forms, there is
no basic change in arrangements for the management and redistribution of family funds; these remain in the father's control
and as before there is no set pattern according to which his wife
may share his responsibilities. Such sharing is pronounced in
Huang Yu-lai's household (J2): most funds are secured in banks
and the Farmer's Association, but in a chest placed in the bed-

Table 20
Worker and Management Roles of
Second Generation Males in *Chia* Groups with
Joint Primary Households, Yen-liao [a]

Birth Sequence [b]	Tobacco Growers (17 families)					
	Farm Manager	Enterprise Manager	Farm Worker	Enterprise Worker	Salaried	Salaried, economically independent
1	14	2	1			
2	2	6	5		3	1
3		3	6		2	3
4	1	1	3		1	3
5		2				1
6			1		1	
	Others (5 families)					
1	1	3		1		
2	3	2				
3	1	1		1		
4		1				1
5						
6						

[a] Managers are often workers at the same time, but for purposes of this table I separate persons with managerial responsibilities from those with work roles only. Three men conscripted into military service are assigned their roles prior to being drafted; third sons in two tobacco-growing families had been farm workers; a fourth son in a family not growing tobacco had been independently earning a salary.

[b] The birth sequence is relative to surviving sons only.

room used by Huang and his wife there is also a considerable amount of money. Both have keys to the chest, which holds cash sufficient to cover one or two day's anticipated expenses and an additional amount to meet emergency or unforeseen requirements; but only Huang adds to the chest, with funds he personally withdraws from the Farmer's Association almost every morning. Huang's four sons turn over to him income from the family enterprises they manage; Huang dispenses funds as required and also directly handles many transactions, especially those involving crops produced on the Yen-liao farm. On one occasion I saw him give a man about NT$90,000 in payment for

.20 *chia* of prime land. Every day Huang's wife buys food with money from the chest, and she or her husband dip into this till when their sons or daughters-in-law ask for cash. In contrast is the household of Yeh Wang-ch'üan (J8), who has two married sons and two still single. Here money is kept in a drawer to which only Yeh has a key; he personally provides funds for all family expenditures, including money he gives his wife for food.

Whatever the extent to which his wife has access to the family purse, the father remains sharply defined as financial manager; and he has final say with respect to investments or other expenditures. In Huang Yu-lai's family, decisions concerning major business expenditures are arrived at jointly by Huang and his sons, for Huang relies on their greater experience in these matters. But in other contexts, Huang does not hesitate to act independently, as when he spent NT$10,000 to purchase the honorific position of "assistant grand director" in a 1963 religious celebration.

The tight control a father can exercise over a joint household economy is exemplified by Fu Ch'ing-feng (J14). Fu has one son in Taipei who drives a truck purchased in 1964 with family funds; but his son's wife and children remain in Yen-liao together with other family members, including four more sons and their wives. The adults constitute a farm work force into which are fully integrated yet another married son and his wife, who live in a nearby hamlet but take most of their meals in Yen-liao. Fu himself is crippled and stays behind the counter of the grocery store he runs. He is well known in the Yen-liao region as a stingy man who drives his family like a tyrant. Owning 4.76 *chia* of land and a 1.7 *chia* tobacco permit, the family is sufficiently well off for Fu to have spent NT$100,000 for the truck. With their large labor force, the Fu Ch'ing-feng family needs only minimal outside assistance. However, only the Fu household was observed to do major farming work on the first day of the lunar new year, which for almost everyone else is a time of visiting and entertainment. In my presence Fu complained bitterly of a spoiled daughter-in-law who refuses to eat the salty (and cheap) food which is the family's daily fare; he protested that another daughter-in-law was sick, forcing him to hire additional labor. Perhaps with some accuracy, local residents tell how Fu is reluctant to give his sons and daughters-in-law money for medicine when they are in need. But it is also commonly acknowledged that Fu's sons fully realize how their father's methods have resulted in the expansion of the estate that they will one day divide among themselves.

The collective economy of the complex household is entirely an expression of practices concerning redistribution and financial management. A common purse is maintained only because the father, in his role as redistributor, can be the sole recipient of the income derived by *chia* members who exploit the estate or contribute outside earnings; the role of financial manager involves monopolization of the power to allocate funds from this purse for the entire group's welfare and the estate's advancement. The strategic importance of the redistributor and the financial manager roles is obscured because in most primary households the father holds both roles while at the same time he also has overall authority over family affairs. These roles are very different from those linked to the particular economic activities of a household; the group and estate of one *chia* can develop along lines different from those of another, and in each there can be unlike constellations of "managers of family enterprises," "family workers," "salaried workers," and the like. But "redistributor" and "financial manager" are important positions with respect to complex family organization as such.

The transfer of redistributive and financial management roles in Yen-liao's complex households has been from father to eldest son only, except that in one stem household a widowed mother holds both roles. Table 21 shows that between father and eldest son there are only three possibilities: father has both roles, son has both, or son becomes financial manager while father stays on as redistributor. Household complexity and the father's competence have an important bearing on role transfer; but the father's age as such is not a significant element, so that such transfers are yet another of the important developments in the

Table 21
Redistribution and Financial Management
in Complex Primary Households, Yen-liao

	Household Form	
Distribution of Roles	*Stem*	*Joint*
Father controls redistribution and financial management; Mother alive	10	9
Father controls redistribution; financial management by eldest son; Mother alive	0	5
Mother controls redistribution and financial management; Father dead; eldest son absent	1 [a]	0
Eldest son controls redistribution and financial management; Father and Mother alive	2	3
Eldest son controls redistribution and financial management; Father dead; Mother alive	1 [b]	4
Eldest son controls redistribution and financial management; both parents dead	0	1

[a] Eldest son works and lives outside; he sends money home.

[b] Father alive, but lives in different household.

family for which the "life cycle" approach provides little or no illumination. In Table 22 I list surviving fathers who are members of Yen-liao complex households by year of birth, household form, and role. Note that in joint households there is no marked difference in age distribution between the men still holding both roles and those who have relinquished one or both; men in the latter category in fact average about one year younger than those in the former (average years of birth 1904 and 1905), and neither can there be seen significant differences if the men holding one or two roles are grouped together and contrasted with fathers who have given up both (but now the average years of birth are 1903 and 1905).

In stem households only two fathers have neither role, and it is hardly meaningful to look for a relationship between age and retirement. But we must consider why positions of redistributor and financial manager are held by ten out of twelve fathers in stem households but only by nine out of 17 living in joint households. In stem households the large majority of fathers keep their positions precisely because these economic roles are

Table 22
Fathers in Yen-liao Complex Household by
Year of Birth and Economic Role

	Stem Households			Joint Households		
Year of Birth	Redistributor and Financial Manager	Redistributor only	Neither	Redistributor and Financial Manager	Redistributor only	Neither
1893–1896	1	0	1	2	0	0
1898–1901	0	0	0	1	2	1
1904–1907	1	0	0	1	2	1
1908–1911	1	0	1	5	0	0
1912–1915	2	0	0	0	1	1
1916–1918	5	0	0	0	0	0
TOTALS	10	0	2	9	5	3

held in a context where the fathers still maintain considerable general authority over family affairs, and their authority is buttressed by several characteristic features of stem family organization. In each of these households the father has at least one son who is still single, and in all but two there is also at least one daughter who has yet to marry. Now the father's control over his unmarried children, especially sons, takes on an added dimension owing to the presence in the household of one adult son. The latter has had full coparcenary rights since his marriage, but it was precisely that event which made his father the guardian and representative of the rights to the estate that all of his remaining sons might eventually claim; and the obligation to provide his daughters with proper weddings is translated into yet another series of claims against *chia* holdings. In other words, while father and married son may be jural equals, the father's representation of his unmarried children reinforces his economic and political power within the household.

Thus the marriage of the first son poses the least threat to the father's general authority, so that his roles as redistributor and financial manager continue to be linked to his control over family affairs in general. In most cases, with such conditions little can be done by a man who feels his father is not competent to manage family wealth.

The examples of the two stem households where role transfer has occurred illustrate some of the circumstances that can lead to a weakening of the father's power. One household is headed by Huang Kuei-ch'un. Huang, born in 1893, was well-to-do during the Japanese period; he owned a farm and was highly regarded and heavily patronized as an architect and builder of traditional structures such as temples, shrines, and ancestral halls. But Huang's love of women, wine, and gambling led to a steady increasing indebtedness that finally destroyed him; he was forced to sell all his land and by the time Japan surrendered he was almost penniless. Huang's oldest surviving son now manages family finances and provides most income. A brick mason, he assumed responsibility at about the time of his marriage in 1960 at the age of 27. He pools his earnings with those of his wife, younger brother, and sister, and he provides his parents and other family members with money for food and other necessities. He lets his father keep money he earns through occasional wood carving and the preparation of religious documents. Huang's son stopped turning money over to his father because he knew that most of it would be used to buy wine, and his father did not protest. In terms of household organization, Huang's tragedy was an extreme form of mismanagement resulting in the loss of the very estate with which he might have been able to maintain control over his oldest son and the household economy.

Yeh Wang-ch'ing's only surviving offspring is a daughter who has married uxorilocally. Yeh was born in 1909; he is neurotic, drinks heavily, and is now quite incapable of seriously assuming any responsibilities. Yeh's son-in-law moved in on the basis of a contract stipulating an alternating use of the Yeh surname and his own in naming the children born of his marriage, with naming sequences established separately for boys and girls. The contract also contains the stipulation that all boys, irrespective of surname, have equal rights to the *chia* estate. In effect, then, the son-in-law stands as the representative of his surname's coparcenary rights, while his wife and father-in-law represent theirs. With a strong claim against the *chia* estate, the son-in-law does not hesitate to work for its expansion and for the benefit of the entire household. He is a vigorous businessman and while he manages the farm he has supplemented its earnings by setting up a candy and vegetable shop on a small plot of family land located in a nearby hamlet on a busy road. The shop is tended mostly by his wife, for he has also become a vegetable wholesaler and spends much time traveling. Yeh dislikes his son-in-law, who is by contract his equal within the *chia* group, but he is unable to stand up against him in almost any context. The son-in-law controls income from the farm, his own business, and the shop managed by his wife; he provides his mother-in-law money for food and other expenses, and is also the only source of cash for Yeh Wang-ch'ing and other family members.

The transition from stem to joint household form initiates developments such that the father's roles as redistributor and financial manager are less closely linked to his overall power within the household. Under these circumstances the father's managerial skills become increasingly important as a buttress to his position within the *chia*, so that in comparison with stem households there is a reversal in the relationship between his role as financial manager and his overall power. The father's diffuse authority becomes weaker as his sons marry and acquire adult status; the father is increasingly forced to use his position as redistributor and financial manager to reinforce his general standing within the *chia*.

The father's fiscal management with respect to the outside world is of greatest importance here. In the past, when the family had been held together by the father's authority, the family's fate was of course largely linked to his managerial skills, but within the family sphere his role as financial manager could not

be threatened by other than complete failure. In joint households, however, sons view the condition of the estate and economy in terms of self-interest. Their father, on the other hand, is
concerned with the *chia*'s very survival; since this is now
largely a function of good fiscal management, he sometimes
may even be the first to conclude that such responsibilities
might be more capably handled by one of his sons. Thus it is
within joint households that the father's personal characteristics
appear most closely linked to his position with respect to management. As a whole, the nine men who still totally run the financial affairs of their families are able, vigorous, and self-
assured; they are truly "strong" fathers precisely because jural
control over the estate supports their leadership to a reduced
extent or not at all, and some of these men may indeed maintain
their positions until their deaths. Within this group are Huang
Yu-lai and Fu Ch'ing-feng (J2 and J14), and we have already
seen the tight control they hold over their families. The two
men are commonly regarded in Yen-liao as the village's
strongest and most domineering family heads; and it is not surprising that Huang Yu-lai's last son has been married for more
than a decade, while of Fu Ch'ing-feng's seven sons only the
youngest has yet to be provided with a wife.

A striking contrast is provided by the three joint-family fathers who no longer manage or redistribute family funds. Yeh
Wang-sheng (J7) is paralyzed and bedridden; Huang Ch'uan-
sheng (J3) and Fu Sheng-feng (J16) are known for their inability
to handle "a family's business," but in the case of Huang, born
in 1899, this is attributed to senility, while Fu, thirteen years
younger, is merely considered "foolish." Fu's household illustrates economic management under such circumstances: his
oldest son controls family finances and manages the farming of
their .80 *chia* farm. Fu's wife and his oldest unmarried daughter
work for wages during the slack period (the family grows no
tobacco); Fu's second son recently married, and the family purchased a motor cart which he uses in a transport business. Earnings from all these sources are given to the oldest son. The two

daughters-in-law rotate between farming and domestic work on a regular basis.

Remaining the head of an intact joint family is more than a matter of a father's pride, for he also knows that in the event of family partition, now an ever-present possibility, he and his wife may undergo one of the most dramatic and complete changes of status involved in Chinese family organization. As a result of partition the father as his family's head can turn into the collective dependent of the new households his sons have established; this is a tragic event for a man, who is now supported not as is his due as a family member, but by means negotiated by his sons as a convenient arrangement of their shared obligations.

Thus if joint household development is marked by the erosion of the father's direct control over the estate, it also sees his emergence as the one adult male who exclusively identifies as his interest the preservation of family unity and the advancement of its welfare. Each son who has attained jural maturity holds such goals insofar as they coincide with the narrower interests of his own *fang;* should there be a divergence of interests, his right to claim a share of the estate is an alternative strategy denied his father.

A father may at his own initiative turn the joint household's fiscal management over to his eldest son, or he may do so when he feels or is informed that such a step is desired by other *chia* members. In any event such transfers of responsibility are common among joint households precisely because the father sees his managerial role mainly as an artifact for the family unity which is his overriding goal. While one of the forces making for *chia* unity is generated by benefits that can be a product of the coordinated efforts of *chia* members, another is produced by the common acceptance of standards by which such benefits are to be distributed. Both forces operate on all joint households, but their impact can be seen most clearly in the five where the father handles redistribution while his oldest son manages family finances; because such an arrangement seeks to lessen the possibility that the eldest son will use *chia* funds for the benefit of his *fang*, it in fact brings into strong relief the ambiguous position of all married sons in the joint household.

The usual pattern is for the son to keep account of household earnings, which he first collects from the others and then turns over to his father; and he likewise takes from his father funds needed for family business or the farm, and for various personal expenses of household members. The father controls the family purse, including bankbooks; he often directly gives his wife or daughters-in-law money for food, and he may give his grandchildren small change for candy; but before handing out money for other purposes he consults with his oldest son and usually prefers that funds first pass through his son's hands.

Although the father's position with respect to redistribution and fiscal management varies from one joint household to another, the fact remains that the eldest son stands as potential or actual successor in all households; this includes four households where the deceased father is survived by his wife and one where both parents are dead. In this connection, we may note that Freedman, speaking of Chinese society in general, remarks that while the "hierarchy of seniority among brothers" was well established, it did not serve to prevent the fraternal conflict fed by the individuated rights to the estate held by male siblings (1966:46). But the pattern of economic organization in Yen-liao joint households reveals an additional facet to the relationship between seniority and conflict; for given the importance of the economic roles we have been discussing, it can be seen that their assignment to the eldest brother on a prescriptive basis precisely serves to remove them from the arena of conflict. Joint households can more readily be maintained intact, after the father's death, because succession to economic management as such does not become a bone of contention among brothers. The Yen-liao data do not permit me to judge the extent to which the eldest son's competence is a factor under such circumstances, but presumably he does not assume such responsibilities if his brothers are not confident of his ability.

That the transfer of financial responsibilities from father to eldest son is linked to the preservation of family unity is further confirmed by the fact that joint family economic arrangements provide the greatest benefits for the eldest of several brothers and are least advantageous for the youngest. The oldest brother marries first, and his children are supported by the resources of the *chia* over the longest period of time; and because of their average age relative to other members of the third generation, at any given point they are usually absorbing more *chia* wealth on a per capita basis than are the offspring of the younger brothers. Likewise, the youngest brother's children tend to receive the least amount of *chia* support. The oldest brother's favorable position within it reinforces his commitment to the *chia*'s unity and increases his dependability as an impartial manager of family finances, while for the youngest brother mismanagement of the family economy can only make it easier for him to feel that his interests might be best served by partition.

The specialization of roles within the family economy tends to restrict management and the handling of funds to men. Men supervise family enterprises, while women shuffle back and forth between the household and the fields. But such a pattern of specialization is also the basis of a system of redistribution and property relationships. Allocations from the redistributor are for specific purposes. Money or other resources under the control of the man with redistributive responsibilities are of course assets of the *chia* estate. Such assets can be earmarked for the support or expansion of existing family enterprises, or they can be invested in new businesses, which become family property. Likewise, income from family enterprises remains family property; only after an enterprise's manager turns the income over to the redistributor can such funds be allocated for different purposes. This includes support in the form of food or money for food, medical expenses, tuition, and so forth. Such expenditures do not create private holdings, but allocations for durable items such as clothing, cigarette lighters, wrist watches, jewelry, and others result in the creation of private property, and must be approved by the financial manager. When the person in control of redistribution is the father, or the oldest of several brothers whose father is dead, he is also the recognized family head (*chia-chang*); but we have seen that in some cases the redistributor is an oldest son whose father is still alive. Nevertheless, the latter remains the family's formal representative during ceremonial and religious events and is provided money for donations to temples, or for the gifts given at weddings, funerals, and birthday celebrations.

In complex as well as conjugal households, men who earn wages or manage nonagricultural enterprises keep "spending money" for such things as cigarettes and entertainment. But male family members managing or working the farm must be provided such funds; without direct access to family money, such men have considerably less day-to-day financial autonomy than do the others. In Huang Yu-lai's wealthy family, for example, the second son, who is the farm manager, must often ask his father for cigarette money, while his three brothers for the most part limit their requests to funds connected with the family businesses. We have noted, however, that in most complex households the farm manager is the oldest son, and as long as his father continues to redistribute and manage family money this man is far less involved than his brothers in the household's financial affairs; there is, then, a very dramatic change in the oldest son's position when he assumes the roles previously held by his father in the family economy.

Most money in the pockets of men is thus family money circulating within a redistributive framework. And it is not at all paradoxical that one expression of men's dominant position in the *chia* economy is their very limited rights with respect to private property. Such rights in fact are curtailed by mutual agreement among the men; they are encouraged to submit to the constraints of collective life precisely because the alternative is *chia* partition.

The growth of a complex household involves the introduction into the family economy of new women whose assimilation contrasts with the process at work among men, for the women are increasingly restricted to farming and domestic work. Such restrictions apply to both the mother-in-law and her daughters-in-law in most households that have diversified into nonfarming activities, so that in the transition of such units from conjugal to complex form we can see a simplification of the woman's economic role. But there nevertheless are differences between stem and joint households in the work roles of mothers and their daughters-in-law. Table 23 shows that in seven stem households the daughter-in-law specializes in farming while her mother-in-law does the cooking and other domestic work. The mother-in-law's position gradually changes, however; in 17 out of 21 joint households she has retired from most labor and assumed a fully managerial role, and in one she is fully retired.

Yet the mother-in-law is the dominant figure even before she turns from working with her son's wife to the supervision of her activities. The purchase of food is her prerogative from the outset, and only if she plans to be absent from the household or in the event of her illness is this responsibility delegated to the daughter-in-law. Again, as the mother-in-law moves about the household, dangling prominently from her trouser pocket are a bunch of keys that give access to the storage rooms where food or equipment are secured; they are duplicates of those held by her husband, and are both symbols and evidence of the mother-in-law's overall control of domestic affairs.

In joint households the daughters-in-law are in the fields part of the time and take up household labor on a rotation basis. The duration of shifts varies from household to household; quite commonly, if there are two daughters-in-law, each works in the kitchen for fifteen days; with three, ten-day shifts are usual; one household with six daughters-in-law assigns women domestic work for one week at a time.

The woman on domestic duty spends most of her time preparing meals for the household and caring for the family's pigs, whose sties are always located only a short distance away. Her first task is to prepare breakfast for household members, and as the food and rice are still cooking, she takes the day's laundry to a nearby stream or irrigation canal. Here she is joined by the

Table 23
Work and Management Roles of Women
Residing in Yen-liao Complex Households

	Stem Households			Joint Households			
	Mothers	Daughters-in-law	Daughters	Mothers	Daughters-in-law	Daughters	Grand-daughters
Work Roles							
Full-time salaried workers			1			6	3
Farming only		7.	3				
Enterprise operation only		1 a					
Miscellaneous wage labor only			2				
Farming & miscellaneous wage labor		1	1	1	2	4	3
Domestic Work							
Full-time (alone)	7		1	1			
Part-time (shared) b	1						
With miscellaneous wage labor, alone		1					
Ditto, shared	1	1					
With enterprise operation, alone				1	1		
Ditto, shared					3		
With farming, alone	1				1		
Ditto, shared		1			33		
With farming & miscellaneous wage labor, shared	2	2	1		12		
Management roles							
Domestic management, only	1			17			
TOTALS	13	14	9	20	52	10	6
Retired	1			1			

a A daughter with a uxorilocally married husband

b Domestic work may be shared by a woman and her daughter-in-law, or on a rotation basis by several daughters-in-law.

wives of her husband's brothers; but while they wash only the clothing worn by members of their own *fang*, the woman on domestic duty also tends to the laundry of her parents-in-law.

After serving breakfast and washing the dishes, her next job is to prepare the pig food. She harvests a day's supply of sweet potato leaves, which are usually grown on fields convenient to the household. She then chops the leaves and cooks them, most frequently in a room near the pigpens that has been set aside for such processing. A hand-cleaver was once used for chopping, but now most families in Yen-liao have a machine for slicing sweet potato leaves and tubers; this device, made of iron, is operated by pushing down on a foot pedal and at the same time stuffing the leaves through a funnel at the top of the machine. These machines make chopping quicker and less toilsome, and they often appear in a girl's dowry; their inclusion in the dowry reflects the absorption of pig-rearing into the domestic routine, for it is an assertion by the girl's natal family of their continuing interest in the girl's welfare. (By 1972, many of the machines were motor-driven.)

Pigs are fed daily in the morning, early afternoon, and late afternoon; for each feeding, the woman prepares one or more buckets of a feed mixture, which includes sweet potato leaves chopped and cooked the day before, soybean cakes, rice chaff, sweet potato tubers, and a variety of commercially prepared foods. The proportions of each ingredient vary with different techniques and with the age of the animals.

The woman on domestic duty harvests from a garden some or all of the vegetables she uses in preparing three meals for her family that day, and she also tends to the family's poultry. While most of the daughter-in-law's domestic work consists of a well-established daily routine, her mother-in-law sometimes assigns her additional tasks such as collecting and binding firewood material. During rice harvest she is frequently joined by her mother-in-law, if the latter is physically up to it, when sunning and winnowing the grain.

When a woman's turn at domestic work is over, she goes back to the fields and comes under the direction of the manager of farming operations. Most farming tasks are undertaken by men and women alike. During rice cultivation initial weeding is usually restricted to women and plowing to men, but both sexes transplant and harvest the crop. There is no sexual differentiation during most phases of tobacco production; the only men's specialties are plowing, duty in the tobacco house while the drying chamber is in operation, and the sorting of tobacco leaves into grades, while both men and women flatten the leaves and bind them into small bunches. Given the wide employment of women in farming, it is not surprising that they are available for labor exchange.

It is precisely the deemphasis of sexual differences in the organization of farming which reinforces the superordinate position of men in the overall arrangement of the family economy. Women in families and households at all levels of complexity participate in a wide variety of activities within the agricultural sector, but they are progressively restricted to this sector as the number of adults in the family work force increases; men also have a general role in farming, but their dominance is expressed with increasing clarity as more become fully occupied with nonagricultural work, and as they monopolize managerial positions on and off the farm.

Sexual status as such is an important factor in the arrangement of economic activities. With a smaller work force sexual segregation can more readily be detrimental to efficiency, which can take priority; but as a family comes to comprise a larger number of adults, sexual discriminations are given greater latitude of expression. Yet numerical increase involves marriage, which results in structural change; as the scope of a woman's participation in the general run of family economic life is reduced, she is provided with new spheres of activity from which men are barred. Let us now turn to consider how such changes in the status of women come about, and their important implications for complex family organization.

CHAPTER 6

Weddings and Women

WE NEED only a simple characterization of marriage when we consider its implications in Yen-liao for family continuity and other demographic matters, or for quantitative changes in family organization; a man is granted exclusive sexual access to his bride, and usually she is incorporated into his family. For marriage so described, the significance of the nuptial ceremonials lies in their proclaiming and validating the new union in the customary manner.

We cannot so lightly dismiss the wedding ceremonials once we turn to the important qualitative changes in family organization that result from marriage, for these changes are in fact brought about by the ceremonial sequence that culminates in the wedding. We have already had to deal with marriage as a creative factor which, by confirming men as adults, redefines the basis of their cooperation within the family; but the formative process also includes the definition of husband and wife as a new social unit within the larger family, and new property relationships and economic roles are created. I shall consider the marriage procedure mainly in terms of its significance for family development; I first provide an overview of marriage practices and then I describe in some detail those elements in the ceremonial sequence which have a direct bearing on changes in family structure and economic organization. Marriage is a public occasion not only in that the ceremonial sequence is arranged to insure its exposure to as many eyes as possible, but also in that the two families party to the wedding must draw upon the support and participation of many other families in order for the affair to be conducted successfully. The many families who actively participate in a wedding are linked to the families of bride and groom within the larger framework of Mei-nung's social system, and I shall try to show on what basis and for what purposes these families are brought into the proceedings.

My summary of the events leading to the establishment of a new husband–wife unit is a synthesis of my observations of the nineteen marriages to which Yen-liao families were party during the period of my fieldwork. Each marriage was between a member of a Yen-liao family and an outsider; Yen-liao families provided brides in ten cases and grooms in nine (but two of the latter had been living outside of Yen-liao before their marriage, and after the wedding they left the village together with their brides). The first of the nineteen weddings was on February 28, 1964, and the last on June 19, 1965; but at any given moment, of course, different families were involved in different phases of the procedure which only culminates on the wedding day (for a general description of Taiwanese Hakka weddings see Liao 1967).

Weddings in Mei-nung have been "modernized" insofar as the principal actors now travel by cab (since about 1955) instead of sedan chair, bride and groom wear western-style attire, and a truck is used to transport dowry and other items. But the structure of marriage is very much in the Chinese tradition and has as its framework the procedure anciently fixed as the "Six Rites," which Freedman has summarized as follows:

> Inquiries are made in a girl's family by a go-between sent by a family seeking a bride; genealogical and horoscopic data are sought by the go-between; the girl's horoscope is matched with the boy's; the betrothal is clinched by the transfer of gifts; the date of the wedding (that is, the transfer of the bride) is fixed; the bride is moved. (Freedman 1970b:181)

Another traditional aspect of weddings is that the movement of persons and goods is structured within a complex ritual framework; it would appear that much of the Chinese religious system in its Mei-nung variant is implicated at one point or another in the ceremonial sequence, for there is worship not only of ancestors, but also of major and lesser deities in the Taoist pantheon.

A family prepared to arrange the marriage of a boy or girl in its charge first contacts or accepts the services of a marriage broker or *mei-jen* ("*moe-gnin*"), who may be a man or a woman. The marriage broker's activities may be limited to serving as a passive go-between for families who have already come to an informal agreement, or the broker can be an active matchmaker, bringing to each other's attention families with persons eligible for marriage. The broker's spouse must cooperate during many ceremonies which at different points call for husband and wife to assume the *mei-jen* role individually or together, and the broker may serve only in such a ceremonial capacity when both parties to a marriage have worked out all the details beforehand.

When two families express interest in a match the broker can arrange the "*k'on se-moe*" ("seeing the girl"), which is first in the sequence of formalized activities culminating in marriage. The young man calls at the girl's home in the company of his parents, other family members, and a few close relatives or friends; a similarly constituted group receives them, with the broker also in attendance, and all are served refreshments by the girl herself. After an hour or so the visitors depart, with the young man leaving a small cash gift (usually NT$60).

The girl's family can reject the match by having the broker return the money; if they keep it the young man's party can simply fail to respond—an almost insulting form of rejection—or they can send the broker to fetch the girl's *pa-tzu* ("*pat-se*"), her horoscope of "eight characters." These are matched with those of the young man by a specialist who determines if they have the compatibility required for a successful marriage. If a man's family has decided against a marriage, an acceptable procedure is to express this by reporting that the two *pa-tzu* do not match;

in a minority of instances the rejection has in fact been the consequence of unfavorable horoscopic diagnoses.

Most persons preparing for marriage will in any event participate in more than one *"k'on se-moe"* visit before they move on to the next major ceremonial event, the *"la ka-moun"* ("visiting the gates of the home"). For this occasion a party representing the girl's family is treated to a banquet-style lunch at the home of her prospective spouse; with the girl's parents are others from her family, the host's relatives and friends, the broker, but never the girl herself. The *"la ka-moun"* is said to give the girl's side an opportunity to inspect the groom's home and surroundings, and while the marriage may still be called off after this point, it is very uncommon.

The events described so far provide a ceremonial framework for the selection of spouses and the negotiation of marriage agreements; there is nothing in the arrangement of the activities themselves that commits a family to a match, and for many the events during this phase do provide an opportunity to search for a satisfactory marriage. Yet precisely the same sequence of activities precedes a marriage sponsored by families who have reached agreement completely on their own. The ceremonies are taken as a totality, and this may be because during their second phase they guide a creative process such that the entire series of events becomes too important to tamper with.

Fixing the betrothal date is a declaration by both sides of agreement to the marriage. A specialist consulted by the groom's family provides the date on a red slip of paper which also sets the timing of the major rituals that follow, including those during the wedding day, thus expressing the betrothal as the first in a series of interconnected and interdependent events. In the morning of the day chosen for the betrothal ceremony (*"kuou-t'in"*), a party representing the groom's family goes by cab to the girl's home; riding with the groom are his parents, other family members, the marriage brokers (husband and wife), and sometimes the groom's close agnates or friends. They bring along many gifts and a large sum of betrothal money (*p'in-chin,* *"p'in-kim"*); when they arrive they enter the ancestral hall while members of the girl's family place the gifts on a table set in front of the tablets and offer wine, burn incense and ritual paper money, and verbally inform the ancestors of the girl's betrothal. Additional guests—mostly the host's kinsmen—are invited to the betrothal feast that follows; and after the meal is over it is the turn of the boy's family to receive gifts, which they take back in the cab.

After the betrothal ceremony the groom's family begins to prepare the room where the new couple will sleep and keep their personal possessions. The date and time for "setting up the bed" (*"on-ts'ong"*) is included in the document which schedules the wedding ceremonials, and is usually a week or more before the wedding. It is held that following *"on-ts'ong"* there should be someone, preferably the man about to marry, who will sleep in the bed every night until bride and groom move in together.

Major ceremonial activity does not resume until the day before the wedding. In the afternoon, the bride's father, or close agnates acting on his behalf, present offerings to their ancestors and sometimes also to one or two of the neighborhood's tutelary earth-god shrines (*"pac-koung"*). The offerings consist of wine, eggs, fowl, cuttlefish, and bean-curd drawn from and then returned to the large stocks purchased for the wedding feast.

The groom's family also worships on that day, but according to a more elaborate procedure known as "honoring the matrilateral ancestors" (*"kin ngoe-tsou"*). The most important in a series of offerings made by the groom are in the ancestral halls of his mother's father and his paternal grandmother's father, but stops at these halls are interspersed with trips to two important temples, one near Yen-liao and one elsewhere in Mei-nung. After the groom returns home, he presents offerings to the village's earth-god shrine and to the "pig-pen diety" (*"tchou-lan pac-koung"*) who guards over the family's animals.[1] These offerings are similar to those at the bride's side, but also include

1. The two temples are religious centers for the Lung-tu and total Mei-nung communities respectively, while the Yen-liao local shrine has similar significance for the village itself. Thus the worship includes recognition by the groom's family of their participation in the hierarchy of community organization discussed in chapter 2.

plates of small sweetcakes made from glutinous rice. At the conclusion of each offering the sweetcakes are distributed to members of the group and bystanders, mainly children, while other items are returned for consumption during the wedding.

The emphasis on cognatic ties expressed in the *"kin ngoe-tsou"* is followed on the evening of the same day by the participation of many agnates in the ritual known as *"van-chin"* or "completing (the worship of the) spirits." This is a long and complicated procedure which commences between 7:00 and 8:00 P.M. and usually continues until well after midnight (one ceremony held during a typhoon was shortened to two hours); first *T'ien-kung*, the Heavenly Deity, is worshipped and then the ancestors of the compound. All families in the local agnatic group sharing the ancestral hall usually participate, and as the *"van-chin"* proceeds, the men, women, and children of the compound repeatedly arrange themselves in front of the offering tables, incense in hand, and bow as directed by the ritual specialist hired for the occasion.

On the morning before the wedding day preparations begin on a large scale at the compounds of both families involved in the nuptials. Arriving at each compound are relatives and neighbors recruited to help the host family; the bride's side usually requests the assistance of between 20 and 25 persons, who remain on the scene until the conclusion of the next day's evening meal; from 40 to 50 persons help at the groom's compound, and they disperse only during the early afternoon of their third day of work. The male helpers at each compound see to the delivery and arrangement of the canopy, tables, benches, and other fixtures needed for the wedding rituals and feast; most tables are set in the compound's courtyard, where they are protected by a large canvas or plastic canopy which roofs the courtyard and is attached to the compound's base and wings.

The helpers, male and female alike, spend most of their time preparing and serving meals; in addition to the major wedding feast, there is feasting on a smaller scale throughout the interval that helpers are at work, for their meals are also provided by the host family. The family sponsoring a wedding feast has as its most important source of assistance the other households in its own compound; cognatic kin or neighbors send helpers when requested, but more persons are contributed by each family within the local agnatic group. At the same time, the kitchens belonging to the different households in the compound are used for preparing the wedding-period meals, and the entire membership of the local agnatic group feasts together with the host family and the other helpers.

A portion of the food needed for the feast and helpers at the bride's side is provided by the groom's family on the morning before the wedding day; a representative of his family delivers the *"tchou-p'ien,"* the "side of pork," which is a cut of meat weighing between 76 and 80 Taiwanese catties (99–104 lbs.). The groom's side delivers at the same time another piece of pork weighing about 20 Taiwanese catties (26 lbs.) and known as *"a-p'o-niouc,"* the "maternal grandmother's pork." This is a gift for the natal family of the bride's maternal grandmother and is said to express gratitude at their having reared the mother of the bride's mother. The bride's side quickly delivers the meat to the appropriate family (if the family has partitioned, the meat is distributed among the derivative families).

Let us for a moment consider the significance of the *"a-p'o-niouc's"* distribution to kinsmen seemingly so remote from the bride's family. Although the *"a-p'o-niouc"* is supplied in the first instance by the groom's side it is in fact a kinship connection to the bride's family that is reaffirmed. *"A-p'o-niouc"* can be viewed in conjunction with the "honoring the matrilateral ancestors" or *"kin ngoe-tsou"* ceremony described earlier, even though it is the groom who worships at the ancestral halls of his mother's father and his paternal grandmother's father. In fact, of course, both ceremonies are testimonials to the relationships created through the marriage of the parents of the bride or groom. The two sets of ceremonies have different kinsmen in the senior generation as their objects of attention, but if these kinsmen are viewed together they very neatly provide for the generation senior to the parents the non-agnatic links needed to incorporate into a combined genealogy their entire set of eight

grandparents, as illustrated in Figure 7; the father's agnatic ancestors receive ample attention during the *"van-chin"* and at
many other points in the ceremonial sequence. Of course, the
"a-p'o-niouc" distribution and the *"kin ngoe-tsou"* do not occur
together as far as any one family is concerned, except during a
very few combined son-and-daughter weddings (these are
known to occur in Mei-nung, but there have been none in Yen-
liao); but most families stage one ceremony and then the other
as their sons and daughters marry.

These ceremonies are not isolated events; they incorporate
into the realm of custom, and therefore provide yet another context for the expression of ties of cognatic kinship, an aspect of
Mei-nung's social structure whose importance we have already
seen from a variety of perspectives. It is not fortuitous that dimensions of the dense kinship network are highlighted during
wedding ceremonials, for through marriage additional strands
are woven in.

The wedding day is both the culmination and the busiest
phase of the ceremonial sequence. The first group to depart
from the groom's home leaves shortly after a truck hired by the
groom's family arrives at their compound early in the morning,
usually before 6:00 A.M. The vehicle remains only long enough
for several men to load onto it a "meat box" and a "vegetable
box" and to clamber aboard themselves. The food the boxes
contain is contributed to the stocks at the bride's home; the
boxes also hold a supply of joss, ritual paper money, and firecrackers. The men on the truck are known as *"ts'ia-long"* or
"wedding porters" as are those who later bring dowry from the
bride's side. The groom's *"ts'ia-long"* are relatives and friends,
some in their late teens, the oldest in their early 30s. They ride
together with four musicians who play traditional instruments
during the trip to the bride's family.

After a short interval the remainder of the groom's party departs by cab. The groom, who wears a western-style suit and tie,
is accompanied by the marriage brokers (husband and wife) and
by his two *"t'oung-hang"* or "co-travelers." The *"t'oung-hang"*
are held to represent and protect the interests of the groom and

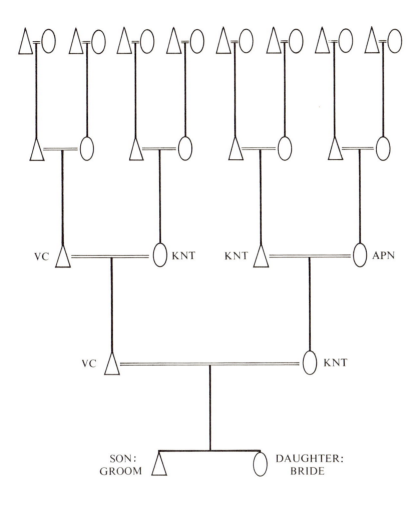

Code: VC="van-chin" and other rites of agnatic ancestor worship
        KNT="kin-ngoe-tsou" ("honoring the matrilateral ancestors")
        APN="a-p'o-niouc" ("maternal grandmother's pork")
        FIGURE 7 KINSHIP LINKS EMPHASIZED DURING WEDDING
                  CEREMONIALS

his family during the proceedings at the bride's home. One is usually a relative or friend who is knowledgeable about wedding procedures and can coach the groom while they are at the bride's home; and men prominent in Mei-nung politics and administration, such as the head of the township or the Farmer's Association, serve as the other *"t'oung-hang"* if the groom's family has kin ties with them or is influential in its own right. Such men have the experience for yet another responsibility of the *"t'oung-hang,"* who must keep the groom sober by drinking most of the wine pressed upon him while he is breakfasting at the bride's house. The *"t'oung-hang"* bring along additional ritual paper money, incense, candles, wine, and candy, and a container, sealed with red paper, known as the *"t'iap-hap,"* the "card box." In the box are eight "red packets" and a slip of paper inviting the bride's family to lunch at the groom's side. The "red packets" amount to somewhat less than NT$300 and are distributed as follows: (1) children of the bride's family, (2) bride's hairdresser, (3) the cook who prepares the wedding feast for the bride's family, (4) women who arranged the flowers later distributed by the bride during the wedding feast at the groom's side, (5) the man who lights candles in the bride's ancestral hall, (6) the woman who shaves the bride's face before the makeup is applied, (7) the tailor who made clothing for the bride, (8) the bride's family.

When the truck reaches the bride's home, the goods are brought into the ancestral hall and arranged on a table before the tablet, while the wedding porters are led to other rooms and offered refreshments and cigarettes. Then the cab with groom, co-travelers, and marriage brokers arrives, and all get out immediately except for the groom, who waits until a young boy from the bride's family invites him out by offering two cigarettes on a tray. The groom places a "red packet" containing NT$5.00 on the tray, emerges from the cab, and is led by the co-travelers directly into the ancestral hall, where he bows with incense in hand toward the tablet together with a man who is a member of the bride's family or a close agnate. After they leave, the food brought by the wedding porters is removed from the offering table and given to the helpers preparing meals, and the tables in the hall are rearranged in preparation for the breakfast, which forms the main wedding feast sponsored by the bride's family.

Among the guests at the wedding feast are a select few who dine in the ancestral hall while the others eat outside at tables set up in the center of the compound under a large canopy. Special attention is lavished on those in the ancestral hall, where there are usually four tables seating eight persons each. To the rear of the hall and to the right of the tablet, there is one table where the co-travelers, the wedding broker (man), and often other prominent guests sit together with the groom; the seat to his right is the most honored of all, and it is usually offered to the eldest male in the bride's compound, who sometimes refuses and leaves it for one of the co-travelers, especially if the latter is a prominent person. Seated at the other tables in the hall are the wedding porters and some of the more prominent or elderly men invited to the wedding feast. One man at each table represents the bride's family; he keeps the guests' winecups constantly filled and offers them cigarettes throughout the meal, while other family members circulate among the tables toasting the guests. The wedding porters receive from their host a special attention later reciprocated by the hospitality the groom's family lavishes upon the bride's wedding porters, and the two families in fact seek to outdo each other as hosts in this respect.

Except for representatives from the groom's side, the persons in the ancestral hall are "paying guests" in common with the larger group eating outside. The wedding invitation is addressed to the family head (*chia-chang*), but another family member sometimes appears in his stead. When a guest arrives he first goes to a table where a man takes his cash gift and records the amount in a small booklet. All guests present money, with closer relatives tending to give more than distant kin, co-residents in the village, friends, or colleagues. The number of guests invited varies from wedding to wedding, but invitations to the breakfast feast held by the bride's side usually number between 75 and 100, while 150 or more are sent out for the noon or afternoon feasts hosted by the groom's family. It is not uncommon for one family to be invited by both sides and to dispatch family members to both meals. By inviting a family to a wedding the host both expresses and exploits a social tie; a family that intentionally ignores an invitation does not simply terminate whatever positive relationship there may have been but inevitably turns it into one of enmity. In most cases the appropriate response is for a family representative to attend the feast, but kinsmen and friends who live far away often send money without making a personal appearance. Money contributed by the guest is for the host family and serves to offset wedding expenses.

The bride remains in her room throughout all the activity described above. Wearing a western-style bridal gown, she finally emerges in the late morning, usually after 11:00 A.M.; following the groom, she is led into the ancestral hall where they both bow low before the bride's ancestral tablet for the final time that day. They then enter a cab where they are joined by the groom's co-travelers and the wedding broker (woman). The bride's co-travelers (also called *"t'oung-hang"*), a group of six or eight girls, follow in a second cab or wait for the first to return. The girls are the bride's friends or relatives who are of her age; they bring along in a basket the flowers used during one of the events at the groom's side.

At about the same time, the bride's wedding porters load dowry onto the truck earlier driven from the groom's side; the vehicle is now filled with cargo, while during the earlier trip it had been relatively empty. The bride's wedding porters, like the groom's, are younger men who are relatives and friends. They crowd into the dowry truck together with the groom's wedding porters and the musicians, and with the departure of the truck the wedding-day ceremonials at the bride's side end.

But major activity at the groom's house only begins when the cab arrives with bride, groom, and the other passengers; all but the bride emerge while she, like the groom earlier, waits until "invited" out by a young member of the groom's family; after she places a "red packet" on the tray he holds she is led from the cab directly to the *hsin-fang* or "new room" prepared by the groom's family, and when her co-travelers arrive they join her there. When the truck comes, the dowry is immediately unloaded by the bride's wedding porters.

By this time guests are showing up, and the procedure for receiving their cash gifts is the same as at the bride's side. But at the groom's side it is not uncommon for richer families to host one wedding feast at noontime and another later in the afternoon or early evening; the second meal is a catered affair mainly attended on a one-person-per-invitation basis by non-kinsmen, for whom commercial, political, or other ties with the host family are maintained in a context much larger than that provided by the Mei-nung local community. The noontime meal, however, is called for by the practices that organize marriage within Mei-nung society, and such meals follow the same format whether or not they are followed by a second feast. During the noontime meal the bride's wedding porters are feted inside the ancestral hall, while special hospitality is also lavished upon her co-travelers, who sit outside the hall, but at their own table. Shortly after the meal has begun, the *"ts'ap-fa"* or "inserting of flowers" begins: the marriage broker (woman), holding the basket of flowers earlier brought by the bride's co-travelers, escorts the bride from the "new room" to the guests seated under the canopy; she leads her from one to another of the older women and at each stop she hands a flower to the bride; the bride fixes it into the hair of a woman indicated by the marriage broker, and each woman so adorned rewards the bride with a small cash gift.

When she has concluded the *"ts'ap-fa,"* the bride returns to the "new room." Most of the guests depart when the meal ends, but pushing their way into the now very crowded "new room" are some men who want to "poke fun at the bride" (*nao hsin-niang*); the men who tease and joke with her are commonly relatives of the groom's family, sometimes joined by a few non-kinsmen.

During the afternoon, the bride emerges at the arrival of a professional photographer; she returns to the "new room" until

her co-travelers are about to leave, when she gives each a hand-
kerchief or a bottle of perfume. At about the same time, the
groom sees off with cigarettes the departing wedding porters,
who go back on the truck, otherwise now empty, which had
brought them with the dowry. During the afternoon the bride
steps outside once more and goes with the groom to the ancestral hall where they bow before the tablets as directed by a
close agnate of the groom; they then bow before this man and
the groom's father. The marriage broker (man) is also present;
the groom bows and presents him a tray with two betel nuts,
two cigarettes, and a "red packet" containing the *mei-jen li*,
which is the marriage broker's "commission," and generally
amounts to NT$220. The entire group leaves and the bride re-
turns to the "new room," where she remains until later that evening.

The last of the day's major ceremonial events is the *"sin-
niong-tsiou,"* or "bride's wine," which usually begins at about
9:00 P.M. Small tables are aligned so as to form one or two
longer ones on which are set candies, cookies, and fruit provided by the groom's family. This event is open to all members
of families invited to the wedding, and individuals from the
bride's new family also participate. The guests usually seat
themselves around the table in shifts; entertainment is first provided for the male guests, who later leave to be replaced by the
women. During each shift, which lasts about 20 minutes, the
bride makes several circuits around the table accompanied by
the marriage broker (woman); the bride first serves betel nuts;
when she next serves cigarettes she also is joined by the groom,
who lights those accepted by the guests; then she offers each
guest his choice of wine or an alternate beverage; she serves
cigarettes and wine once more, and finally tea. As the guests at
each shift get up to depart, they leave the bride a cash gift.

After the *"sin-niong-tsiou"* the groom once more burns incense in front of the ancestral tablet while the bride goes directly to the "new room." The groom joins her after a few minutes and begins the *"sia-fa,"* the "removal of the flowers"
which had been pinned to her hair as part of her wedding

makeup. The marriage broker (woman) and several women from the bride's new family help her change into ordinary attire and then serve her the first meal she has had that day. Soon all the women leave except for the marriage broker, who says: *"pac tze ts'ien soun, van nian fou koui"* ("may you have innumerable sons and grandsons, may you have eternal prosperity"); the marriage broker then departs, leaving the couple to themselves.

The day following the wedding continues to be organized by ritual events, which begin early in the morning when the bride and groom enter the family kitchen and burn incense before the picture representing the Kitchen God; the bride leaves behind a "red packet" with anywhere from NT$2.00 to NT$10.00, said to symbolize the bride's apologies for not preparing all of the day's meals for her new family. She then sets out on a "return visit" (*"tchon-moun"*) to her parents' home, accompanied by the marriage broker (female), the groom, and one or both of his parents.

The *"tchon-moun"* party goes by cab and takes paraphernalia for worship in the host family's ancestral hall, including firecrackers, incense, candles, a bottle of wine, and some candy. The noontime feast that follows the hall ritual brings together members of the new kindred created by the marriage; in addition to the *"tchon-moun"* party, the bride's parents invite agnatic kin and cognates through other marriages. The marriage broker's husband attends, arriving through his own devices, and often a few friends of the bride's parents, but the affair is primarily one for relatives new and old.

Early in the afternoon the *"tchon-moun"* party returns to the groom's home, by which time items borrowed for the wedding have been returned and other chores connected with the previous day's activities have been taken care of by the helpers, who have also had their final meal (noontime) at the groom's family. The preparation of supper on the same day marks the first time that the bride cooks for her new family. She first bathes, using a pail of hot water prepared by a younger person in the family whom she rewards with a "red packet" with NT$5.00 or NT$10.00. Then it is her turn to prepare hot water for the family members, who as usual use one or two small washrooms in succession. By the side of each pail of hot water she places a pair of sandals provided by her natal family. These sandals, the *"t'iap-kioc hai,"* are sent with the dowry for all family members on the groom's side old enough to walk. The bride distributes the sandals as an expression of her new loyalties and obligations, but she gets paid when she gives out another category of footwear, the *"hao-vi hai,"* after that night's supper or at some point during the next two days. Twice more the bride's return is a time for her natal family to host members and relatives of her new one; the events are called *"chip-gni-gnit"* ("twelfth day") and *"man-gniet"* ("full month"), but they frequently occur earlier than the days they are named after. These visits are the last of the activities required by the wedding procedure and they are among the least elaborate, for travel is often by bicycle, there are no offerings in the ancestral hall, and only a small number of guests at the meals.

We now turn to the sequence of economic activities organized by the ceremonials that commence with betrothal; money and goods are transferred between the families of bride and groom, and other transactions also involve nonfamily members, mainly kinsmen. All 19 weddings I observed in Yen-liao were organized such that bride and groom are the ultimate recipients of most wealth circulating within the wedding framework. This includes each of three weddings where the groom, having been economically autonomous before marriage, was joined by his bride in reverting to the same condition after their wedding; two men returned to their primary households in Yen-liao for the wedding ceremonials and then went back to Taipei, while one who married a Yen-liao girl likewise temporarily returned to his natal home elsewhere in Mei-nung.

But the pattern of wedding transactions has additional implications for family development in the 16 cases where the new couple joined others in the same household. There are cash payments to the bride which bestow upon her rights to hold and independently dispose of her own wealth, and at the same time there are other allocations that define husband and wife as a property-owning unit; and there is still the category of family property, also expressed during the wedding transactions. These are the spheres of property that provide a framework for elements of economic organization unique to complex households and to complex *chia* groups which are economically inclusive. In discussing the allocations that create the new property spheres, I propose to follow generally the order in which transactions occur within the sequence of wedding ceremonials; but I think it more illuminating if the different payments that establish a woman's independent rights are considered separately, and I therefore take up these allocations only after dealing with the others.

The first transfer of gifts linked to the endowment of bride and groom is during the betrothal and reinforces the commitment of both sides to the marriage. The most expensive individual item is the betrothal money presented by the groom's family to the bride's. The "standard" fee is said to be NT$12,000, but the amount actually given varies somewhat; NT$12,600 is the highest fee to come to my attention. Included within the comparatively narrow range of variation from the "standard" are payments made by the richest and one of the poorer families in Yen-liao. The betrothal money is often given in two installments, one part during the betrothal ceremony and the remainder a few days before the wedding. This fee is in no way a form of "brideprice," for its effect is to *partially* subsidize the wedding expenses later borne by the family of the bride; in most cases the dowry brought by the bride costs more than the betrothal money her family receives. In that the betrothal money represents no economic gain for the girl's family it is not a permanent allocation and may be differentiated from the remaining engagement gifts.

One category of goods distributed within the framework of marriage rituals includes food and other items consumed during the ceremonies themselves. During betrothal the most important goods in this category are the betrothal cakes, between 120 and 160 of which are presented by the groom's side. After receiving the cakes, made from glutinous rice flour and with candy and nut fillings, the bride's family returns a small quantity and both sides distribute them to friends and relatives, usually giving one cake and two betel nuts to each family. This cake presentation is especially important for the bride's side, for it serves as a substitute for the distribution of printed invitations to the wedding feast they will host. The remaining goods given during betrothal to the bride's family as a unit are also in the category of consumables, as are gifts from the bride's side to the groom's family group.

In the second category of wedding goods are items that survive the betrothal and later ceremonies; some, such as tiepins or rings, are more durable than clothing or soap, but all become "property" for periods of time. During the betrothal ceremony only the bride or groom as individuals or as a unit are recipients of second-category gifts. The bride receives gold jewelry as a personal gift from the groom's family, and from the bride's side the groom gets a wristwatch and the western-style suit he will wear on the wedding day; the bride's side also supplies pillows and sometimes other items for the bride and groom as a unit, but these gifts have far less value than those given the groom himself.

Following betrothal the process of endowing the new couple continues with the establishment of a new room (*"on-ts'ong"*), which is a responsibility of the groom's family. The room can be a newly built extension of the compound where the family resides, or if an old room is used it is completely refurbished. The groom's family also provides some of the room's furnishings, including a desk, a bureau for clothing, a trunk, a mosquito net, and a wooden bed. The bed is an elevated platform which extends from wall to wall and takes up the rear portion of the room; the bed is covered with *tatami* (Japanese-style mats), and has sliding doors which likewise extend to both walls and can thus close the platform off from the rest of the room.

The cost for the groom's family of the new room's preparation represents a transfer of family wealth to the new couple. The *"on-ts'ong"* marks out the private domain of bride and groom, for access to the new room and its furnishings is restricted to them. It is safe to say that the personal items given bride and groom during betrothal have greater value than any they had ever before received at one time, but because these are personal items they are qualitatively no different from earlier allocations. With the *"on-ts'ong,"* however, bride and groom are defined as a unit in that they share rights to certain holdings which are distinct from family property and the individual possessions of family members. In this connection it can be noted that a new room provided by reoutfitting an old one will have previously been serving as a storage area or as sleeping quarters for family members not yet married. I know no cases of one couple moving out to make way for another, for the former would in fact be giving up their property.

The dowry transfer makes up, in value and bulk, the largest of the transactions incorporated into the wedding procedure, but like the betrothal gifts the dowry is in fact a set of allocations to different parties. The groom's family as a whole receives from the bride's side such household items as a radio (or, since 1965, a television set), tables and chairs, an electric fan, a fluorescent lamp; farming equipment (such as a rice-threshing machine) may also be included. The new couple receive additional furnishings for their room, bedding, a bicycle (or a motorcycle if the bride's side is rich) and other items. The clothing and other items meant for the bride's personal use greatly exceed in value and variety those received by the groom, who already had been provided for by the bride's side during the betrothal.

From the betrothal through the wedding day, the bride receives the gifts that establish her rights to independently own and dispose of wealth. The gift-givers include her older brothers and men who are the heads of the families in her local agnatic group; otherwise the contributors are females, including her sisters, other women and girls in the compound who have married in or have yet to marry out, the sisters of her parents and grandparents, and more distant cognatic kin. Friends give gifts they have purchased, but they are far outnumbered by relatives, who generally give the girl cash. One bride received gifts from 35 persons outside of her family; 29 kinsmen, including six men, gave her money as did one girlfriend, while five gave her other presents.

Although cash gifts manifest formal obligations of kinship, the other presents are a more intimate and personal expression of friendship. And if for the first contributions to her purse the bride relies on her family's position within a matrix of kinship relationships, it is the location of the groom's family within their own kinship network that provides her additional cash income. During the "inserting of flowers," held while the noontime wedding feast at the groom's side is in progress, each woman having a flower pinned into her hair by the bride reciprocates by placing a NT$5 or NT$10 "red packet" into the flower basket held by the marriage broker. The women who give money are the groom's married senior kin, both agnates and cognates. In one wedding the bride received cash from 26 of the groom's relatives, as follows:

From outside compound		*From own compound*	
Link to groom	*Number of persons*	Link to groom	*Number of persons*
elder si.	4	mo.	1
fa. si.	6	fa. br. wife	1
si. mother-in-law	4	fa. fa. fa. br. so. wife	1
fa. si. mother-in-law	2	fa. fa. fa. br. so. so. wife	1
fa. mo. br. wife	2	fa. fa. fa. br. so. so. so. wife	1
fa. mo. fa. br. wife	1		
fa. fa. si.	1		
fa. mo. si. daughter-in-law	1		

The bride's rights to her purse receive strong confirmation when part of the money is supplied by two groups of kinsmen now linked by her marriage, and among the contributors are many male kin of the groom's family who in the evening attend the "bride's wine," which provides her additional funds. They are joined by neighbors of the groom's family and most significantly by members of that family itself, as can be illustrated by classifying the 64 persons who attended one "bride's wine" as follows:

Men's shift	*48 persons*
Bride's new family	4 persons
Other compound members	14 persons
Outside cognatic kin	13 persons
Other residents of Yen-liao	16 persons
Outside friend (of groom)	1 person

Women's shift	*16 persons*
Bride's new family	2 persons
Other compound members	2 persons
Outside cognatic kin	9 persons
Groom's fa. *"siong-gnin"* [2] (fictive) br. wife	1 person
Other residents of Yen-liao	2 persons

NT$10 or NT$20 is the usual amount a "bride's wine" participant leaves the bride; but among those I have listed above was the bride's father-in-law, who gave NT$100, while two of the groom's brothers each gave NT$10, and a third NT$20. Because the men in her new family attend the "bride's wine," the event highlights the difference between her new position and that of male family members. The men contribute to her private purse what is in fact family money, for the organization of the family economy does not provide them their own funds. Yet the money goes to the bride according to the "bride's wine" format, as gifts given individually by each man who attends. Her family thus expresses support of the "bride's wine" as an occasion when the bride can attract additional contributions—some from kinsmen, but others from persons who come not out of obligation

---

2. Most *"siong-gnin,"* or fictive kin relationships, represent a formalization and intensification of a preexisting friendship. Persons acknowledging each other as *"siong-gnin"* are obligated to act as kinsmen in ceremonial contexts, which serve to affirm and publicly demonstrate what is in fact a permanent social tie.

but because they in fact wish to be entertained. The participation of her new family on the same basis as outsiders is a public demonstration that the family accepts the limited but well-defined economic rights of the new member of their group.

The final event during the wedding sequence which brings the bride income is the distribution of the shoes called *"hao-vi hai";* provided by the bride's natal family and sent with the dowry, the shoes are "sold" to all members of her new family senior to herself and her husband. The bride's earnings depend on the number of family members qualified to receive shoes and on the "prices," which had been negotiated earlier and are about double the store cost. One girl was the first to marry into her father-in-law's family, and could only "sell" him and his wife *"hao-vi hai"* at NT$150 for each pair. Her total earnings of NT$300 were only NT$60 less than those of another bride marrying into a family where six persons "bought" shoes as follows: father-in-law, NT$100; mother-in-law, NT$100; husband's brothers (2), NT$40 each; their wives (2), NT$40 each.

If in the course of "bride's wine" the bride's rights to her own purse are confirmed by her new family for the benefit of the outside world, they are given further recognition within the family when the girl's seniors accept and pay for the shoes. As with "bride's wine" income, her *"hao-vi hai"* earnings are given over by individual members of the family, but in many cases they use family money allocated to them for that purpose. The bride's natal family takes a great interest in the shoes, which they supply only after consulting with the groom's side regarding those qualified to get the footwear, the sizes and styles desired, and the "prices" the recipients are willing to pay. The shoes provide a ceremonial means by which the girl's natal family can determine transfers within her postmarital domestic unit such that family funds become the girl's private holdings. The ceremonials thus emphasize what in the usual course of events becomes one of the enduring features of the relationship between the two families, for the family from which the girl marries is interested not only in endowing her with a private fund, but also in seeing that their new affines respect and act in accordance with the status definitions which, as we shall see, allow a girl to maintain this fund and even increase it.

After the transfer of *"hao-vi hai"* the only remaining wedding transactions are those linked to the "twelfth day" and the "full month" visits of the bride to her natal home. These visits are comparatively inexpensive for the bride's family, and it is safe to say that each usually costs less than NT$400. I have not been able to include them in Tables 24–26, where I outline the economic transfers during one wedding, which created a new husband–wife unit within a Yen-liao primary household. The natal families of the bride and groom in this wedding include farmers, and the groom's side in Yen-liao has income and holdings that place it at about the middle of the rich-to-poor continuum as found in the village.

The families of both bride and groom received less than they paid out in the course of the transactions summarized in Table 26, and this was true for all weddings during my stay in Yen-liao, save one. The latter involved the marriage of a man from one of the wealthiest families in the village. Another member of this family is an important government official, who sent out over 600 wedding invitations, many to farmers having no social ties to his family but who were within his sphere of economic and bureaucratic influence. As a result, the cash gifts received by this family yielded a profit of over NT$6000. The guests invited to the other weddings were already connected socially to the host families in one way or another, and while their presence confirmed existing ties, their cash contributions served to partially subsidize the wedding ceremonials. Most of the losses borne by the families sponsoring weddings must be considered as expenditures for the endowment of bride and groom as individuals or as a unit within the larger family organization. Table 26 shows how in one case about 71 percent of the losses were matched by allocations to the bride and groom from their families or from others participating in the wedding ceremonies hosted by these families, while about 63 percent of the losses were direct allocations to the bride and groom from their families.

Tables 24–26 show how events listed as "pre-wedding pre-

Table 24
The Economy of a Wedding:
Allocations During Wedding Sequence, Groom's Family

Ceremony/event	Item	Value	Object/purpose
Betrothal	Consumables: betrothal cakes and ritual paraphernalia	NT$1,016	Distribution to appropriate persons; use in ancestral hall.
	Alarm clock	250	Bride and groom
	Gold jewelry	1,370	Bride
	Betrothal money	12,200	Bride's family
"On-ts'ong" ("setting up (the bed")	Refurbishing and furnishing of "new room"	3,869	Bride and groom
Wedding period (3 days)	Consumables: food-stuffs, ritual paraphernalia, and other items	14,442	For holding of wedding cere-monies and feasts
"Kin ngoe-tsou" ("honoring the matrilateral ancestors")	motor cart hire	100	For trips to places of worship
Wedding	Printing invitations	100	Wedding guests
	Slaughter of two pigs (including tax). Weight (of whole animals): 480 catties (624 lbs.)	5,751	Bride's family: 76 catties pork Bride's mo.mo. family: 20 catties. Remainder: for wedding consumption
	Dowry truck hire	350	Transfer of goods and persons between homes of bride and groom
	"T'iap-hap" "red packets"	260	NT$ 82: bride's family NT$ 178: other appropriate persons
	"Red packets" distributed by groom.	50	Appropriate members of bride's family and others

Ceremony/event	Item	Value	Object/purpose
Wedding	Cash gifts from guests invited to feasts	15,660	Groom's family
	"Ts'ap-fa" ("inserting flowers"): cash gifts from relatives of groom's family	170	Bride
	Payment to marriage broker	220	For performance of role
	Payment to ritual specialist	70 '	For services rendered
	Payment to cook	100	For services rendered
	"Bride's wine": payments by family members with family funds	130	Bride
	"Bride's wine": payments by family members with non-family funds and payments by others	1,010	Bride
Wedding and "tchon-moun" ("return visit")	Cabs	315	For transport of persons between bride's and groom's families
Wedding	Cash gifts returned to guests	510	"Special guests," [a] cook, marriage broker, ritual specialist
	Payment to musicians	650	For services rendered
	Bride's wedding gown	300	Rent
"Hao-vi-hai" (presentation of shoes)	Cash payments from family	360	Bride

[a] "Special guests" include persons, such as the township head, invited because of their political or social prominence in Mei-nung. Such people attend numerous weddings, and it is understood that their cash gifts would be an impossible financial burden if not returned. But they may refuse to take back the money if the wedding involves their own relatives, close friends, or political associates.

Table 25
The Economy of a Wedding:
Allocations During Wedding Sequence, Bride's Family

Ceremony/event	Item		Value	Object/purpose
Betrothal	Consumables: foodstuffs		NT$1,000	Engagement feast
	Wrist watch, clothing, etc.		2,573	Groom
	Pillows, handker-chiefs, etc.		231	Bride and groom
	Perfume		14	Bride
Pre-wedding presentations	Cash given by relatives and friends		1,240	Bride
Wedding period (including "*tchon-moun*" or "return visit")	Consumables: foodstuffs, ritual para-phernalia, and other items		2,838	For holding of wedding cere-monies and feasts
Wedding	Dowry: radio-phonograph		4,531	Grooms' family
	console	2,200		
	records	32		
	round tables and eight stools	700		
	small table and four chairs	620		
	electric fan	470		
	electric tea pot	95		
	light fixture	100		
	tea pot, cups	70		
	miscellaneous items—serving trays, flash-lights, ashtrays and, others	244		
	Dowry:		2,763	Bride and Groom
	bicycle	1,300		
	blanket	460		
	curtains	150		
	chairs (2)	180		
	miscellaneous items for the "new room"—pillows, screens, locks, mirrors and others	421		

Ceremony/event	Item	Value	Object/purpose
Wedding	toiletry items— tooth paste, brushes, soaps, ointments, washbasins, and others	252	
	Dowry:	4,720	Bride
	sewing machine	1,000	
	wrist watch	400	
	iron	45	
	clothing	2,520	
	miscellaneous items for personal use—needles, thread, yarn, lipstick, etc.	355	
	cash for making additional clothing	400	
	Dowry: cash for personal use	1,000	Bride
	Dowry: handker- chiefs (9)	54	Bride's "*t'oung-hang*" ("co-travelers")
	Dowry: shoes and sandals ("*t'iap-kok- hai*" and "*hao- vi-hai*")	598	Members of groom's family
	Dowry: money attached to various items	260	Groom's family
	"red packets" presented by bride	68	Members of groom's family and other appropriate persons
	cash gifts presented by guests at feast	3,080	Bride's family
"*Tchon-moun*" (return visit)	Money given to groom's relative's children	285	Children coming with "*tchon-moun*" party

Table 26
The Economy of a Wedding: Summary of Allocations and Overall Wedding Expenditures

Groom's family:	A. Value of allocations	NT$42,413
	B. Value of allocations received from bride's family (not including consumables)	4,791
	C. Value of allocations received from other sources (not including consumables)	15,660
	D. Total wedding expenditures (B and C subtracted from A)	21,962
Bride's family:	A. Value of allocations	20,935
	B. Value of allocations received from groom's family (not including consumables)	12,282
	C. Value of allocations received from other sources (not including consumables)	3,080
	D. Total wedding expenditures (B and C subtracted from A)	5,573
Bride & groom:	A. Allocations to bride and groom as a unit (goods only)	
	From groom's family	4,119
	From bride's family	2,994
	B. Allocations to groom as individual (goods only)	
	From groom's family	—
	From bride's family	2,573
	From others	—
	C. Allocations to bride as individual (goods only)	
	From groom's family	1,370
	From bride's family	4,734
	From others	—
	D. Allocations to bride as individual (cash)	
	From groom's family	490
	From bride's family	1,000
	From others	2,420
	E. Total allocations to bride and groom	19,700

sentations," "dowry," "*ts'ap-fa*," "bride's wine," and "*hao-vi hai*" yielded the bride a total of NT$3910, of which NT$2420 came from nonfamily sources. The amount accumulated by the bride varies from wedding to wedding, especially with respect to cash given as "dowry"—i.e. by her natal family—but this dowry payment is generally the largest of the individual cash gifts. The bride's natal family, in other words, to a large extent determines the size of the purse she brings to her new home. Thus another bride received from dowry NT$5000 out of total wedding earnings amounting to NT$8720.

Marriage usually means that the bride's family loses an economically productive family member while the groom's side gains one. Nevertheless, the wedding transactions cannot be regarded merely as "payment" for this transfer of a woman. We have noted that men living outside of Yen-liao can return for their weddings, which will still be subsidized by their *chia* groups. In most cases both sides lose money, although it is true that the greatest expenses are borne by the groom's family, but in any event the wedding allocations are geared to the endowment of a new couple. The terms "payment" or "sale" only apply under circumstances of extreme poverty, where there are practices such as the marriage of girls to mainlanders, who in some cases present the cash and other gifts expected from the groom's side, but receive very little in return; but with such conditions the issue is not the function of wedding allocations as such.

The economic elements in the marriage ceremonials are behind qualitative changes introduced into family or household organization when with the arrival of a bride domestic form changes from conjugal to stem; and in all complex domestic groups, each couple's wedding ceremony endows them as the very economic and social unit that ultimately will make up the focus of a new family. We have noted how certain allocations during the wedding endow a new category of property—the "new room" and its furnishings collectively owned by the new couple. This property-owning unit is the *fang*, known in Hakka as the "*fo*"; the terminological distinctions made in Mandarin

between *fang, chia,* and *hu* ("household") are paralleled in
Hakka (*"fo," "ka,"* and *"fu"*).

Although wedding allocations create a new sphere of property rights involving both husband and wife, there are also the
cash gifts given to the bride alone; these differentiate her as an
independent property-holder with her own rights of disposal,
and within the *"fo"* these rights are not fully shared with her
husband. Her money is known as *"se-koi"* ("private money"),
while the Mandarin term is *szu-fang-ch'ien* ("private room
money"). *"Se-koi"* is not liable to the financial manager's control in the bride's new family, nor to her husband's. In fact, the
bride is quite reluctant to let her husband know exactly how
much money she has, and it is considered in very bad taste for
him to ask. The bride's secretiveness was manifested on one occasion when I was attempting to gather data on the subject of
"private money." The woman in question had returned to Yen-
liao with her husband for the "twelfth day" feast. When I
brought up the subject of *"se-koi"* she immediately walked out
of the room where we had been sitting with her husband. Following her out, I had to promise not to reveal to him anything
she said regarding this matter.

This secrecy is an aspect of the bride's independent management of her "private money." If her husband or other family
members were to find out how much money she has, they might
attempt to get control of it. At the time of marriage the bride and
groom are well endowed with many personal effects, and there
is little or no need to use *"se-koi"* or even family funds for personal purposes. By using the "private money" for investment
outside the confines of her new family she preserves it from
possible encroachments and also is able to get some sort of return.

In a household that has just turned from conjugal to complex,
the wife with her *"se-koi"* is the only individual who has property rights extending beyond the category of personal belong-
ings acquired through the financial manager's allocations of
family funds. It is she alone who has her own individual cash,
which may be used for productive purposes without reference

to the larger family economy; anything she purchases with her money remains hers, and if the cash is invested, the income is added to her *"se-koi."* Thus the arrival of a bride with individualized property rights marks a qualitative change in family economic organization.

The important position of men in the household economy and redistributive system is backed by their very limited rights to private property. The situation of a woman who married into a household is far more ambiguous; she is not by role exclusively a participant in a redistributive arrangement, so that the product of her labor is linked to the family economy through special controls placed on her activities. Other family members seek to insure that as a producer she contributes primarily to the family she has married into and not to her *"se-koi."* Her daytime labor belongs to the family, be it domestic work, farming, wage labor, or such other tasks as may be demanded of her by family members with managerial positions.

There are several areas of economic activity possible for a woman over which family controls do not extend. She can work for her own money during her spare time: this commonly includes the periods before breakfast, after lunch (which is siesta time), after supper, and also whenever there is no family work for her to do. At present, embroidery is the most popular non-agricultural work, though in the past there was a greater variety of activities. In any event, the equipment needed for such work is either supplied from dowry or purchased with "private money." In most joint households, each of the daughters-in-law is allotted a small vegetable plot which she is responsible for maintaining. When it is her turn at domestic work the vegetables from this plot are used in preparing meals, but at other times she is free to sell them and keep the money. Income derived in this way is steady if not considerable. Some women use their *"se-koi"* to buy piglets and pay poorer families to raise them.

Another minor source of funds is the annual distribution of cash gifts during the lunar new year. All family members who are old enough to walk get something from the financial man-

ager. The sum I observed given to each of the daughters-in-law
in one family was NT$200, which appears to be a standard
amount among Yen-liao families, except perhaps for the poorest.
The women's children also get money; in one case the youngest
ones, of preschool age, each received NT$10. This they imme-
diately gave to their mother, who kept the money for herself; I
am told that this is also a standard practice. The daughters-in-
law in some families are given small sums of money after each
year's tobacco sale while in others payments are also made after
pig sales. The two daughters-in-law in one joint household independently grow and sell bananas, which are therefore known
as *"se-koi-tsiao"* (*"tsiao"* means bananas). They estimated for
me that during a one-year period (1964–65) their income from
sources other than investments was as follows: one daughter-in-
law earned NT$240 from bananas, the other NT$110, and each
made about NT$300 by selling vegetables; the family's finan-
cial manager (an eldest brother who is the husband of one of the
women; their mother-in-law is a widow) gave each of them
NT$200 during the lunar new year period, another NT$200
following the tobacco harvest, and yet another NT$200 after the
sale of some pigs.

But a woman's most important economic activity relates to the
investment of *"se-koi"* originally accumulated during her wedding. The bride sometimes immediately places the money in
the custody of her father or a brother and asks him to invest it
for her, but more generally she handles the money herself or
asks her husband to make specific investments on her behalf.
Yet the woman still keeps her spouse uninformed as to the total
amount she has.

Many *"se-koi"* investments are maintained over time, as is
the investment pattern; part of the money is invested locally in
"rotating grain associations" (*"tchon-kouc-fi"*) and part is
loaned out to individuals; interest from the personal loans is
used for the biannual payments required to maintain membership in the associations (see Fei 1939:267–74 for a description of grain associations and similar groupings). Investments in
grain associations are most attractive; pegged to a staple, there

is not the risk that they will be lost during a period of inflation (and many people did suffer during the inflation that followed Japan's surrender in 1945). Loans are often made to close agnates, especially if they share residence at the same compound site with the woman's family through marriage. Owing to the large number of complex families in Yen-liao, the tendency of women to invest their "private money" makes an impact on the local economy, although I have not been able to determine the extent of this in regard to personal loans. Women play an active role in grain associations, even though they do not attend the feasts or other session meetings. Although a grain association in session appears to be entirely a man's world, many of the men are in fact representing their wives. In June 1965, I counted eighteen grain associations organized in Yen-liao, and I believe these included most, if not all, in the village at that time. There were a total of 174 shares and 43 of these, or almost 25 percent, were held by women as *"se-koi"* investments. I do not include as shareholders the eighteen organizers, for they borrowed rather than invested funds.

Women use their "private money" for a variety of purposes. This includes personal support, as sometimes occurs when the financial manager is unwilling to supply funds requested for such things as medical expenses. In the family of Fu Ch'ing-feng, whose penuriousness I have already noted (chapter 5), the daughters-in-law on several occasions reportedly used their *"se-koi"* to supplement family funds when ill. These women, constantly pressed for cash, have a reputation for being among the hardest-working vegetable growers in Yen-liao.

Children can also be the objects of a mother's support. Women commonly report that the main use to which they put their available *"se-koi"* (as opposed to that locked up in investments) is to provide their small children with refreshments; many mothers use the money to buy their children clothing or food in addition to what is provided with family funds. As far as the preschool child is concerned, the mother is already a redistributor, for we have noted how a child gives his mother money he receives on new year's day. But throughout his life as a

dependent member of a complex family he may on many occasions rely on his mother's "private money" for one purpose or
another. As does the woman herself, the dependent often relies
on the money when the financial manager makes available in-
sufficient funds or none at all in response to a specific request.
In one case the man in charge of family finances refused to give
his nephew money for a wristwatch when the boy was about to
leave home for a period of apprenticeship, and it was the boy's
mother who finally provided him the cash. In another joint
household, a boy who failed the college entrance examinations
used his mother's money to attend "supplementary sessions" in
Taipei; this was after family funds, controlled by his grandfather, were refused him.

"Private money" may also be used for social purposes; prominent in this category are the very gifts of cash that provide the
"*se-koi*" of other women. In some families women use a combination of "*se-koi*" and family funds, while in others "*se-koi*" is
used exclusively. Many managers of family money make a clear
distinction between family payments as invited guests and personal gifts given by daughters-in-law during the wedding ceremonies.

During the early years of marriage the controls placed on the
woman by her family seem effectively to keep the family's
funds from becoming part of her "*se-koi*." And while it appears
that the woman can conceal the exact amount of her "*se-koi*"
holdings, she cannot refuse all requests for money without jeo-
pardizing her relations with her husband or other family members. However, such transactions are considered as between
separate property holders. One man told me that he "borrowed"
money from his daughter-in-law to repay debts accumulated as
a result of her wedding.

In some cases, however, other family members may come to
the aid of a woman in financial trouble. For example, a woman
appealed to her father-in-law to save part of her "*se-koi*." She
had made a loan to the head of another family in the same compound who came to her and said he was unable to repay; instead he would give her a free share in a grain association he

was about to organize. But the woman knew that the interest from her remaining funds, loaned out to others, would not be enough to make payments at future meetings of the association. She asked her father-in-law to take over the share and pay her for it, which the man did.

For a variety of reasons, a woman's money may be greatly reduced or even lost altogether, but she does not then lose her independent status with respect to property rights. For example, one woman asked her father to buy her some land with money she had obtained through participation in a grain association; the man complied and it was agreed that her father-in-law should till the land and give her rent. No rent was forthcoming, however, and the woman still complains bitterly. Yet there is no doubt in anyone's mind that the land is hers.

A woman's disposition of her own funds can for long periods remain independent of the circulation of family money. But there may develop certain links, such as when her father-in-law uses her money for family purposes. Such transfers are usually bitterly resented by the woman, and in all cases that have come to my attention it is invariably her husband who gets the cash for his father. Sometimes the husband asks his wife for money he plans to use for personal expenses; the men who most commonly make such requests appear to be family farm managers or workers, and we have seen that these men, unlike the managers of non-farm enterprises, often have no direct access to family funds.

A more important connection between *"fo"* and family is established when the husband begins to give his wife family money without the financial manager's approval. In wealthier families, husbands often hand over to their wives some of their "spending money," which is added to the original *"se-koi"* and is invested. *"Fo"* connected with family funds in this fashion may become rich. In one very large joint family, where there are *"fo"* in the first, second, and third generations, many of the women not only own shares in numerous grain associations, but also have large holdings of land (*"se-koi-t'ien"*) and bananas. It is probable that some of Mei-nung's *"se-koi-tiam"* (*"tiam"* means shop) are also supported through the transfer of family funds. Such a shop can be any kind of store owned and capitalized by a married woman with her own money. Although such establishments are well-known in the Mei-nung region, none have been set up by Yen-liao women.

Now it is often of some importance that while a woman's individual financial affairs and those of her family can be linked in a variety of ways, the connection is always through her husband. Husband and wife are a *"fo,"* yet the husband is also firmly integrated into the family economic organization; changes in his economic relationship with his family must at the same time alter the economic connection between him and his wife. In that there can be seen different patterns in the economic relations between the spouses, we are brought back to the theme earlier discussed in the context of conjugal family organization; at all stages of family development economic relationships between husband and wife are variable while the husband-wife unit consistently remains clearly differentiated within a larger family context.

The woman remains the redistributor even in wealthy *"fo"* into which family funds are flowing. Furthermore, husband and wife both make an effort to maintain the secrecy of the financial operations, so that transfers of funds between women belonging to different *"fo"* and to different families are talked about more than seen. However, once I did chance upon just such a transaction: there were two women behind a tobacco house, one counting out a large amount of cash and the other waiting to receive it. Both were wives of men who were not in charge of the finances of their respective families, but it can be added that it is not unknown for financial managers, if one of several brothers, to give their wives money to add to their *"se-koi."*

Note the dramatic contrast between the wife as *"fo"* financial manager–redistributor and the daughter-in-law as family worker. The number of roles assumed by daughters-in-law in the family economy is minimal. The expansion of family enterprises takes place in conjunction with a growing specialization among the married men; in many families these men are available for such roles precisely because there is a large working force of women for the fields. The daughter-in-law receives funds for support only, and in the context of the family economy she certainly is in no position to make allocations. Within the *"fo,"* however, the wife can assume as many separate economic roles as her *"se-koi"* and her limited time allow. She has the rights of a redistributor, she can run enterprises, she can obtain returns, reinvest them, or use them for other purposes.

There is another important difference between *"fo"* and family. The family provides most of the support its members receive, so that the use of their own funds does not prevent most women from continuing to keep at least part of their money in investments; and the investments can be expanded in those cases where family funds begin to enter the *"fo."* In general, then, the *"fo"* is significant for domestic economic organization in that the activities of the wife duplicate in miniature the economic system of the family. But from the standpoint of future developments, the importance of the *"fo"* is that it serves to maintain or bank resources over long periods of time.

The relationships defining the *"fo"* are connected to the fact that the woman ultimately shares her rights with her husband. In reality *"se-koi"* is *"fo"* property, the property of the husband–wife unit. I have shown that the initial definition of this kind of property occurs at the time of the wedding, with the establishment of the "new room." But in the context of the redistributive system of the family, the husband has no property rights in terms of role; that is, he is able to create only additional family property. The woman can indeed create property, but within the limitations placed upon her as a member of the family work force. Thus it is role, and not ultimate rights of access, which differentiates husband and wife as property-holders.

That the husband and wife ultimately share rights to *"fo"* resources can be seen under two sets of circumstances. One relates to family division and is discussed in the next chapter. However, there have been cases where the husband or wife has died while their *"fo"* was still part of a complex family.

One woman had been married for less than two years, and had already given birth to a daughter, when her husband was killed by lightning. After a short period, remarriage was arranged by her parents, and she left the family of her husband, taking with her the contents of the "new room" and her *"se-koi,"* and leaving the daughter behind. Here, the *"fo"* was destroyed and the rights to its property were asserted by the woman. Another woman died of leukemia six years after she had married into a joint household. Within her *"fo"* she was survived by her husband, two sons, and a daughter. At that time, some of her money was invested in a grain association and some loaned out to individuals. Her husband claimed her share in the association, took over the loans, and continued to use the furnishings in the "new room." It was understood that the investments were being held by him in trust for his children. He thus assumed the role of his wife within the *"fo,"* while maintaining his propertyless role within the family.[3]

It can be added that after he remarried, his new wife lived with him in the same room, whose furnishings were now expanded to include what she brought with her as dowry. This kind of match is unpopular among families where there are girls eligible for marriage, for the woman is expected to treat her stepchildren as her own. Yet an element of tension is immedi-

---

3. Margery Wolf, in commenting on these two cases (as they are described in my preliminary report on Yen-liao family organization [Cohen 1968]), has this to say: "Myron Cohen conceives of this money in Hakka society as . . . the property of the new conjugal unit, but from his own description I think it might more accurately be described as money belonging to the woman's uterine family. A widow who remarries takes the total amount with her, and . . . a young husband . . . is allowed to keep his deceased wife's private money *in trust* for her children (Wolf's italics [M. Wolf 1975:135])."

I fail to see how my "own description" supports Wolf's assertion that the money really belongs to the woman's "uterine family," by which Wolf means a woman and her own children (see M. Wolf 1972 for her detailed discussion of the subject); the widow *dissolved* her "uterine family" by leaving her daughter behind, a fact I noted in my 1968 article, while the man who took over his dead wife's "private" property was by Wolf's own definition not even a member of her "uterine family." Of course he had to hold the money in trust if he was to keep it at all; in a complex family there is no "men's money," only women's money and family money. (For more on this matter, see pp. 210–11.)

ately introduced into the situation, for the husband generally does not make his dead wife's *"se-koi"* available to his new spouse; he suspects that her commitment to her stepchildren will not be so intense as that which she will later feel toward her own. Widower remarriages thus often lead to the development of *"fo"* where there are internal cleavages; the husband looks after the interests of the *"fo"* as a whole, but he is often especially concerned about his dead wife's children and feels that those borne by his living wife are receiving most of her attention. The second wives of widowers commonly are from poorer families, who receive the standard payments from the groom's side but provide a much reduced dowry, which merely supplements what had been in the groom's home since his first marriage. For such families the economic advantages outweigh whatever may be their distress at placing the bride in a very unpleasant situation; and the girl's predicament is made all the more difficult because her natal family's poverty makes it highly probable that she will enter her new family with far less *"se-koi"* than that brought in by most brides.[4]

I do not know of an earlier study of Chinese family organization that has attempted an extended treatment of a married woman's special economic role in a complex family and the creation of this role in the course of the wedding process; and I fear many readers of the preceding pages may conclude, quite erroneously, that the situation in Yen-liao is a local or at best a Hakka peculiarity. I therefore think it important to present evidence showing that we have been concerned with arrangements which were in fact generally characteristic of complex family organization in China.

First, I would note that McAleavy, summarizing Japanese scholarship on the subject, has discussed aspects of *"fo"* or *fang* autonomy:

> . . . the son and his wife, with their children, form a unit of their own within the framework of the family. This unit is called a *fang*

4. Here Margery Wolf's idea of "uterine family" (see note 3 above) has applicability, insofar as it concerns the closer emotional ties between a woman and her own children.

. . . and owns property of its own, quite distinct from family property. (1955:545)

In the same article he notes that the *fang* is endowed in the
course of the wedding ceremony:

. . . a clear distinction was made between articles of pure personal
adornment making up the trousseau proper, and land and other
property. The former . . . was the property of the wife. As to the
latter, . . . it became the property not of the wife. . . . but of the
fang and it was the husband who had the power of management
over it. (*ibid:*546)

McAleavy's interpretation of the husband's power within the
fang conflicts in some ways with my observations in Yen-liao.
Of course, "the power of management" might refer to the husband making investments on behalf of his wife, or, say, collecting rents from *fang* lands; and we have seen that after a period
of time the husband may give his wife family money and direct
her in its utilization. But the wife can also give the husband her
"se-koi," known in Mandarin as *szu-fang-ch'ien;* this is a kind of
property not noted by McAleavy.

It is clear to me from the documentary evidence and from
conversations with many Chinese of diverse origin that *szu-
fang ch'ien* was tied in with complex family organization
throughout China. In Taiwan, *szu-fang-ch'ien* is found among
the Hokkien majority, where it is called *sai-khia,* and several
persons who are natives of the southeastern portion of continental China have told me that the terms *sai-khia* and *"se-koi"* are
also used in the Hokkien and Hakka districts of the mainland to
describe women's money. *Szu-fang-ch'ien* is noted in studies of
villages in Kiangsu (Fei 1939:62), Kwangtung (Kulp 1925:175)
and Yunnan (Fei and Chang 1949:110–11).

In at least two discussions of *szu-fang-ch'ien* in mainland
China there is explicit recognition of the role this form of property plays in maintaining *fang* autonomy. In describing the
"rural economy" of Ku-shih County, in Honan Province, Chu Yu
includes the following remarks:

In families with a large number of people, with many brothers, sisters-in-law, sisters, wives, sons, and daughters, it is difficult to

avoid using some pocket money. Clothing, food, and residence are shared in common; but as to pocket money, since the disposition and pleasures of each person are unlike, there is the saving of *szu-fang-ch'ien*. Land given as dowry, money received as gifts upon marriage, money given on new year's day, . . . interest from loans, as well as money that has been saved through economizing accumulate into a sum from which interest may be derived. A little turns into a lot, capital and interest increase and become a large sum which can be used as the foundation for the establishment of a new family (*chia*). Most borrowing of money [in the countryside] . . . involved *szu-fang-ch'ien*. (1962:135)

Mention of *szu-fang-ch'ien* is in M. Yang's description of a village in Shantung:

The daughters are given a dowry at the time of their marriage, to which they add any money they may have earned and saved while in their parents' home. The young wife can either invest this sum in small home industries or lend it at interest to fellow villagers. When the sum is sufficient, she can buy land with it and this land will belong to the small family unit including herself, her husband and children, and not to the large family of her husband. . . . This kind of property . . . is legally recognized but not encouraged by the family at large. (1945:79)

There is an interesting description of functions of what is obviously *szu-fang-ch'ien*, although it is called by a different name, in a report on a 1929 survey of rural credit in Ting County, Hopei Province:

In families owning more than 50 *mou*, especially in rich families, there are, in addition to loans made by the family head, the somewhat smaller number of loans made by many women. This is because in most prosperous large families fathers, sons, brothers and daughters-in-law live together, and for the women in each *fang* to accumulate private holdings has become a common phenomenon, colloquially known as "keeping *li-chi*" (*ts'un li-chi*). In families owning from 50 to 20 *mou*, about 20 percent of the women also keep *li-chi*, but there are very few women able to keep *li-chi* in poor households with less than 20 *mou*. In this region there is a very special custom whereby a daughter-in-law's family practically takes no responsibility for her and her children's clothing and pocket money. These kinds of expenses are provided for by the daughters-in-law's natal families or through their own devices. Thus they strive to keep *li-chi*; some surreptitiously keep private funds independently; some cooperate with their husbands in building up savings; some have close kinsmen from their natal families manage and loan out [funds] on their behalf; some leave the management to trusted middlemen but keep the receipts [promissory notes] themselves; and there are only a few who personally loan out the funds. The amount loaned each time is from several dollars (*yuan*) up to ten or twenty; ordinarily the interest is two percent [monthly], but the guarantor assumes full responsibility in the majority of cases. Because this miscellaneous lending is not carried out very publicly, it is not very easy to investigate matters concerning the number of families making loans, the number of loans, the sums involved, or the circumstances of the lenders. (Feng 1935:880–81)

I suspect that the field investigators who noted the "very special custom" mentioned in the above quote took the remarks of the women they interviewed a bit too literally. Women in Yen-liao who use their "private money" to supplement family funds commonly complain that they do not receive family money to meet legitimate expenses, and that they are forced to turn to their natal families for help; if I were to have taken such complaints at face value, and not as expressions of the tension generated by the presence of different and sometimes conflicting foci of economic activity within one household, I would have reported that in Yen-liao there is exactly the same "very special custom." But also note the remark that "lending is not carried out very publicly"; this is also true in Yen-liao, as we have seen, and it is safe to say that in both places the reasons for the secrecy are the same.[5]

5. Margery Wolf (1975) insists that in Taiwan women's money is more important in Hakka families than among the Hokkien. Yet her reference to the Hakka is based on my preliminary report (Cohen 1968) on Yen-liao's families; in this report I introduced much of the evidence I have now presented here, showing that women's private property was incorporated into complex family organization throughout China. When Wolf asserts that "although Hokkien women also have a private fund of money . . . it is not likely among peasant women to survive the first year of marriage" (M. Wolf 1975:135), she seems to be treating the matter as a difference between Hakka and Hokkien customs. But because women's private money is a characteristic of Chinese complex families in general, it is not surprising that members of joint families in several Hokkien areas in south Taiwan provided me with descriptions of the uses and importance of

Within the complex family, the *"fo"* emerges as a unit with its own property and economic organization. Created and endowed through the wedding ceremonies, it can maintain autonomy throughout its existence as part of a larger domestic group. It is not a family; its basic subsistence needs are met through participation in a redistributive arrangement that can involve the coordinated efforts of many more persons. The unit for subsistence and economic advancement is the complex family as a whole, which is better suited than the conjugal family to take advantage of the varied opportunities present in a society predominantly agrarian but with a highly differentiated economic system. This greater potential for economic survival and progress is most emphasized in joint families, and is a force keeping *"fo"* contained within the larger organization. But the *"fo"* is also the focal point of the joint family's weakness, and we must now examine this situation in greater detail.

women's money which matched and confirmed my findings among the Hakka of Yen-liao.

   I have shown that the wedding which creates the complex family endows the bride with her private property and confirms her rights to it. Evidence that this applies to Hakka and Hokkien alike is in fact found in Margery Wolf's earlier book published in 1972. The book deals with the psychological ramifications of women's subordinate status, and it does not discuss a married woman's special economic position in the complex family; nevertheless Wolf notes, *en passant,* how "at the end of the [wedding] feast the bride and groom are led to each senior relative to bow and accept [a "red packet"], the contents of which are considered the bride's property" (M. Wolf 1972:138; see also M. Wolf 1975:134–35).

CHAPTER 7

A House Divided

PARTITION is usually the final event in the history of a Chinese complex family. In my discussion I first deal with changes in the pattern of family organization that characteristically anticipate division, then describe the process as such and the social context that regulates it in Mei-nung. Finally I turn to some of the factors having a bearing on the differential longevity of families in Yen-liao.

Relevant to our consideration of family division are social relationships which constitute an area of family life to which I have made scarcely more than passing reference up to now. But these relationships loom large in the sociological literature on the Chinese family, and it seems safe to say that Chinese and foreign observers alike have found Chinese family life a fascinating subject largely because of the contrasting, perhaps even contradictory, social relationships that are involved in family organization. The relationships that have received the most attention are between father and son, brother and brother, husband and wife, mother and daughter-in-law, and among the daughters-in-law themselves. A given relationship can involve dominance, submission, unity, division, solidarity, or competition; through time such qualities can replace each other as the main element in a given relationship, and at any given point in time some or all of these qualities may variously characterize the different specific relationships that make up the total network of intrafamilial ties.

Some of the most important changes in the quality of such social relationships are linked to the dissolution of family unity and the imminent onset of formal partition. These changes are in fact characteristic of the final phase of joint family life, and their significance is most readily apparent when the terminal pattern is contrasted with the antecedent arrangement of relationships in the family. But in the earlier literature the importance of these relationships is not seen in the context of family partition; rather, a major theme is how such relationships are differentially patterned between families of different form (see Fried 1953; Hsu 1943; Lang 1946; Levy 1949). Freedman takes the discussion a step further when he suggests that there is a change in intrafamily social ties during the course of family development, and before turning to the Yen-liao material it would be helpful to have a brief summary of his analysis with respect to China in general (the quotes are from Freedman 1966:45–47).

Freedman focuses on three relationships which are "crucial": a unified complex family is supported by a relationship between father and son that is "overtly one of severe dominance and submission"; the fraternal relationship "is one of competition, and potentially of a fierce kind," but it can "preserve some solidarity" if it is controlled by the father; and such paternal control also means that there is a husband–wife relationship where the men pay "little attention to the affairs or interests of their wives." When a father has little power over his sons, the latter come into competition and each identifies more closely with his spouse.

Freedman links the "quarrelsomeness" of sisters-in-law to the larger arrangement of relationships within the family; each woman is forced to act as the sole representative of the interests of her own conjugal unit when she is isolated from her husband while the father is able to keep the family intact; but her isolation is replaced by husband–wife solidarity in a poor family, or in a rich one that is disintegrating. Freedman's interpretation of the context encouraging conflicts among women follows the argument in his earlier book, where he says that a woman is "forced . . . into the struggle which essentially turned on the rivalry between her husband and his brothers" (1958:21).

Freedman makes some vital points which are confirmed by the Yen-liao data. Most significant is the general interconnection he finds between the imminent fragmentation of a complex family and changes in the relationships between its members; particular developments in Yen-liao families that accord with Freedman's description are a change in the husband–wife relationship from one of distance to one of solidarity, and the competitive relationship between brothers during the terminal phase of a joint family's existence; more generally, the Yen-liao data confirm that there is an interconnection between conflicts among daughters-in-law, the quality of the husband-wife tie, and the onset of family fragmentation.

The major discrepancy between Freedman's interpretation and what I have found in Yen-liao concerns the brother–brother relationship in a united joint family; from this discrepancy it follows that the father–son and husband–wife relationships must also differ in important ways from Freedman's description, precisely because Freedman properly sees all three relationships to be interdependent. In chapter 5 I focused on the jural equality of married brothers as the most important support for the joint family's economic arrangements and therefore for its survival. Jural equality describes the status of brothers, and not the social relationships between them, but this equality also provides the context for the different relationships the brothers in a joint family may have. Conflict is no more inherent in the fraternal tie in Yen-liao joint families than is solidarity, for each of these contrasting qualities describes the relationship between brothers during different phases of family development. There is a consistency to the quality of the fraternal link only in that it results from the positions taken by brothers vis-à-vis one another as each works to best serve his own interests. During a joint family's unity phase the fraternal relationship is one of intense solidarity, but as we shall see, this is transformed into hostility when partition is imminent. Fraternal solidarity manifests itself as a sentiment, among other ways, but it is a function of the control that married male siblings exercise over each other's behavior while they are together.

In sharp contrast to the solidarity of brothers in a united joint family is the ill will among their wives; a hostile sister-in-law–sister-in-law relationship is in fact as fully characteristic of family life during this phase as is the strongly positive quality of the fraternal tie. As far as sisters-in-law are concerned, we might first note that in Yen-liao it is almost inevitable for persons of either sex to blame women for the domestic discord that causes the partition of families. Although accusations are encouraged by the circumstance that women indeed play the major roles in conflicts that endure long enough to become notorious, such conflicts are provided with their context precisely by the unity of brothers; for when brothers turn against each other partition occurs not long after. Thus it might seem to follow that through a simple process of elimination, conflicts lasting for relatively longer periods could only be those in which none of the married men participate. Yet it must also be understood that the situation of men which defines the elimination process also provides positive encouragement for the women-oriented conflicts that are long-lasting.[1]

The very commitments and sharing practices that express continuing solidarity among brothers are those which at the same time constrain each from acting on behalf of the particular interests of his *"fo."* A brother's wife is thus sharply defined as the isolated guardian of *"fo"* welfare, and she is drawn into conflict with her sisters-in-law owing to redistributive practices within the joint family which assure that each *"fo"* will fare differently from the others. Joint family redistributive arrangements impose upon family members what we might call a "consumers" equality, which involves the pooling and distribution

---

1. In seeing women as disrupters of domestic peace, Yen-liao seems typical of China. For evidence concerning the country as a whole, see Freedman (1958:21f.; 1966:46f.), who in the context of his own analysis is also able to turn upside down the popular Chinese notion of the connection between women and family strife.

of family wealth according to criteria of individual need as well as the advancement of the family as a whole. The application of such criteria maintains family unity precisely because there is no provision for the *"fo"* as a separate economic unit. Consumers equality is very different from the jural equality of male siblings. Jural equality is economically expressed only in that the brothers have rights to arithmetically identical fractions of the estate, whose composition and total value can change for better or worse. Consumer equality focuses on individuals and is expressed through down-to-earth management and redistribution organized to sustain all family members. If fraternal equality is a fact expressed in mathematically ideal terms, consumer equality is rather an ideal that cannot be attained when it is based on one person's fiscal management and his evaluation of the needs of other family members.

Consumer equality is an adjustment to the fact that while brothers are equal it is in the nature of things that the *"fo"* each heads cannot be arranged to equalize their demands on the family economy or their contributions to it. Brothers marry in sequence; by the time of the wedding of the youngest, some children of the oldest may be students. In addition, the brothers' wives bear or raise to maturity differing numbers of offspring. As a result, at any time each of the *"fo"* coexisting within a family will comprise a different assortment of consumer requirements, demands, and tastes—differences that will become more prominent as the children in the several *"fo"* begin to mature. Each child increasingly tends to enter into a particular pattern of life influenced by his individual history of encounters with forces at work in the outside world, and also by the decisions made by those who manage the family's affairs. Thus the inequality of *"fo"* as units of consumption may be highlighted by the contrasting circumstances, say, of a boy in one unit who works the family farm following an unsuccessful effort to gain admittance to senior middle school, and of a young man in another who has already entered college with full family support.

In the context of an unequal distribution of family wealth

among its constituent *"fo,"* each sister-in-law finds herself de-
fending the relatively advantageous position of her particular
unit or protesting what she sees as the preferential treatment ac-
corded other *"fo"* at the expense of her own. In any event, a
woman usually justifies her own stand by comparing her needs,
and those of her children, with what she takes to be the lesser
requirements of other members of the joint family; and she will
also emphasize the contribution of her and husband to the family economy and belittle the efforts made by the others. A man
who wishes the family to remain together cannot involve himself in such arguments with members of other *"fo,"* and by leaving their wives to fight among themselves the male siblings are
provided another means of affirming their own solidarity.

Yet the conflicts among daughters-in-law have as their context
an isolation of each from her husband which is more than a
reflex of the refusal of the man to represent the interests of his
"fo," for the conflicts are further reinforced by the positive
estrangement of the husband from his wife. The tensions between husband and wife reflect the potential access that each
has to resources commanded by the other; the wife deploys her
"se-koi" secretly because she is threatened by her husband's
commitment to the family as a whole, to be sure, but she em-
ploys secrecy in the absence of any clear-cut demarcation of
claims between herself and her spouse. In the same way, the
husband resists his wife's claim on his loyalties because it constitutes a threat to family unity; and it is a threat because the
husband's position in the family economy gives him access to
family resources and the nature of the ties between him and his
wife provides an ever-present possibility for the deflection of
these resources to the *"fo."* Such deflections sometimes do
occur, but do not necessarily compromise family unity or cement the husband–wife relationship, for joint family unity im-
poses controls on the economic ties husband and wife may
have.

In a joint family the relationship between husband and wife
is characterized by the authoritarian role of the husband, by
emotional and social distance between the spouses, and by a

tension frequently manifested as arguments and sometimes by the husband's rebuking or insulting his wife in public. The altercations between the spouses frequently are over family affairs directly involving their different commitments. Often, a quarrel between husband and wife is provoked by the man's reaction to a dispute between his spouse and his brothers'. He is encouraged to verbally or even physically assault his own spouse because among the contending women she is the only person he may so deal with without threatening family unity. And as far as he is concerned, the merits of the case are only that it is this unity which is being disturbed. Given the stress infusing the relationship between husband and wife it is easy for them to be provoked into a confrontation by matters that may be only distantly or not at all related to their major domestic concerns.

We have seen how the unity of a stem family is expressed by the married son's submission to his father's authority, which is buttressed by the father's control of the estate as representative of the interests of family members still jurally minor. Stem family unity is compatible with solidarity in the relationship between the son and his wife, and this solidarity is often reinforced because stem family unity is not compromised by hostility between the father and his married son.

The transition to joint form brings changes in the "balance of forces" supporting unity such that tensions in the husband–wife relationship are now encouraged as far as married couples in the second generation are concerned. In the second generation it is of course only the eldest son and his wife who experience married life in both stem and joint family contexts, and the readjustment of their relationship introduces tensions of the sort which are felt by a younger brother and his wife at the outset of their marriage. The adverse impact of joint family life on the relationship between spouses is thus most readily apparent with respect to the oldest son and his wife, and in Yen-liao it is indeed commonly recognized that the second son's marriage worsens the ties between his older brother and the latter's spouse; but as might be expected, the popular view has it that relations between the spouses sour because of the characteristic inability of daughters-in-law to remain on friendly terms.

Strains in the husband–wife relationship that are a manifestation of a joint family's unity are exacerbated by the joint family's continuing success. Time is one factor, for the tensions between the sisters-in-law, and among husbands and wives, feed upon each other and at the same time increasingly encourage the men to isolate themselves from their spouses. Increasing complexity itself may cause the husband–wife relationship to become progressively strained. The emphasis on fraternal solidarity is heightened as more brothers marry, and when all have wives, the force of their solidarity is most powerful. The husband–wife relationship also comes under greater pressure as the wives are increasingly confined to farming and domestic work while the men take on new responsibilities; this sort of occupational specialization tends to decrease contacts between the spouses during the working day, and thus provides reinforcement for their structural and emotional separation; at the same time, the women must work together more than before and this can only increase their mutual antipathy.

In a joint family, where the balance of forces favors unity, father-son solidarity tends to be linked to fraternal variety and the mother is prone to have with some or all of her sons' wives hostile relationships that are similar to those among the wives themselves. But the relationships that concern the father and mother need only be considered briefly for our present purposes, for unlike those we have discussed earlier they are not vital to joint family organization and to a much greater extent their characteristics vary from case to case. We have seen how important the father's managerial skills can be for family unity; a father who still manages family affairs and finances will maintain authority over his sons as well as a solidarity with them. But the important connection under such circumstances is that the father's handling of family affairs supports a situation such that brothers are encouraged to stay together, and this kind of arrangement includes the common acceptance by the brothers of their father's authority. We have also seen, however, that the father may transfer his responsibilities to the eldest son, again, to support family unity. And it is not unexpected that with such a transfer the nature of the father–son relationship alters considerably and is less emphasized.

The mother-in-law's authority over her sons' wives is supported by a context in which family unity is emphasized, for the mother-in-law shares her husband's commitment to keeping the family intact, and by supervising her daughters-in-law in the kitchen she exerts a strategic control over family consumption. Conflict between the mother-in-law and the women under her control is a common but not regular feature of joint family life; it may be encouraged insofar as the mother-in-law acts as her husband's agent by curtailing family consumption in order to provide additional family resources for the estate. The mother-in-law must also uphold consumer's equality, and she may especially provoke the wrath of the women for whose *"fo"* this kind of equality is most disadvantageous; on the other hand, there are at least two Yen-liao joint families where the mother-in-law has made common cause with her eldest son's wife, and we have seen that the latter's *"fo"* stands to gain most from redistribution within the family.

I have tried to show that the prominence of women is characteristic of a particular kind of conflict which in fact testifies to the inability of females to threaten family unity. Women are accused of harboring a mutual antipathy which threatens the relationship between the men when actually it is the men who by keeping the family together set the women against each other. In all joint families the brother–brother, husband–wife, and sister-in-law–sister-in-law relationships are arranged in a characteristic fashion because fraternal solidarity provides the basis of unity, and because the other two relationships feel the consequences of this solidarity.

There is an equally characteristic rearrangement of relationships during a joint family's fragmentation phase, and there are other events unique to this period. Included is a particular kind of verbal conflict known as *"nao oi poun"* (*nao fen-chia*, "agitation for partition"). It is a commonly expressed view in

Yen-liao that this type of conflict, which includes men among the opposing parties, is quite different from the type involving women only. But when people discuss "agitation" they continue to focus on women as the threat to family unity. According to their view, the two patterns of conflict are linked in that continuing antagonism among women finally turns their husbands against each other.

"*Nao oi poun*" refers to demands for partition openly voiced by men in a family; but the phrase is also a general label for the circumstances during a complex household's terminal phase, including fraternal strife and the solidarity of the husband–wife unit. A conflict between brothers, whatever its initial form, will very rapidly be expressed by some or all of the parties concerned as a demand for partition. Such conflict is a denial of the close identity of interests brothers must have if they are to preserve unity, for it is obvious that brothers at odds are no longer controlling each other's behavior and have therefore ceased supporting the joint family situation each had previously viewed to be in his own interest. More precisely, each had viewed the larger family's unity as being in the best interest of his own "*fo*," but under the changed circumstances the man's perspective now coincides with that held by his wife; during the terminal phase of a joint family each "*fo*" as a unit seeks to maximize the benefits forthcoming from family partition.

All brothers are quickly drawn into a conflict that at first may have involved only some, for during "agitation" endemic hostility is encouraged by the very collective arrangements that had previously unified the family economy. Each of a joint family's constituent "*fo*" is encouraged to assert and protect its claim to a share of the estate, but at this stage any claim can only be expressed as an abstract fraction of undivided and diverse assets. The different parties concerned may be in conflict about the proportion of the estate due each, and such conflicts can of themselves lead to a general heightening of tension. But the conflict is sharpened and the tension even further intensified by the fact that each "*fo*" must also express its claim with respect to family property through an assertion about the composition of the estate in its entirety.

Conflicts during *"nao oi poun"* have as one major theme the property status of different items; frequently, land, commercial holdings, farming equipment, or household items may be claimed by a man as his individual possession, or as his wife's *"se-koi,"* or as *"fo"* property such as that commonly kept in a married couple's private room. Such a claim may be countered by another claim that the items in question belong to the estate. During "agitation" a man fights for the inclusion of as much property as possible within the estate and also resists any effort to incorporate into the estate property he claims as belonging to his *"fo"* or to any of its members. There is thus a generalized hostility among the family's constituent *"fo,"* which is encouraged by the heightened vigilance of each individual unit. In the final analysis the hostility is generated by the preexisting property arrangements as such and is not linked to the fact that for each instance of *"nao oi poun"* the specific items that become objects of property status disputes make up differing proportions of the total body of holdings owned by the family and its component *"fo"* or individuals. The "agitation" involves the competing *"fo"* in frequent confrontations, which usually become increasingly bitter; for one thing, they simply keep getting into each other's way; for another, by the very nature of its activities each *"fo"* proclaims its suspicions of the others.

It is common for each *"fo"* in a family on the verge of breakup to organize on its own an elaborate inventorying operation; the husband often spends much time between the family's fields and the local Land Office as he checks and rechecks the details of family land ownership and other farm assets, and should there be several family enterprises he will be busily investigating those managed by his brothers or by anyone else not in his *"fo."* Accumulating data on family effects within the household is usually the wife's job, and often she counts, one by one, dishes, utensils, and other items. If the investigations of husband and wife overlap, this certainly does not lead to conflict between them, but rather to a comparison of mental or written notes. They also work closely together when staking out a claim to what they consider the property of their *"fo"*; in some cases their efforts to gain control over certain items includes concealing them from other family members. In fact, cooperation between husband and wife during "agitation" manifests a solidarity which is probably stronger than during any other phase of family development.

"Nao oi poun" is clearly different from the general run of conflicts that may occur in a family, especially conflicts among the women in a large, complex family. Such long-lasting conflicts testify to the unity of a family, for when people tolerate an unpleasant situation they are strongly motivated to stay together. The motives of those involved in "agitation" are quite different and must be explicitly expressed precisely because *"nao oi poun"* is not the only kind of family conflict.

Family division in Yen-liao has often been preceded by flagrant departures from the roles which economically integrate a complex family, and it seems clear that a deliberate effort to force partition is involved when a family's sharing practices are increasingly compromised by the refusal of some individuals to contribute their labor and time, or by the outright embezzlement of family funds. The most obvious campaign to initiate partition to come to my attention involved several brothers who had already convinced each other to separate, but still required their father's consent. This consent was forthcoming only after the brothers demonstrated their determination when together with their wives and children they evacuated the household en masse; their parents required only one night of solitude before the father agreed to the family's partition.

There were many economic deviations during the final year of one joint family's existence as an integrated unit. First, the family workers, men and their wives, refused to participate in the rice harvest. The financial manager, one of four brothers, desperately tried to hire more labor at the last minute; he finally succeeded, but by then part of the crop had sprouted. Then women in the family had begun charging personal purchases to the family, and the merchants were demanding payment from the manager-brother. This man was a meat retailer at the time, and some erstwhile members of his family later claimed that he was then giving his wife a portion of his earnings.

Although there can be long-standing conflicts or tensions in a family, these may have little or no impact on the family economy; but when some family members deliberately undermine sharing arrangements, the others perceive a threat to their very subsistence. Those who attack the family economy still obtain family support, the family continues to eat together, and there is still available a common purse. But at the same time the family functions less efficiently as a unit geared to provide its own livelihood, and in extreme cases it stops functioning in this respect altogether. In some cases the family economy can remain reasonably intact during "*nao oi poun*" and up to the time of partition; but both "agitation" and then partition will surely result if the family economy is undermined.

My analysis has considered the consequences of joint family unity for a concentrated *chia* group or for the joint primary household of one that is dispersed. We know that the common understandings of jurally adult brothers can preserve as a unit a *chia* group which may be residentially dispersed, and that not all members may participate in the *chia* economy. But fraternal solidarity has a different significance under such circumstances, and I do not propose to deal in detail with the impact of variations in residential and economic arrangements on the three relationships with which we have been primarily concerned. I would only note that the greater freedom siblings allow each other removes much of the tension among wives living apart and between each of them and her husband. There is much more that could be said on the subject, but for present purposes it will have been sufficient to consider the pattern of relationships when fraternal solidarity supports maximal economic and residential unity.

If the onset of "*nao oi poun*" is marked by a demand for partition voiced by one or more of the men in a joint family, its termination is signaled when all the men agree that formal partition proceedings should be initiated. While the bitterness and recrimination characteristic of "agitation" continues even during the course of the partition deliberations, the usual procedure provides for each of the parties directly involved some assurance that his particular set of claims will weigh as heavily as those of the others in determining the distribution of estate holdings. Most important in this regard is the practice of requesting outsiders to oversee the property distribution. Such persons constitute what we may call a partition council, and they are selected by mutual agreement among the men in the family. One of the council members also serves as the amanuensis (*tai-pi-jen,* or *i-k'ou tai-pi-jen*) who writes out the contract that records the details of the partition agreement.

If family members have already agreed informally as to the main conditions of partition, the council's duties may involve little more than serving as a body of witnesses, or perhaps the members of the council may help work out some minor details. But with stronger disagreement within the family the council's role becomes more active, and it may be forced to bring opposing parties together and hammer out a settlement. In any event, the council's presence brings outside forces to bear on the partition process, which is thus expedited.

Analysis of partition council composition indicates that the members of such groups have a variety of social ties with the family seeking to divide. All of them are of the kind crucially important within the framework of Mei-nung society. I have information concerning the make-up of 11 councils convened between 1950 and 1963, a period when there were 19 cases of family partition in Yen-liao. The 11 councils each consisted of between two and seven persons; some individuals participated in more than one council during this period, but for present purposes they are counted once for each council they were on, yielding a total of 49 councilors. The connections between the council members and the families they helped dissolve may be categorized as follows:

close agnates (worship at same ancestral hall)	18
other close agnates	2
same surname	14
cognatic kinsmen	6
others	9
TOTAL	49

I list under "other close agnates" one councilor who was the brother of three men who separated; he had long since formed his own family to the south of the Mei-nung area. The other councilor in this category is a man from one of the two Yeh A compounds (which worship in separate ancestral halls, see chapter 2), who was asked to be present at the other compound for the partition of one of its families. The emphasis of the agnatic principle extends to those included under "same surname." They are identified as "lineage members" in most of the partition documents, which use for these men terms that are also applied to close agnates (*tsung, tsung-tsu, tsung-ch'in,* or *t'ung-tsu*). A man prominent as the manager and religious leader of a nearby temple is in one document called "lineage head" (*tsu-chang*). Now neither this man nor the family concerned belonged to any agnatic group other than those focusing on their respective ancestral halls, so that in fact the title he received was bestowed in recognition of his considerable influence in local affairs.

Eight of the eleven councils had one or more men with more than ordinary weight in the affairs of Yen-liao and elsewhere in the Lung-tu area, and in some cases throughout Mei-nung. Two councils included men important in temples and religious life in general; five others had as a member one of two men active in Mei-nung Township politics, while three boasted the head of Yen-liao's wealthiest family. Forty members of the councils under consideration were from Yen-liao; two of the outsiders were close kinsmen, but the remainder were invited to serve as councilors because of their importance in Lung-tu society.

Thus when a family divides it involves in the process persons with whom it has frequently overlapping ties of kinship and co-residence in Yen-liao; influential persons can be from other parts of Lung-tu because a man must operate in this larger community in order to establish for himself a position of significant prominence (see chapter 1). Such men of influence play the most active role in inventorying assets and liabilities, computing shares, and working out the text of the partition document, so that they are in demand because of their expertise as well as their prominence. These men view their participation in partition councils as one of the services they must provide in order to maintain and expand their sources of support within the community. Councils in which prominent men do not participate will in any event include local people known to be technical experts in the preparation of partition documents.

There are important reasons for the preponderance of agnates among the kinsmen serving as council members. An agnate will have more or less equally close ties with each of the men involved in family partition. This is most obvious as far as agnatic ties defined solely on the basis of common surname are concerned; and in seeing this kind of agnatic connection used in the recruitment of partition councils we may recall its use, especially during the pre-Japanese period, in the formation of large lineages (chapter 2). The neutral position of close agnates is clearest when brothers divide: their father's brother, say, has equivalent genealogical connections with all of them, as do other members of their local agnatic group. The situation is more complex when sons separate from their father. In each of two such cases among the 11 partition councils, a father's brother served as councilor, and in genealogical terms, the ties between brothers are closer than those between uncles and nephews; but persons with brothers and nephews about to separate usually are their immediate neighbors in the compound, so that the future course of day-to-day relationships and cooperation can be influenced by the outcome of the partition proceedings. Such close agnates are strongly motivated to see that as little hostility as possible is generated between them and each of the parties to the separation, and while close agnates might therefore be encouraged to entirely absent themselves from the partition proceedings, they are actively sought out by the parties concerned. Of course, most other men within a local agnatic group have a similarly strong interest in maintaining friendly ties with the new families.

The position of cognatic kinsmen is quite different. The six that were included in the 11 partition councils were in each instance related to the parties involved through matrilateral ties three to five generations removed, although in one case there was an additional connection in that the council member was also the brother, adopted out (through affinal adoption, see chapter 2), of the three men who separated. Affines, important during many events, are conspicuously absent during partition proceedings. A woman's close relatives are avoided, for they are held to be biased in favor of her husband.

The different connections implicated during partition serve to expedite the process, for failure to reach agreement reflects not only on the family concerned, but is also a rebuke administered to the council. Most persons are motivated to reach an understanding so as not to threaten their ties with kinsmen, neighbors, and men of influence. As we have seen earlier, their desire to complete the division process often is reinforced by what may be the dysfunctional state of the family economy at that point. To my knowledge, family partition councils in Yen-liao have succeeded in every instance in obtaining agreement during the first meeting, even though most such occasions are marked by bitter altercations among family members, and often last until the early hours of the morning. In the larger Lung-tu area I know of one instance, though there probably have been similar ones, where five council meetings were needed to settle the dispute. Many council members refused to attend succeeding sessions and new ones had to be found. Finally, a local specialist in legal matters and family division was hired to preside; after meeting with the family and other council members for nine hours, he succeeded in obtaining agreement at 4:00 A.M., thereby earning for himself a sizable commission.

The partition proceedings, attended by the council and adult

male family members, take place during and following a meal
in the dining room or ancestral hall of the unit about to divide.
First, the council determines all family holdings and debts and
obtains agreement as to their value. The assets and liabilities
are then divided into shares of equal worth. Often the men
draw lots for the shares, but some or all of the estate may be distributed by mutual agreement, especially if much nonagricultural property is involved. The details of the partition agreement are recorded in a document that serves both as contract
and deed. To the document are affixed the seals of the council
members and the parties to the division, and copies are made
for each of the latter. I am told that in the past it was customary
for an additional copy to be taken to the ancestral hall and burnt
before the ancestral tablet, but in recent years this procedure
has been followed only in a minority of instances.

The *"fo"* emerges as an independent unit at the time of partition. If it had been part of a larger *chia* group living in one
household, it now establishes its own kitchen and conducts its
own economic affairs; if a *"fo"* had been autonomous, formal
separation involves receipt of a share of the *chia* estate and the
termination of the commitments and mutual claims which we
have seen to be characteristic of *chia* organization. When a *"fo"*
turns into a *chia* a woman's *"se-koi"* is merged with that portion
of the estate received by her husband through partition. He
takes control of grain association shares, loans, and the woman's
cash, which he usually uses to purchase such items as farm tools
or kitchen utensils, for building a new kitchen stove, and to
meet other costs of setting up a new family.

Family development comes full-circle when the husband assumes control of his wife's *"se-koi,"* a transfer of wealth that
reveals the wife's independent property rights are an artifact of
the *"fo"*'s membership within a larger family unit, and following which the woman begins to assume the kinds of roles we
saw her hold when we discussed conjugal family organization.
It is customary and expected that the wife should surrender the
"se-koi" to her husband when they form their own family unit,
even if her finances had previously remained completely in-

dependent. Thus, when I would ask men about their wives' money they would claim not to know the total sum involved; but many would add: "when the family divides I'll find out." The wife is encouraged to part with her "private" wealth by the domestic climate preceding partition, which we have seen to be characterized by the unity of husband and wife as they fight for their interests, and those of their children, in opposition to the other *"fo"* within the disintegrating *chia.*

Another event associated with the partition process also bears mention. Shortly after the formal proceedings have been completed, each of the new families holds a feast attended by guests who present cash or items of use in outfitting the new domestic unit. The guests are the man's close friends or his affines; agnates or the man's matrilateral relatives do not attend, for they have identical ties with each of the new families. Agnates predominate in partition councils because they are kinsmen who are neutral with respect to the contending parties within the *chia;* but after partition there is expressed the closer relationship between a man and his affines, who help him meet the material requirements of his new household.

Family partition is a contractual undertaking recorded in the documents that are drawn up at the conclusion of most partition proceedings. Though these documents must be used with caution, as I shall show, they are still an invaluable source of data for analysis of the principles and claims involved in the division of the *chia* estate. A selection of these documents from Yen-liao is included in Appendix B and they are cited here where relevant; they follow the same format and are basically identical to published material in the same category from other areas of China (cf. Johnston 1910:152; Lin 1948:125). While family partition in Yen-liao has as its dominant principle the equal rights of brothers, persons other than brothers do have certain claims, so that there is a fairly straightforward division of the estate into equal shares only when the family consists of siblings, their wives, and children.

If one or both parents are alive when the family divides, they must be taken into account. In some cases the father is one of the parties to the division and a son, usually the eldest, the other. Division Document A, which records an agreement between father and son, is worthy of comment in several respects. (This document and the family partition that produced it date from after the period mainly dealt with in this book; I obtained the document and additional information during a revisit to Yen-liao in the summer of 1966.) First of all, from the document's title and preamble, it would appear that the division was initiated and ordered by A-T'ien, the father. In fact it was Te-lai, the eldest son, who agitated for separation to the point that communal living became intolerable for all concerned. Such a situation is not different from one in which one of several brothers demands division following the death of the parents. It is true that if a father is alive his consent must be obtained before the family can divide, and that sometimes he may demand division, but precisely the same applies to adult brothers. In Document A, there are only three men classified as adults: A-t'ien, the father; and Te-lai and Kuang-t'ien, the eldest and second sons. Note, however, that the names of the third, fourth, and fifth sons also appear; though having rights to shares of the estate they were not yet married at the time of division and so did not have rights of partition and independent management. Document A, then, represents a case where the father divides the estate with his eldest son, in the name of his remaining sons, with the second of these indicated as the nominal representative of the second party to the division. This document also misrepresents the role of the father in that he seems to disappear from the picture with the completion of division. A-t'ien, in fact, remained the family's head once the eldest son withdrew his portion of the estate.

The role played by the father in family partition proceedings is associated with his former position in the family. If he has already retired as active family head, or if all his sons have married, he will not take part in the separation proceedings as a de facto shareholder, in opposition to other shareholders. The negotiations, rather, are confined to his sons, and the father's role is limited to perhaps demanding special considerations for himself and his wife, for the general principle is that sons when separated still retain collective responsibility for supporting parents and subsidizing their funerals. Most commonly the parents (or the surviving parent) become what I have already described as the "collective dependents" of the new families established by their sons. The sons undertake to distribute among themselves responsibility for support and the parents keep a room to themselves and eat in rotation among their sons' families. Although the agreement to jointly support the parents is often noted in the division contract, the technique, rotational board, is usually left unstated (see Document B, clause 5). The rotational technique is a standard one and is favored because, among other reasons, it leaves little room for any of the sons not to live up to their commitments. Division contracts serve to clarify and stipulate in detail arrangements that otherwise might be ambiguous, but the specific means by which a general agreement is implemented need not be put in writing if it is not liable to future misinterpretation.

An alternative to rotational support of parents is an agreement whereby one son incorporates them into his household and receives compensation from the others. This may be in the form of stipulated payments (see Document C, clause 14) or through the assignment of additional land to the party undertaking the parents' support. The latter arrangement is sometimes associated with the notion of *chang-sun t'ien*, "eldest grandson's field." This concept seemingly departs from the otherwise accepted idea that all sons have equal rights to the estate, for it provides that the eldest son of the eldest son can obtain an additional share apart from those distributed among his father and uncles (see Freedman 1966:50–51). The additional land is rarely if ever freely awarded, however, for the party receiving it assumes obligations not borne by the other parties to the division. Document D indicates how in one case a condition to the allocation of land was that the recipient undertake to be the sole support of his mother (clause 4). The "eldest grandson" who nominally receives the land is almost always still a member of his father's *chia* and the land is actually an increment to the family as a whole. In Document D, then, the land is under the management of Wang-te, not his son Shao-hsiang. A *chang-sun t'ien* is not demarcated unless all parties to the division agree, which almost inevitably assures that the recipient will also assume additional obligations.

The responsibility of the family to pay for the weddings of its members can take the form of a claim upon the *chia* estate if the sons who are parties to the division have unmarried brothers or sisters. In Document E, this obligation is expressed in the form of an extra cash payment to one of three brothers, a widower planning to remarry. Money is often likewise set aside for a sister, who usually lives with one of her brothers during the period following partition but before her marriage.

Document F, which dates from an earlier period than those noted so far, illustrates how in the context of stem family division many of the different procedures and claims involved in partition may be invoked concurrently, and how these claims may reduce the married son's share of the estate. There is the outcome of negotiations between father and eldest son, phrased in the preamble as if it were the father's command; in clause 3 there is a claim on land for purposes of supporting marriages; in clauses 4 and 5 there is described the utilization of property for father's support and funeral expenses. Obligations such as those due parents are not necessarily included in the texts of partition documents. These obligations are most likely to be put into writing when they are transformed into claims by one party against another; in this case the obligations shared by a group of brothers are borne by only some, who are compensated for taking on additional responsibilities. By the terms of Document F, then, Ting-jen, the eldest son, is no longer bound to join in the support of his father Ch'ing-feng, or subsidize his funeral, or help pay for his younger brothers' weddings. It can be seen, then, that even very fundamental ties between father and son can be modified through written agreement.

The above discussion has dealt with division where the families involved were formed through the usual pattern of virilocal marriage and patrilineal descent. But we have seen that in the absence of surviving male offspring, the family line may be maintained by adoption or uxorilocal marriage. Should a *chia* contain both adopted and true sons, they hold equal rights to the estate, but the status of sons born from uxorilocal marriage is determined according to the conditions of the marriage agreement. The usual procedure is to distribute both surnames equally among the children, with the oldest son and daughter receiving their mother's surname, the second child of each sex the father's, and so forth. But sons bearing their father's surname have only minimal rights or none at all to the *chia* estate, unless the original marriage agreement stipulates otherwise. Since men willing to marry uxorilocally are usually landless and quite poor, they have little bargaining power in arranging the terms of the agreement; in most cases they must settle for the assurance that they themselves will have land to work and that some of their sons will bear their surname, though without any inheritance. Document G was penned in such a context; the first name appearing as signatory is the mother's, followed by the four sons with her surname, the father, and the three sons whose surname he shares. In this case, like others noted earlier, there were only two parties to the actual partition—the parents and their eldest son. The document does not list the land he received, which was only .10 *chia,* but rather places the entire estate ultimately in the hands of the Yeh brothers; the final division of the estate, along with the dispossession of the Kuo, is yet to come.

All but one of the documents in Appendix B were written after 1950; they are included not merely to illustrate points raised in the preceding pages, but also to offer concrete evidence of the strength of customary practices of family partition. Document H is in a somewhat different category, for it is indeed a true will; in its frankness, it points to the tenuous relationship between this body of customary procedure and the national legal system. At one point in the will "false registration" is mentioned, the purpose of which was to protect land from compulsory purchase under the Land Reform Law. Elsewhere, the will is called a "legal document" and there is a threat to call upon "law officers" should its instructions not be obeyed. Now this document does have what might be called "legal force" in the context of the local community, and its stipulations conform to local practices, which consider a will as evidence to be used during partition proceedings that can alter property distribution, but I doubt if it would ever be introduced in a court of law. Local procedures do not follow along lines set by the national legal system, but are enforced by the diffuse sanctions operating within the local community itself.

In turning to the question of differential endurance of complex families, I would first note that in Yen-liao the continuation of family unity is certainly encouraged by situations where the advantages, especially economic, derived from such unity outweigh those forthcoming for the parties concerned in the event of partition. But the significance of the economic elements must be viewed in the context of family development, because different sets of factors may appear most important when the partition of a family that has endured for many years is contrasted with the division of one that has held together for only a short period. I can illustrate the relationship between a family's longevity and the decisive elements in its partition by arranging families on a scale according to the degree that their economic activities encourage or impede fission. At one hypothetical extreme, circumstances are such that at least for some of the units within a joint family it is positively advantageous to separate. For example, in one such family division might involve little overall loss from the standpoint of the youngest of several brothers. Loss of the efficiency of a larger working force, or the advantages of a larger body of collectively owned resources, would be more than compensated for by certain gains; married but not yet a father, the youngest brother would be able to work his own land and plan for having children and providing them educations. After partition, he would no longer have to work for his nephews' support; their welfare and education had been consuming much of his family's wealth, thus preventing the expansion of family holdings and undermining future opportunities for his own children. Under such or similar circum-

stances, family division can be explained without reference to
its inevitability in all joint families. The same is not necessarily
true when families at the polar opposite of the continuum are
considered. Here division may be an economic disaster for all
concerned; each has specialized roles and the family advances
as a unit in a way impossible for any of its parts alone. Yet this
family also divides, and at this end of the continuum we cannot
appeal to the family's particular economic situation as such but
must look at features of family economic organization.

I would suggest that latent weaknesses in the arrangement of
redistribution assure that in any event all families ultimately
divide. We know that as long as the father is able to serve as
manager of family funds he usually tries to act as a disinterested
party with reference to the *"fo"* of his different sons; but upon
the father's death or retirement, redistribution comes under the
eldest son's control. While the father's commitment to family
unity is given, the same is not true of his eldest son. In terms of
family structure, the latter is in an ambiguous position; he oc-
cupies a pivotal position with regard to distribution within the
family, but at the same time he has access to resources within
his *"fo."* He is able to give his wife funds he has received from
other family members or from the family enterprises under his
management; he can keep family money tied up in banks or in
the fund kept at home, to which only he has direct access; finally, he is in a position to distribute funds in favor of his own
enterprises or his own children.

Under such potential circumstances the management of family funds takes on a public character if the eldest son shares
with his younger brothers a desire to maintain the family intact.
A brother in charge of finances is at pains to justify his activities
thoroughly, and he is under far closer scrutiny than was his father. In each of at least two Yen-liao joint families the oldest
brother keeps detailed account books, which are frequently in-
spected by other family members. Lang (1946:160) notes that
the same procedure for demonstrating a continuing loyalty to
the family was sometimes employed in mainland China if a
brother cared for family money. With a brother in control a fam-

ily may indeed remain united for many years; but in the process
of receiving and disbursing family funds the brother, while he
may be guided by the opinions of his siblings, must make the
final decisions regarding investment and consumption; and
there remains the fact that with consumer equality the *"fo"* of
the oldest brother tends to enjoy greater family support. Since
the oldest son, unlike his father, is in the final analysis concerned with the best interests of his *"fo,"* it becomes increasingly difficult for the younger brothers to remain convinced that
their sibling is acting on behalf of the family as a whole, even if
he should in fact believe that his *"fo"* is better off remaining in
the larger family. Partition is therefore likely sometime during a
brother's tenure as family fiscal manager.

If all complex families fragment at one point or another, it
nevertheless seems clear that the main factor behind their differential longevity is the degree of interdependence that characterizes the family economy; that is, the degree to which the
coordination of effort results in economic gain. Interdependence is relative, for all cases of family separation probably involve some economic loss, yet interdependence is emphasized
to varying degrees by different economic activities.

The economic interdependence of a tobacco-growing family
is heightened because of the heavy labor requirements of the
crop and its high return, so that the economic value of the family worker is increased. Tobacco-growing has had a direct impact on family development in Yen-liao, with the result that as
of May 1965, 17 out of the village's 22 joint households grew
tobacco, as did 7 out of the 14 stem households, and 13 conjugal
households out of 32. Tobacco cultivation is more suitable for
families with comparatively large numbers of productive
members and some families started growing the crop when they
had already assumed joint form; but the important point is that
the joint phase of the family developmental sequence is prolonged once the cultivation of the crop is undertaken. The 1965
figures reflect a general tendency for tobacco-growing families
to stay together for longer periods of time than others, and division sometimes occurs at a stage of development advanced

enough to result in the formation of additional joint or stem families. Table 27 compares sequence of family development among tobacco-growers and others starting in 1940, the year six Yen-liao households for the first time planted "Bright Yellow," the type still grown today. The table shows how tobacco-growing families are more complex at formation, maintain themselves as units for longer periods of time, and are more prone to develop into joint forms than families not cultivating the crop.

Table 27

Sequences of Family Development Terminating in Partition, Major Agnatic Groups, Tobacco-Growers and Others, Yen-liao, 1940–65 [a]

	Development sequences	*Cases*	*Average number of years between partitions*
Tobacco	Conjugal to joint	8	42.0
growers	Conjugal to stem	1	2.0
	Stem to stem	1	7.0
	Stem to joint	1	15.0
	Joint to joint	5	15.4
	Overall average		27.3
Others	Conjugal to stem	3	15.3
	Conjugal to joint	4	26.0
	Conjugal to fraternal joint [b]	4	3.2
	Overall average		14.8

[a] Not all families began to grow tobacco at the same time; if cultivation was begun during a family's development sequence, it is placed in the tobacco-growing column.

[b] Younger brothers separated from older ones shortly after marriage (parents dead).

Another convenient measure of this tendency is the relationship between marriage and family partition. Since 1940 there have been among Yen-liao's major agnatic groups 45 new family units created through the partition of tobacco-growing families; 31 of these, about 69 percent, resulted from the division of families in which the brothers party to partition remained together until all had married. For families not cultivating tobacco the respective figures are 23 and three, the latter being a mere 13 percent of the former. There are also important differences if partition is viewed with respect to the father–son relationship. Twenty-six tobacco-growing families, about 58 percent of the total, were formed through partition following the father's death, and the same is true of eight noncultivating families, about 35 percent. But these figures actually refer to very different situations, as can be seen if both measures of family unity are combined, as I have done in Table 28. Among

Table 28
Family Partition Among Yen-liao's Major Agnatic
Groups, Tobacco growers and Others, 1940–1965

| | | Partition When Father Alive | | Partition When Father Dead | |
		Number of cases	Number of families resulting	Number of cases	Number of families resulting
Partition when all brothers have married.	Tobacco growers	2	5	8	26
	Others	1	3	0	0
Partition before all brothers have married.	Tobacco growers	6	14	0	0
	Others	6	12	4	8

tobacco-growers, when partition follows the father's death it invariably occurs only after all the brothers have married; among other families, however, the father's death has been followed by the partition of brothers, some of whom have yet to obtain spouses. Thus linked to the greater complexity of tobacco-growing families is a situation where there is a greater emphasis of the forces encouraging the unity of fathers and brothers.

One impact of tobacco production on the family economy is that after partition the problem of conflicting demands on the family labor force is more serious than would otherwise be the case. This can be seen in the division of work into domestic and agricultural tasks. In all Yen-liao complex families, pigs are raised as an agricultural sideline and domestic work is a full-time job. The system of rotating daughters-in-law is a way of distributing domestic labor equitably; even in times of heaviest field work, such as rice harvest, domestic labor is considered more onerous than farming. The demands of domestic labor are somewhat more variable in conjugal families, but when pig-rearing is incorporated into the daily schedule, the woman of the household is kept at home for all or most of the day, so that domestic work frequently conflicts with other demands on time.

Thus the partition of Huang Ch'ing-te's tobacco-growing joint family into conjugal units in 1963 led to a reduction of economic activities. At that time Huang, one of four brothers, was a butcher; he bought pork from the Farmer's Association and retailed the meat in Yen-liao and adjoining areas. Huang kept up this work after separation, and he also continued to rear pigs as another sideline; like most other pig-growers, he sold the animals live to the Farmer's Association. Huang, like his brothers, also continued to grow tobacco. With his wife as the only other productive family member, Huang was hard put to carry on these diverse lines of activity. During the tobacco season, if his wife worked in the fields Huang would have to balance time between cooking and tending to pigs at home and selling pork outside.

For a while Huang entered into a variety of ad hoc arrangements in order to continue all enterprises. For example, he convinced the grocery store manager to sell pork on his behalf (the grocery store would attract more customers, Huang said). But the family in any event depended heavily on hired labor to cultivate their tobacco and do other work. Often the workers were only partially supervised by Huang's wife, who was not able to spend much time in the fields. During my residence in Yen-liao, Huang complained bitterly: workers were untrustworthy, pig production at home was less than satisfactory, and conflicting responsibilities were losing him customers. About six months after my departure in 1965 Huang finally gave up his outside business.

Agricultural work as such can also involve conflicting claims on the family labor force, but such conflicts occur only during short periods of peak labor demand if tobacco is not involved; if tobacco cultivation is undertaken, the duration of such periods

is greatly extended. The relative weight of the demands of tobacco and rice on the family labor force may be illustrated by
referring to the joint family of Huang Ch'uan-sheng, one of the
poorest in Yen-liao. Huang and his wife are both retired from
major productive roles, and the family work force consists of
three married sons, their wives, and a son and daughter who are
still single. The family land amounts to .70 *chia*, and in 1965
they planted .60 *chia* of tobacco. All told, 104 days were spent
by one or more family members at work related to tobacco production, including work meeting labor exchange obligations,
but labor exchange was utilized only during harvest. Otherwise
reliance was exclusively on family labor except for one worker
hired during an exceptionally busy harvest day. Family labor to-
taled 391 workdays and its utilization can be summarized as
follows:

Number of family workers per day	*Number of days*
1	15
2	8
3	20
4	20
5	28
6	11
7	2

The two rice crops during 1964–65, each .50 *chia*, required
much less effort. Data are available for labor involving more
than one family worker per day:

Number of family workers per day	*Number of days*
2	1
3	2
4	—
5	—
6	2
7	2

Tobacco production, not to speak of rice, has not fully absorbed the labor force of eight persons. The surplus, however,
has been made productive; the unmarried son has been hired

out as a full-time servant to another family in the compound, while the married sons manage to get a variety of miscellaneous jobs, especially during the tobacco season. During the 1964–65 agricultural year the family spent approximately NT$40,000 for various purposes. Of this amount, NT$10,000 was acquired as wages, NT$26,000 was from tobacco sales, and most of the remainder from pig-rearing. The family is unable to expand its estate because its income is barely sufficient to maintain present holdings and provide subsistence, and it has been in debt for the past several years, mainly to relatives and neighbors.

If Huang Ch'uan-sheng's family were to partition on the basis of present constituent *"fo,"* three new families would form and two more women would be forced into daily domestic work. The number of persons able to engage on a full-time basis in other than domestic work would be reduced from seven to five. Now, the busiest period on the family farm is precisely when the brothers are able to find daily employment with other families who grow tobacco. Though wages vary, the minimum for any tobacco-associated work was NT$25 per day during the 1964–65 season. If during 1964–65 those now constituting the family work force had been reduced to five persons, there would be 41 days during the year requiring full mobilization for tobacco work. In addition, for 11 days the three families would be short one worker and for 2 days would be short two. But the loss in 1964–65 would not have been nearly so great as during the preceding five years, when the Monopoly Bureau had temporarily increased the family's quota to .90 *chia.* The unmarried son, who was 19 in 1965, had been taking part in tobacco work during the four years before quota reduction, but with reduction the family was more than able to spare his labor. Compared to tobacco, the losses division would cause relative to rice production are small indeed. If reduced to five workers, there would be four days during the year where there could be a maximum loss totaling six workdays.

Tobacco production creates greater interdependence in the families of agriculturalists, but a similar effect results from a family's diversification into nonagricultural enterprises. As an example of interdependence in a diversified economy, we may refer once more to the family of Huang Yu-lai (chapter 5); it will be recalled that one of his sons both manages and works the farm while the other three attend to the brick factory, the trucking business, and a student dormitory in a town to the south of Yen-liao. The man who runs the dormitory lives there with his wife, but the other three women rotate between the farm and domestic work. One man in the family says that the farm, with a 1.50 *chia* tobacco quota, and the other enterprises during the past several years have been yielding a combined annual profit of NT$100,000 (I suspect the actual figure is higher).

In any event, a good deal of money is available for investment, and the family plans to develop new enterprises. Assuming that they were now to partition, their capital would be split four ways. None of the resultant families would have the wherewithal to make the contemplated investments on its own. It is safe to say that the limited investment possibilities remaining to each unit would not bring total returns as great as those derived from the unified investments of the family as now constituted. Division would also mean a reduction in total income from the present enterprises, and tobacco production would be affected. Deprived of common income, the enterprises such as the brick factory and the tobacco farm, which periodically require large sums of money for the purchase of raw materials, would probably have to resort to short-term loans from outside sources. Interest payments, more salaried workers, and the loss of fluid capital would all contribute to a decrease in total income. Furthermore, the utilization of the managerial talents of the grandsons now maturing would be restricted.

The argument so far has been that in joint families diversification and tobacco cultivation both tend to increase interdependence. But in a way, there is a contradiction; diversification removes persons from agriculture, tobacco growing keeps them in. Yet, as I have tried to indicate, the pull of tobacco is exceptional when compared with other crops grown in the Yen-liao region, and we have already seen in chapter 5 that joint families not growing tobacco display a greater degree of diversification away from agriculture than those which do cultivate the crop. Thus all Yen-liao joint families manifest an interdependence, linked to economic activities, which sets them apart from rice-growing agriculturalists. The particular course of each family's development has resulted in a different profile of economic activities, but common to each family is the fact that the component *"fo"* are headed by men who know that they need each other; their consciousness of interdependence and therefore their dedication to family unity are far more pronounced than among the men in an agricultural family that continues to rely on rice and other crops instead of tobacco.

CHAPTER 8

Family in Yen-liao and China

ALTHOUGH some readers may be skeptical about an anthropologist's generalizations beyond his own fieldwork, I think it important to see how my findings in Yen-liao may further our overall understanding of the Chinese family.

Previous treatments of the subject have felt the heavy weight of orthodox views of the ideal standards of family life, as promulgated by the "Confucian" literati and bureaucrats of imperial China. Descriptions of families living according to these standards are in the dynastic histories and other documents; the *i-men* or "righteous families" (literally: "righteous gates"; see Ch'ü 1959:19–20), are so named because they lived together harmoniously for many generations. This is how the Ch'en family is described in the *Sung History:*

> The family of Ch'en Ch'ung after many generations had not separated. The T'ang emperor Hsi-tsung ordered that they be given a testimonial of merit; in Southern T'ang they were once again declared a righteous family (*i-men*) and exempted from corvée. In the family of [Ch'en] Ch'ung's son [Ch'en] Kun and [Ch'en] Kun's son [Ch'en] Fang, thirteen generations lived together; including young and old, they numbered 700 persons. There were no maidservants or concubines, and strife was not be to found. At each meal they gathered in a large dining hall, with the children eating separately. The family had over a hundred dogs; fed together in

> one kennel, the dogs would not begin eating until the last one
> showed up. . . . (Wang 1963:33, quoting the *Sung History*)

Such families were preposterously rare, if they existed at all.
Yet I think it is fair to say that the modern analysis of Chinese
domestic life has been muddled by the large-family ideal. This
development may be traced back to the early part of this century, when the first avowedly sociological descriptions of the
Chinese family fastened upon the large or joint family as the
common form of domestic organization throughout China (see
Fried 1959). The earliest discussions were followed by the publication of community studies, social surveys and household statistics, which revealed that the joint form of family was in fact
comparatively rare, and that among the common people the
conjugal or stem family was the likely arrangement (see Hsu
1943).

If the earliest interpretations misunderstood the relationship
between family ideals and practices, they nevertheless succeeded in making this relationship the major focus of subsequent analyses, which in some cases have suffered as a result.
First of all, Chinese family size has remained a peculiarly sensi-
tive subject for many scholars; some time ago Freedman was
moved to remark that "It has become customary during the last
decade to begin discussions of the Chinese family system with
a round denunciation of the older view that the 'large' or 'joint'
family is the typical family of China. The point has by now
been well enough made for writers on Chinese society to pass
quickly over it" (Freedman 1958:19). Alas, the denunciations
show no sign of abating (see, for example, Levy, 1965:9). While
the history of the earlier misconception is clear enough, the
reasons for the passions the subject continues to generate remain to be explored.[1]

Scholars have commonly reacted to the original misunder-

1. In a manner reminiscent of the revisionist discussions of Chinese family
size, Laslett (1972) critically and interestingly reviews earlier ideas as to the
prevalence of the large family in preindustrial Europe and elsewhere. In the
same article he presents useful schemes for the classification and graphic representation of household structures.

standing of the social impact of the large-family ideal by applying the joint-family model to the social sector that seemed to accept this ideal most readily. Fei Hsiao-t'ung, one of the first to
introduce the peasant–gentry distinction, wrote that "It is often
believed that in China the family unit is large. There are big
houses in which a large number of kin live together, but this is
found only in the gentry" (1946:2). For Fei and other scholars,
the ethnographic facts cannot be reconciled with the gentry or
elite view of society, and it follows that the gentry must have
been talking about themselves only. However, it seems to have
occurred to no one to ask why the gentry, inaccurate in their
representation of China as a whole, should be regarded as competent ethnographers when describing their own sector of society. Instead, it has been taken as given that the joint family is a
function of gentry or elite status, of wealth and political power,
and that simpler families are representative of peasant status
and varying degrees of poverty. Thus, analysis has largely been
confined to seeking connections between joint family characteristics and features of gentry society.

Here I can only briefly refer to some of the most important
scholars who have followed this line of analysis. Fei himself
emphasized the economic and political elements that differentiated the gentry from the peasantry and that supported what he
took to be the prevalent family organization of each class (Fei
1946). Fei's ideas have been further developed by Morton
Fried, who links the different economic and political interests
of gentry and peasantry to different "subcultures," each with its
characteristic family arrangement (Fried 1952; 1962). In
Maurice Freedman's writings on the Chinese family the dichot-
omy between the rich and the poor remains crucial, for "there is
a very general pattern in Chinese society by which wealth and
social standing are associated with family complexity" (1970a:3;
actually Freedman is commenting on my article, Cohen 1970a;
see also Freedman 1958:28ff.; 1966:47ff.).

Some scholars view norms as more important than economic
elements in the relationship between family structure and
gentry–peasant contrasts. According to Francis Hsu, the joint

family is a status or prestige symbol differentially distributed across class lines; this form of family requires a strong father–son relationship, regarding which there is among peasants an "indifference" (1943:561) or between gentry and peasantry a "differential adherence" (1959:129). On the other hand, Marion J. Levy asserts that the joint family was an ideal pervading all of society, but one the peasantry were unable to achieve and among whom therefore "an inherent social element of frustration was to be found" (1949:59).

Now in traditional China there obviously were wealth differentials and elite ways of life, but the Yen-liao situation indicates that the uneven distribution of family types may be understood without assuming differences in domestic behavior between gentry and peasantry. It is of course true that in China people might live under very dissimilar social and economic circumstances; within one village or town economic activities could vary greatly among families. In dealing with economic life in Yen-liao I have tried to show that different activities can be compared in terms of the economic interdependence they bring on in the family. But such comparisons are possible only if the units involved are similarly structured, as is the case with the Chinese family. The arrangement of familial economic roles, such as redistributor, manager, or worker, and the pooling and redistribution of resources are characteristics of family life adaptable to a great variety of economic activities.

I would suggest that it is precisely the basic uniformity of practices most important for family organization that has not been sufficiently emphasized by scholars. All Chinese families were under a constant tension produced by the conflict between unifying forces and those making for fragmentation. Where there are at least two men able to go their separate ways, the basic question is why in some families they stay together for longer periods than in others. If the "gentry" or "Confucian" ideal were uniformly distributed, then such an ideal does not explain variations in family form, but must be considered one of the reinforcements for the uniformity of the family pattern. There are also problems of explanation if it is assumed that "staying together" was more important for an elite group than for others. It is safe to say that during the traditional period the norms regarding the pooling of income and the joint ownership of the *chia* estate by males were adhered to by far more than the elite portion of the population, however that group is defined. Those who separated early did so by following the same rules as those who stayed together longer. To explain joint families by appealing to the monopolization of ideals or norms by the elite is in fact tautological unless it can be shown that these people had different principles of family organization.

In dealing with the impact of social and economic differentiation on family form in China it is more useful to emphasize once again that it was crucial to *chia* organization that ties between persons were associated with common ties to an estate, which could vary in size and value. Great poverty could indeed deprive the *chia* of the minimum material endowment necessary for its cohesion, so that a contrast stressing the presence or absence of an estate is more useful than one emphasizing gross difference in family organization between gentry and peasantry. Indeed, the traditional gentry have long since disappeared from the scene both on Taiwan and on the mainland; on Taiwan, however, it is the survival of the family farm and other forms of private enterprise that provides the context for the continuing development of joint families in rural communities, which can in no way be considered elite by present or traditional standards. And I would suggest that in the People's Republic of China the joint family has lost its viability far more because of the collectivization of land and most other productive property than because of attacks on elite ideology and the destruction of the elite class (for an incisive and up-to-date analysis of family life in the People's Republic see Parish 1975).

Let us now review the particulars of several recent ethnographic accounts from Hong Kong and Taiwan in light of the general points I have raised. Barbara Ward's field work in Hong Kong (Ward 1965) was among the "Tanka," or "Boat People," who are about as remote from the elite as any group in Chinese society; it is an understatement to say that they are looked down upon in contemporary Hong Kong, and during the imperial period they were for many centuries classed as "mean people" and barred from participation in the examinations. Yet Ward found that among the Tanka fishermen the joint family was in fact quite common, and she concludes that the Tanka desire and are able to approximate the gentry's behavior. Here the heavy weight of previous analyses may have had the interesting effect of deflecting an economic explanation when one would seem most called for. The problem is why the inshore purse-seiners, in particular, live in joint families. The issue might be clarified if the assumption that an elite ideology is the main factor is replaced by an acknowledgment that family labor is less expensive than hired; for we are told that "inshore purse-seining . . . could not be carried on by a nuclear family alone; the additional complement may be made up with hired men, but this is unusual; Kau-Sai purse-seiners all house families of the patrilocal extended type or parts of such families" (*ibid:* 119–20).

Again, the possibility that family partition might have to involve ruinous cash settlements, because of the indivisibility of a boat, surely must have had some influence in maintaining families intact. Perhaps one reason why Ward chose to emphasize the "prestige" interpretation relates to the tradition of anthropological and sociological scholarship in this area. The earlier economic approaches to the problem left no room for consideration of family complexity apart from class, so that the appearance of joint families among Tanka boatmen could only be regarded as testimony to the power of the gentry ideal.

It is a tribute to Margery Wolf's literary and descriptive skills that *The House of Lim* (1968), her richly detailed case study of a Hokkien-speaking joint family in a village near Taipei, can in fact be used to confirm that Chinese families are organized according to a uniform pattern. The completeness of Wolf's portrayal of the Lims allows us to see how they typify a Chinese domestic unit, even though Wolf stresses what she considers to be their special qualities. One of her major themes is the ability of the Lims to endure while other families in the village divide, and she links their staying together to a uniqueness that is in part pride:

> There is no formula for human behavior that takes the pride of the Lims into account. The very fact that most village families divide their household within a few years after their sons marry was a strong incentive for the Lim family not to do so (1968:145).

According to Wolf, the distinctiveness of the Lims has another element—the special influence of the man who had founded the family and who had been dead for a decade when Wolf lived with the surviving members: "The strength of his personality and of his memory held them together for many years" (1968:148).

Wolf takes up in turn different members of the Lim household, and we are all the more able to see them as the individuals they are precisely because we see how each responds to the family situation they share in common. Wolf of course does not imply that the family life of the Lims is organized in a special manner, which somehow is the collective expression of what is unusual about each member of the household. But neither does she arrange her description so that it is clear which aspects of life in the household are characteristic of the Chinese pattern and which are unique to the Lims. Although she emphasizes as typical of Chinese family life the divisiveness generated by the claims of the men in a *chia* to equal shares of the estate, she does not identify as such the economic elements that typically serve to preserve unity.

But Wolf nevertheless includes the important economic circumstances in her portrayal of the Lims. Note her description of how they obtain their livelihood through a "careful division of labor":

> the eldest male, and therefore the head of the family, . . . serves as general manager, deciding when and how the family income is to be used, and . . . he also manages the family business, the cement bag factory that employs from four to twenty village girls. [The oldest son of the family head's deceased younger brother] . . . takes primary responsibility for farming the family's . . . land,

arranging for the sale of its produce as well. [The farm manager's wife and the family head's wife] share the . . . task of cooking, each woman taking the responsibility for five days at a time. [The younger brother's widow has as her] main responsibility gathering, chopping, and cooking food for the family's dozen or so pigs. (M. Wolf 1968:34)

In the Lim household, then, we find a familiar situation: a joint family with diversified holdings and with management arranged such that the married men have their specialties. And Wolf indeed notes that "This division of labor enables the family to support itself more efficiently than if they were divided into small nuclear family units" (1968:34). Thus it is clear that if division was delayed by the Lims' pride and the founder's personality, it was only because these were the circumstances under which the Lims could succeed in providing for themselves the kind of economic foundation that in their society a family must have if it is to last longer than most others.

Norma Diamond, who studied K'un Shen, a fishing village in South Taiwan, offers a somewhat eclectic interpretation of the factors associated with variations in family form; she says these are "in part a result of economic circumstances and in part the working out of values surrounding household and family" (Diamond 1969:62). Although "nuclear" and stem units prevail, within the community there are examples of the "complex extended family," which "for some families . . . is an ideal that cannot be realized, and for others . . . neither the reality nor the ideal" (*ibid.*). But the ideal, once again, is the "Confucian joint family," and Diamond explicitly denies a uniform relationship between this ideal, economic standing, and family complexity (*ibid*).

Now Diamond's analysis raises the important question of the relationship between ideology or norms and behavior. It would appear that the economic organization of families in K'un Shen is according to the common Chinese pattern, insofar as income is pooled and usually under the father's control (1969:65–66). As to the family's estate, Diamond says that "theoretically, each son receives an equal share in the family property, with a slightly larger amount set aside for the eldest son" (1969:64), but "in reality, the father often bequeaths his pond or raft and fishing equipment to one son" (*ibid.*), while his brothers can go into a variety of occupations. Yet she also notes that "if the household elders are forceful personalities," they may preserve unity until their death, "completing the process which began as soon as the sons were deployed into different occupations" (1969:65–66). According to Diamond, K'un Shen's inheritance practices are linked to the fact that most families do not have property that is "divisible, . . . permanent . . . [or] capable of supporting complex households." Fishing rafts especially are "neither divisible, nor permanent" (1969:64), for the bamboo poles out of which they are constructed must be periodically replaced (1969:12). Thus with family estates small, impermanent, and not readily divisible, the major process at work seems to be the father's management of his sons' careers, although it would be most interesting to know if those brothers not receiving a portion of whatever property the family might have are compensated with cash payments or in some other fashion.

In any event, it seems clear that in K'un Shen behavior most closely linked to family organization is standardized. With the pooling of income, the family is an integrated economic unit, so that the men have the usual option provided by the Chinese pattern of family organization—to stay together or to divide—and in most cases there is little reason for them to stay together.

Throughout Taiwan improved sanitation and modern medical practices have greatly increased the potentiality for joint family formation because most families now have more than one son surviving to maturity. But under these circumstances the prevalence of joint families is not inevitable. Bernard Gallin found joint families in only five percent of the households in Hsin Hsing, a farming village in central Taiwan, while 29 percent of the families were stem and 66 percent conjugal. It is clear from his account that the preponderance of simpler families results mainly from division (Gallin 1966:138). Gallin's village was Hokkien, and it might be argued that the joint family emphasis is an aspect of Hakka "culture." Yet Burton Pasternak's study of

Tatieh, a Hakka village about 30 miles south of Yen-liao, reveals that these two communities in the south Taiwan zone of Hakka settlement differ greatly in the distribution of family types. Only 4.9 percent of the Tatieh families were joint in 1964, while 35.6 percent were stem, and 55.7 percent conjugal (3.8 percent are listed as "others"); in Chungshe, a Hokkien village he studied, joint families amounted to only 1.6 percent of the total in 1968 (Pasternak 1972:81). Gallin and Pasternak provide comparable data, and in conjunction with the Yen-liao material they highlight one interesting result of Taiwan's improved health situation: variations in family complexity are now more purely a result of the more or less rapid onset of partition than was traditionally the case. Thus we are able to bring into clearer focus those forces encouraging family division and those impeding it.

The forces holding Yen-liao families together are revealed by comparing families that endure, and that grow tobacco or are diversified, with short-lived families unable to bring tobacco to their farms or combine farming with other enterprises. It is safe to say that families similar to those which do not last for long in Yen-liao had as their members the bulk of the Chinese population during earlier times. Their farms were neither so commercialized nor so demanding in labor as those of the Yen-liao tobacco-growers. Given the limitations of farming, the heightened interdependence characteristic of the Yen-liao joint families could not so commonly emerge in the traditional environment, because it would have to be in the form of diversification. Many families lacked sufficient manpower even to make a start toward diversification, and a good many of those with the manpower could not find profitable nonfarming employment. Under such circumstances, it is likely that with the maturation of more than one son the onset of family division would be comparatively rapid. Diversification was more characteristic of wealthy families, which were larger and able to invest in many directions.

The majority of Yen-liao's population lives in close approximation to ideals of family life given official encouragement during imperial times, but none of the village's joint families would have been socially qualified to join the traditional elite. What the few that are poor obtain from tobacco sales provides for little more than subsistence, while the Land Reform laws have prevented the wealthier families from making the investments in land and landlordism that were so attractive to the old gentry. In that all Yen-liao joint families include dirt farmers, they contrast with the traditional elite; in the organization of family life, however, we see one system in operation.[2]

2. The major interconnected elements in the Chinese family system—women's property, husband and wife as an economic unit within the larger domestic group, a collective economy with redistribution under one person's control, and division of the estate among brothers—were in fact characteristic of family organization over much of continental Eurasia. For the joint family system in India see Goody and Tambiah (1973); for the prerevolutionary Russian joint family see Shanin (1972:219-27).

APPENDIX A

Yen-liao Primary Households: Sources of Income

Stage 1 Conjugal Households

Chia group	Farm size (chia)	1965 tobacco quota (chia)	Other enterprises	Sources of wages	Services
C1	.51	.40			
C2	.75	.40			Butcher
C3	0			Miscellaneous wage labor	
C4	.30			Miscellaneous wage labor	Chicken broker Chanter (religious)
C5	.45			Miscellaneous wage labor	
C6	.10			Miscellaneous wage labor	
C7	0			Miscellaneous wage labor	
C8	.55	.30	Rice grinding machine		Veterinarian
C9	.61	.30	Tailor shop		
C10	.52	.60			
C11	.76	.60			
C12	.63			Office clerk	

Stage 1 Conjugal Households

Chia group	Farm size (chia)	1965 tobacco quota (chia)	Other enterprises	Sources of wages	Services
C13	2.78		Grocery store		
C14	0		Barber shop		
C15	0				Carpenter (no shop)
C16	0		Candy and refreshment shop	Miscellaneous wage labor	
C17	.05			Miscellaneous wage labor	
C18	1.13	.50			
C19	.10	.30			Blacksmith
C20	0		Western drug store		

Stage 2 Conjugal Households

Chia group	Farm size (chia)	1965 tobacco quota (chia)	Other enterprises	Sources of wages	Services
C21	.96	.40		Miscellaneous wage labor	
C22	.57		Beauty parlor	Military nurse	
C23	.10			Miscellaneous wage labor	
C24	3.00	1.00			
C25	.12			Miscellaneous wage labor; truck driver	
C26	.10			Miscellaneous wage labor	
C27	.18		Chinese drug store	Clerk	
C28	1.47	.65		Miscellaneous wage labor	
C29	.60	.30			
C30	1.00	.40			
C31	.40		Male breeder pig	Servant; Miscellaneous wage labor	Musician (traditional)
C32	0		Motor cart; candy shop		

Stem Households

Chia group	Farm size (chia)	1965 tobacco quota (chia)	Other enterprises	Sources of wages	Services
S1	1.45	1.20	Truck		
S2	1.54	.50			
S3	.05			Miscellaneous wage labor	Brickmasonry; Woodcarving
S4	2.75	1.20		Salary (public official)	
S5	1.25	.90		Salary (Government clerk)	Blueprint drafting, etc.
S6	.80		Candy and vegetable shop		Vegetable wholesaler
S7	1.40				
S8	1.50	.50		Salary (Government clerk)	
S9	.55	.30	Motor cart	Salary (Government clerk)	
S10	.98	.50		Salary (clerk in Chinese drugstore)	
S11	.60			Miscellaneous wage labor	Wood chopping
S12	.44			Salary (truck driver)	
S13	.56		Truck		
S14	.00		Truck	Salary (truck driver) [a]	

[a] One family member drives the family truck, another is a salaried truck driver working elsewhere.

Joint Households

Chia group	Farm size (chia)	1965 tobacco quota (chia)	Other enterprises	Sources of wages	Services
J1	1.62	.55		Salary (truck driver)	
J2	5.71	1.50	Dormitory; brick kiln; lumber mill; two trucks	Salary (government official)	

Chia group	Farm size (chia)	1965 tobacco quota (chia)	Other enterprises	Sources of wages	Services
J3	.70	.60		Salary (servant); miscellaneous wage labor	
J4	1.85	1.20	Gasoline shop; timber land		
J5	2.54	.65			
J6	2.87	.85		Salary (government clerk)	
J7	2.39	.90	Power tiller [a]		
J8	1.12	.85	Carpentry shop		Fish-net weaving
J9	1.47	.85	Bicycle sale and repair shop	Salary (Air Force Officer)	
J10	2.53	1.70	Grocery store; rice mill; power tiller		Brickmasonry
J11	5.45	1.80			
J12	.94		Chinese drug store	Miscellaneous wage labor	
J13	.84		Carpentry shop; battery service and electrical repair shop	Miscellaneous wage labor	
J14	4.76	1.70	Grocery store; truck		
J15	.93	.80	Power tiller		
J16	.80		Motor cart	Miscellaneous wage labor	
J17	1.14	.90			Portrait painting
J18	1.73	.60		Salary (truck driver)	
J19	3.09	1.70	Power tiller; Chinese drug store		
J20	1.83	2.60	Tile kiln		
J21	1.40		Brick kiln		
J22	2.30		Brick kiln; lumber mill; grocery store; truck		

[a] I include power tillers as enterprises only if they are hired out to other families.

APPENDIX B

Family Partition Documents [1]

A

We all know it is a principle of nature that a big tree should grow many branches and a long river flow into many tributaries. Today, being your father and advanced in age, I ask only that you brothers each establish your own household and plan for your future. I have invited some of our kinsmen here to act as councilors and set down the terms for the distribution of my land and other property. Each and every one of you must act in accordance with these terms and establish his own family and livelihood, so as to shed lustre on our ancestors. Such indeed is my most earnest wish. The details of the distribution are as follows:

1. .7548 *chia*, which is plot A, covering the area bounded at the north by Lien-lai['s field], and extending all the way to the east and west, shall belong to Te-lai.
2. .7127 hectares, which is plot B, extending from the boundary with [the field belonging to] Ping-ch'ang all the way to the two ridges to the north and south, shall belong to Te-lai.
3. The remaining land, after removing that given to Te-lai,

[1] All names have been changed, consistent with the usage employed in this book, addresses omitted, and field registration numbers replaced with capital letters.

shall belong to Kuang-t'ien, Sheng-t'ien, Ching-lai, and Feng-lai.

4. The tobacco house, the drying chamber, the three small sheds, and the vacant land by the eastern shed shall belong to Te-lai.

5. The house in which we are currently living, the veranda, and the side shed all belong to Kuang-t'ien, Shen-t'ien, Ching-lai, and Feng-lai.

Everyone must adhere to the terms of the distribution established above. Two copies of this certificate have been drawn up, and each party shall keep one copy as proof of the transaction.

1965

DISTRIBUTOR:	Father	Huang A-T'ien
RECIPIENTS:	Eldest son	Huang Te-lai
	Second son	Huang Kuang-t'ien
	Third son	Huang Sheng-t'ien
	Fourth son	Huang Chin-lai
	Fifth son	Huang Feng-lai
COUNCILORS:		Huang Yu-lai
		Huang Fa-lai
AMANUENSIS:		Yeh Wang-hsing
POSTSCRIPT:	All five sons shall assume full and equal responsibility in paying for all funeral expenses at the time of their father's death.	
RATIFIERS OF THE POSTSCRIPT:		
	Eldest son	Huang Te-lai
	Representative of the other sons	Huang Kuang-t'ien

B

In compliance with our mother's command we four brothers shall equally divide among ourselves all property inherited from our ancestors and all present property so that each of us may establish his own family and livelihood, and enhance the prestige of the family and shed lustre upon our ancestors. The complete details of the distribution of the family estate are as follows:

1. The old shop by the dike and the plot on which it stands shall belong to Hsin-feng; the tobacco house shall be jointly owned by the four brothers, who shall also share equally in the planting of tobacco; the two rooms at the lower level of the tobacco house as well as its foundation land belong to Te-feng.

2. The two rooms at the western end of our original house and the four rooms at the southern end of our house by the road plus their foundation land belong to Hsi-hung; the four rooms at the eastern end of the original house, the bamboo pig-pen at the northern corner of the road-side house and their foundation land belong to Yüan-hung.

3. As compensation for construction expenses, the sum of NT$10,000 shall be removed from the common estate and given to Te-feng.

4. Hsi-hung, Te-feng and Yüan-hung shall assume equal responsibility for the payment of all outstanding debts and taxes. Hsin-feng shall have nothing to do with these payments.

5. All four brothers shall assume full and joint responsibility for caring for their grandmother and mother, who are still living. They should pay for their living expenses, medical expenses, and for future funeral expenses. Moreover, the four brothers must take turns in making [paying for] offerings to their ancestors.

6. Of our .73 *chia* plot of land, .20 *chia* shall be given to Hsin-feng, and what remains shall be equally divided among Hsi-hung, Te-feng, and Yüan-hung; the .16 *chia* plot of land shall be owned by Hsi-hung, Te-feng, and Yüan-hung.

7. From this day on, all four brothers shall take turns in descending order of birth in meeting the expenses of the annual celebration of their grandmother's and mother's birthdays.

In compliance with our mother's command, we brothers have invited some of our kinsmen to help us arrive at the above terms of division. Four copies of this document have been made, and each of us shall keep one copy and forever abide by the terms agreed therein.

MOTHER: Ch'en A-chin
CLANSMEN: [1]   Huang Hsin-feng
                                 Huang Hsi-hung
                                 Huang Te-feng
                                 Huang Yüan-hung
                                 Huang A-t'ien
                                 Huang Yu-lai
                                 Huang Lien-lai
                                 Huang Fa-lai
RELATIVE: [2]   Yeh Wang-hsing
AMANUENSIS: Huang Ch'ing-yün
1958

                                                                C

We two brothers Fu Ch'ing-feng and Fu Ch'i-feng, the participants in this division of our family estate, often recall the way
in which some people have lived harmoniously in one family
over many generations, some for as long as nine generations.
The customs handed down to us by Chiang Kung are admirable
indeed, and the loyal and fraternal spirit of the T'iens still remains fresh in our minds. However, our forefathers have also
reminded us that a large tree naturally forms many separate
branches and that, as the years go by, a large family will ultimately divide into many separate households. Although we two
brothers do not have the hearts of Kuan and Pao, we nevertheless still have the determination of Wu and Yüeh. Hence, we
have agreed today to invite several councilors to assist us in distributing our family estate. We sincerely hope that after partition each of us will do his best to build his future so as to bring
glory to the family and promote the traditions handed down to
us by our ancestors. The terms of the division are as follows:
[clauses 1–7, detailing land distribution, are omitted]
[clauses 8–12, detailing distribution of buildings, and distribu-
    tion of farm tools, are omitted]

   13. It is agreed that each party shall take turns at managing
       the [fish and water buffalo] pond in front of the old an-
       cestral hall for a period of two years.

1. *(tsung-ch'in)*   2. *(kung-ch'in)*

14. It is agreed that the NT$6000 we have lent out shall be equally divided among the parties. However, the interest shall be given to our parents for their use. Moreover, the future funeral expenses of our parents shall be shared equally by both parties. (It must be further pointed out that Ch'ing-feng must donate 300 Taiwanese catties of rice each season to help support father. No objection to this agreement should be raised).

15. [omitted]

16. Two copies of this certificate have been drawn up, and each party shall keep one copy as evidence.

1953

PARTIES TO THE DIVISION: Fu Ch'ing-feng
                             Fu Ch'i-feng

COUNCILORS: The head of the ward (*li-chang*), Yeh Wang-hsing

The head of the [administrative] neighborhood (*lin-chang*), Huang Yu-lai

The township representative (*chen tai-piao*), Liu Shuang-lin

Lineage uncle (*tsu-shu*), Fu Ting-wu [1]

Lineage younger brother (*tsu-ti*), Fu An-feng [1]

Lineage younger brother (*tsu-ti*), Fu Sheng--feng [1]

D

[clauses 1–2 omitted; they deal with distribution of land and buildings]

3. Outstanding debts:

   [a.] Ten thousand Taiwanese catties of rice owed the grain association [a rotating credit association]; payment to be shared equally by both parties.

   [b.] Both parties share equally in repaying the 1000 Taiwanese catties of rice borrowed from Mrs. Shunch'ang as well as the interest.

   [c.] The money borrowed from the Farmer's Association,

1. A member of the local agnatic group to which the parties to the division also belong.

from Ch'ing-yün, and from Ch'un-mei shall be repaid by Wang-te.

[d.] Money borrowed from Shuang-ch'un, Ch'ien-ch'un,
Shuang-kuei, Chien-an, and Yü-ti shall be repaid by
Wang-ch'üan.

4. Plot A, .28 *chia*, shall be allocated to Shao-hsiang, the eldest son of Wang-te. (While mother is still living, the
products from this land shall constitute the source of her
living expenses.)

5. All remaining household articles shall be placed in our
mother's charge and she will determine their proper allocation.

6. All remaining buildings and building ground shall be
owned equally and jointly by both parties. These properties may be divided in the future if necessary.

7. Two copies of this certificate have been drawn up, and
each party shall keep one copy.

PARTICIPANTS: Yeh Wang-te
                                  Yeh Wang-ch'üan
COUNCILORS   Yeh Wang-hsiang
                                  Liu Shuang-lin
                                  Yeh Wang-ch'ing
                                  Yeh Wang-cheng
                                  Yeh Shang-lin
1955

E

In compliance with our parents' command, we three brothers
shall each set up his own household and develop his own livelihood, so as to shed lustre upon our ancestors. Our entire family
estate shall be equally distributed among the three parties,
and the term of the division are as follows:

[clauses 1–4 omitted; they deal with property distribution]
[clause 5 omitted, stipulates joint responsibilities to parents]

6. It is a great misfortune that Ch'üan-jung has lost his be-
loved wife. In profound sorrow, his elder and younger
brothers agree together to donate NT$6000 to pay for his
remarriage and related expenses.

[clause 7 omitted; stipulates joint responsibility for payment of taxes]

[concluding paragraph omitted]

FATHER:	Yeh T'sai-yung
MOTHER:	Kuo Fan-mei
ELDEST BROTHER:	Yeh Kuo-shu
SECOND BROTHER:	Yeh Ch'üan-jung
THIRD BROTHER:	Yeh Po-pin
CLANSMAN:	Yeh Wang-hsing
AMANUENSIS:	Huang Ch'ing-yün
1960	

F

I, Yeh Ch'ing-feng live at . . . with my four sons, who are, in descending order of birth, Ting-jen, Ta-jen, Hsing-jen and Ch'ang-jen. Knowing that a large tree will naturally divide into many branches and realizing further that this very same principle is also applicable to human life, I conclude that if I invite, while I am still alive, some of our kinsmen to come here as councilors and assist in the distribution of all the moveable and non-moveable properties which I bequeath to my sons, future conflicts among my sons could perhaps be avoided. If all agree to this plan no one shall ever raise objections in the future or cause any disturbances after the final distribution. It is for this purpose that I prepare this document; there are two copies, of which one shall be kept as evidence by my eldest son Ting-jen, and the second by my three other sons, Ta-jen, Hsing-jen, and Ch'ang-jen. The complete details of the property division are as follows:

1. Plot A, consisting of .02 *chia*, plot B with .265 *chia*, one share in the *Sheng-t'ing hui* [an association] and one share in the *Tien-hsüeh hui* [an association] shall forever belong to my eldest son Ting-jen.
2. Plot C, consisting of .395 *chia*, and plot D, .313 *chia*, shall be allotted to Ta-jen, Hsing-jen, Ch'ang-jen, and forever owned by them.
3. The .143 *chia* building ground and all buildings now

located on plot E should be set aside for the marriage expenses of Ting-jen, Hsing-jen, and Ch'ang-jen.

4. Plot F, comprising .175 *chia,* and plot G, .19 *chia,* as well as all household utensils and domestic animals such as cattle, pigs, chickens, and so forth shall be used for paying up our present debt of approximately 1000 yen and also for the living expenses and then the funeral of father, Yeh Ch'ing-feng.

5. Ting-jen, Ta-jen, Hsing-jen and Ch'ang-jen shall jointly possess [a lineage association share].

6. The land rented from Hsiao Yün-chin, comprising .88 *chia,* shall be allocated to Ting-jen for cultivation. He must pay the rent. Moreover, the security for this land, 210 yen, and one share in the Trust Company, must be returned by Ting-jen to father, to pay for father's living expenses.

My testimony concerning the division of my father's property is hereby established.

1939
PARTIES TO THE PRESENT TESTIMONY:
                                Yeh Ch'ing-feng
ELDEST SON: Yeh Ting-jen
SECOND SON: Yeh Ta-jen
THIRD SON: Yeh Hsing-jen
FOURTH SON: Yeh Ch'ang-jen
AMANUENSIS: Yeh Kuei-jung
COUNCILORS: Yeh Wang-hsing
                                Lo Ting-ch'uan

G

In obedience to our mother's command, we now divide the land and houses inherited from our ancestors among the two surnames, Yeh and Kuo, so that each may live separately, establish his own livelihood, and thus give glory to our common ancestors. The details of the division are as follows:

1. Of the family houses, those located to the right of our ancestral hall, the side house with eight rooms, and three more rooms at the end all belong to Kuo.

2. All land belongs to the descendants of the Yeh.
3. From the .833 *chia* obtained through the Land Reform shall be removed .45 *chia*, to be given at once to the Kuo for their cultivation. However, once the agreed-upon time limit has expired, the rights of registration must be turned over to the Yeh.
4. All land adjoining the buildings belongs jointly to the two surnames, for their common use as a construction site. The Yeh assume full responsibility for all land taxes, except that imposed on land given over to the Kuo for cultivation.

All the above conditions have been agreed upon by the Yeh and the Kuo, who have prepared a written record with the help of their kinsmen. A copy of this certificate shall be kept by our parents, and all should abide by its terms.

[address]　　　　　　　　　　Yeh Chia Li-mei
　　　　　　　　　　　　　　　Yeh Kuo-ting
　　　　　　　　　　　　　　　Yeh Ts'un-t'ien
　　　　　　　　　　　　　　　Yeh Hsin-chin
　　　　　　　　　　　　　　　Yeh Mei-man
　　　　　　　　　　　　　　　Kuo Shun-lai
　　　　　　　　　　　　　　　Kuo Hsin-ch'un
　　　　　　　　　　　　　　　Kuo Hsin-chin
　　　　　　　　　　　　　　　Kuo Hsin-ho
COUNCILORS:　　　　　　　　　Yeh Te-yüan
　　　　　　　　　　　　　　　Huang Ming-ch'ao
AMANUENSIS:　　　　　　　　　Huang Ch'ing-yün
1958

H

Since human beings are not metal and stone, how can it be possible that they should exist forever in this world? Life is but an illusion, which shall inevitably vanish. I am now fifty-five years of age, and the shadow of death has already begun to haunt me. This is the reason why I have decided to write this will, so that I may instruct my descendants.

I have seven sons altogether; these are, in descending order of birth, Chin-ho, T'ien-ho, Kung-ho, Kuang-hsiung, Ch'ing-hsiung, Shih-hsiung, and Huo-ch'eng. Among them, the elder brothers have matured; the younger ones, on the other hand, are still quite young and require constant care by their father and elder brothers so that they may grow up. Therefore, the responsibility of caring for the younger brothers and eventually seeing them marry falls upon the shoulders of their elder brothers. In fulfilling such responsibilities, the older brothers will render invaluable help to their parents in managing the domestic affairs of the family and will be regarded as filial sons and worthy descendants.

Now, I shall briefly list the registered land. Plot A, .4877 *chia*, and Plot B, .2374 *chia*, are registered in Chin-ho's name; Plot C, .138 *chia*, in T'ien-ho's name; Plot D, .448 *chia*, in Kung-ho's name; and Plot E, .4293 *chia*, in Kuang-hsiung's name. Although, in principle, the land noted above has been registered in the names of you brothers, the transactions in reality shall not go into effect as of yet. The purpose of this false registration lies in my desire to keep the land. In addition I have a total of 1.579 *chia* in my name, as well as rights to .22 *chia* of jointly registered land at plot F.

I only hope that you elder brothers will be diligent and frugal, persevering yet creative, ever working together in winning success for our family and seeing that your younger brothers received a proper education, attain maturity, and eventually marry. After you have fulfilled all these responsibilities, you may claim the land to which you are entitled and set up your own households. At the same time, .30 *chia* shall be removed from the land registered in my name and given to T'ien-ho. The remaining 1.279 *chia* of my land, and the .22 *chia* of jointly registered land shall be equally divided among Ch'ing-hsiung, Shih-hsiung and Huo-ch'eng. Moreover, my interests in the enterprise I own jointly with Lai-ting shall be divided into seven shares. Every year you brothers must take turns in assuming the costs of ancestor worship. Finally, the remaining hill and forest land, buildings, tobacco houses, farm implements, household articles and tools shall be divided into seven equal shares.

From the time of the writing of this will, whoever is found

unfilial in his behavior, provoking cleavages or disturbances in the family, impairing our family reputation, or even attempting to set up his own household, let him be expelled, without any property, from this family. Though some land may have been registered in his name, he shall not be permitted to receive or cultivate one inch of it.

This will has been written in the presence of our invited kinsmen. Moreover, it has been ratified by their personal seals and signatures. Hence it fulfills all the requirements of a legal document. I sincerely hope all of you will closely observe the instructions contained herein. Should anyone attempt any illegal acts, such as violating the instructions of this will, officers of the law shall be informed immediately so that they may apprehend and punish the transgressor. Moreover, our relatives shall be invited to serve as witnesses in such cases; together we shall attack the evil-doer. This will purify the public morality and alert the masses so that there will be no unfilial son in any family and the nation will consist of law-abiding citizens. This will indeed be a family's fortune and a nation's blessing. Now, two copies of my will are drawn up; my wife and I each keep one copy as my instructions to our descendants.

1955

WRITER OF THE WILL:	Kuo Feng-an [address]
COUNCILORS FROM OUR LINEAGE:	Kuo Yu-an [address]
	Kuo Ta-hsing [address]
	Kuo Chi-hsiang [address]
	Kuo Hsiu-teng [address]
COUNCILORS, KINSMEN:	Huang Te-lai [address]
	Huang Yu-lai [address]
	Huang Ch'ing yun [address]
AMANUENSIS:	Yeh Ts'ai-yung

References

Ag. Cen. Kaohsiung. 1963. *Report on the 1961 Census of Agriculture, Taiwan, Republic of China, Individual Farm Households, Kaohsiung Hsien.* Taipei: Committee on Census of Agriculture.

Ag. Cen Taiwan. 1963. *General Report on the 1961 Census of Agriculture, Taiwan, Republic of China, Individual Farm Households.* Taipei: Committee on Census of Agriculture.

Ahern, Emily M. 1973. *The Cult of the Dead in a Chinese Village.* Stanford: Stanford University Press.

Baker, Hugh D. R. 1968. *A Chinese Lineage Village: Sheung Shui.* Stanford: Stanford University Press.

Barclay, George W. 1954. *Colonial Development and Population in Taiwan.* Princeton: Princeton University Press.

Buck, John Lossing. 1937. *Land Utilization in China.* (Reprinted 1956, New York: Council on Economic and Cultural Affairs.)

Chang, Chung-li. 1955. *The Chinese Gentry.* Seattle: University of Washington Press.

Ch'en Shao-hsing. 1964. *T'ai-wan-sheng t'ung-chih-kao, chüan erh, jen-min chih, jen-k'ou p'ien* (Provisional Gazetteer of Taiwan Province, Vol. 2, Population). Taipei: T'ai-wan-sheng wen-hsien wei-yuan-hui.

Ch'en Shao-hsing and Morton H. Fried. 1968. *The Distribution of Family Names in Taiwan.* Vol. 1, The Data. Taipei: Chinese Materials and Research Aids Service Center.

Chow, Yung-teh. 1966. *Social Mobility in China.* New York: Atherton Press.

Chu Yu. 1962. *T'ai-wan yü chung-yuan wen-hua hsieh-t'ung ti kuan-hsi* (The Cultural Affinities between Taiwan and the Central Plain). Taipei: privately published.

Ch'ü, T'ung-tsu. 1959. *Law and Society in Traditional China.* Paris and the Hague: Mouton.

Chung Jen-shou. 1970. *Liu-tui hsiang-t'u k'ai-fa shih* (History of the Development of the Liu-tui's Homeland). Nei-p'u (Taiwan): privately published [mimeo].

Cohen, Myron L. 1967. "Variations in Complexity among Chinese Family Groups: The Impact of Modernization." *Transactions of the New York Academy of Sciences*, 29, no. 5, pp. 638–44.

———. 1968. "A Case Study of Chinese Family Economy and Development." *Journal of Asian and African Studies*, 3, nos. 3–4, pp. 161–80.

———. 1969a. "Agnatic Kinship in South Taiwan." *Ethnology* 15, no. 3, pp. 167–82.

———. 1969b. "The Role of Contract in Traditional Chinese Social Organization." In *Proceedings VIIIth International Congress of Anthropological and Ethnological Sciences, Tokyo and Kyoto, 1968*. Vol. 2, Ethnology, pp. 130–32. Tokyo: Science Council of Japan.

———. 1970a. "Developmental Process in the Chinese Domestic Group." In *Family and Kinship in Chinese Society*, ed. Maurice Freedman. Stanford: Stanford University Press.

———. 1970b. Introduction to *Village Life in China*, Arthur H. Smith. Boston: Little, Brown and Co. [Reprint of 1899 edition].

Diamond, Norma. 1969. *K'un Shen: A Taiwan Village*. New York: Holt, Rinehart, and Winston.

Elvin, Mark. 1970. "The Last Thousand Years of Chinese History." *Modern Asian Studies*, 4, pt. 2, pp. 97–114.

Fei, Hsiao-tung. 1939. *Peasant Life in China*. London: Routledge.

———. 1946. "Peasantry and Gentry: An Interpretation of Chinese Social Structure." *American Journal of Sociology* 52, no. 1.

Fei, Hsiao-tung and Chang Chih-I. 1949. *Earthbound China*. London: Routledge.

Feng Ho-fa, ed. 1935. *Chung-kuo nung-ts'un ching-chi tzu-liao* (Materials on the Chinese Rural Economy), Vol. 2. Shanghai: Li-ming-shu.

Fortes, Meyer. 1949. *The Web of Kinship among the Tallensi*. London: Oxford University Press.

———. 1958. Introduction to *The Developmental Cycle in Domestic Groups*, ed. Jack Goody, Cambridge: Cambridge University Press.

Freedman, Maurice. 1958. *Lineage Organization in Southeastern China*. London: Athlone Press.

———. 1961–62. "The Family in China, Past and Present." *Pacific Affairs* 34:223–36.

———. 1966. *Chinese Lineage and Society: Fukien and Kwangtung*. London: Athlone Press.

———. 1970a. Introduction to *Family and Kinship in Chinese Society*, ed. Maurice Freedman. Stanford: Stanford University Press.

———. 1970b. "Ritual Aspects of Chinese Kinship and Marriage." In *ibid.*

Fried, Morton H. 1952. "Chinese Society: Class as Subculture." *Transactions of the New York Academy of Sciences* 14:331–36.

———. 1953. *Fabric of Chinese Society.* New York: Praeger.

———. 1959. "The Family in China: The People's Republic." In *The Family: Its Function and Destiny,* ed. Ruth N. Anshen. New York: Harper.

———. 1962. "Trends in Chinese Domestic Organization." In *Proceedings of the Symposium on Economic and Social Problems of the Far East,* ed. E. F. Szczepanik. Hong Kong: Hong Kong University Press.

Gallin, Bernard. 1960. "Matrilateral and Affinal Relationships of a Taiwanese Village." *American Anthropologist* 62:632–42.

———. 1966. *Hsin Hsing, Taiwan: A Chinese Village in Change.* Berkeley: University of California Press.

Geertz, Clifford. 1963. *Agricultural Involution: The Process of Ecological Change in Indonesia.* Berkeley: University of California Press.

Goody, Jack and S. J. Tambiah. 1973. *Bridewealth and Dowry.* Cambridge: Cambridge University Press.

Ho, Ping-ti. 1962. *The Ladder of Success in Imperial China.* New York: Columbia University Press.

Hsieh, Chiao-min. 1964. *Taiwan—Ilha Formosa: a Geography in Perspective.* Washington: Butterworths.

Hsu, Francis L. K. 1943. "The Myth of Chinese Family Size." *American Journal of Sociology* 48:555–62.

———. 1959. "The Family in China: the Classical Form." In *The Family: Its Function and Destiny,* ed. Ruth N. Anshen. New York: Harper.

Hu, Hsien-chin. 1948. *The Common Descent Group in China and Its Functions.* New York: Viking Fund.

Johnston, R. F. 1910. *Lion and Dragon in Northern China.* New York: Dutton.

Kuhn, Philip A. 1970. *Rebellion and Its Enemies in Late Imperial China.* Cambridge, Mass.: Harvard University Press.

Kulp, Daniel H. 1925. *Country Life in South China.* New York: Teachers College, Columbia University.

Lang, Olga. 1946. *Chinese Family and Society.* New Haven: Yale University Press.

Laslett, Peter. 1972. "Introduction: The History of the Family." In *Household and Family in Past Time,* Peter Laslett ed. London: Cambridge University Press.

Levy, Marion J. 1949. *The Family Revolution in Modern China.* Cambridge, Mass.: Harvard University Press.

———. 1965. "Aspects of the Analysis of Family Structure." In *Aspects of the*

Analysis of Family Structure, ed. Ansley J. Coale. Princeton: Princeton University Press.

Liao Su-chu. 1967. *"T'ai-wan k'e-chia hun-yin li-su chih yen-chiu*, A Study of Matrimonial Ceremony of the Hakkas of Taiwan." *Taiwan Wen Shian* 18, no. 1, pp. 19–87.

Lin, Yueh-hwa. 1948. *The Golden Wing: A Sociological Study of Chinese Familism*. New York: Oxford University Press.

Lu Nien-tsing, ed. 1962. *T'ai-wan-sheng tso-wu tsai-p'ei tiao-ch'a t'ung-chi*, Statistics of Crop Cultivation in Taiwan. Taipei: Bank of Taiwan, Department of Research and Development.

Ma, Fengchow C., T. Takasaka, and Ching-wen Yang. 1958. *A Preliminary Study of Farm Implements Used in Taiwan Province*. Taipei: Joint Commission on Rural Reconstruction.

Man Szu-ch'ien, et al. 1958. *English-Hakka Dictionary*. Taichung: Kuang-ch'i ch'u-pan-she.

McAleavy, Henry. 1955. "Certain Aspects of Chinese Customary Law in Light of Japanese Scholarship." *Bulletin of the School of Oriental and African Studies* 17:535–47.

Osgood, Cornelius. 1963. *Village Life in Old China: A Community Study of Kao Yao, Yünnan*. New York: Ronald Press.

Parish, William L. 1975. "Socialism and the Chinese Peasant Family." *Journal of Asian Studies* 34:613–30.

Pasternak, Burton. 1972. *Kinship and Community in Two Chinese Villages*. Stanford: Stanford University Press.

Potter, Jack. 1968. *Capitalism and the Chinese Peasant*. Berkeley: University of California Press.

Shanin, Teodor. 1972. *The Awkward Class, Political Sociology of Peasantry in a Developing Society: Russia 1910–1925*. London: Oxford University Press.

Shen, T. H. 1964. *Agricultural Development in Taiwan Since World War II*. Ithaca: Cornell University Press.

Simon, G. E. 1887. *China: Its Social, Political, and Religious Life*. London: Sampson Low, Marston, Searle and Rivington.

Skinner, G. William. 1964–65. "Marketing and Social Structure in Rural China." *Journal of Asian Studies* 24:3–43, 195–228, 363–99.

Smith, Arthur H. 1970. *Village Life in China*. Boston: Little, Brown and Co. (Reprint of 1899 edition.)

Taeuber, Irene B. 1970. "The Families of Chinese Farmers." In *Family and Kinship in Chinese Society*, ed. Maurice Freedman. Stanford: Stanford University Press.

Van der Sprenkel, Sybille. 1962. *Legal Institutions in Manchu China*. London: The Athlone Press.

Wang Jen-ying. 1963. *"T'ai-wan nung-ts'un chia-t'ing chih i'pan*, The Rural Family on Taiwan." *Taipei Wen Hsien* 6:20–47.

Ward, Barbara. 1965. "Varieties of the Conscious Model: the Fishermen of South China." In *The Relevance of Models for Social Anthropology*, ed. Michael Banton. A.S.A. Monographs 1. London: Tavistock.

Wolf, Arthur P. 1966. "Childhood Association, Sexual Attraction, and the Incest Taboo." *American Anthropologist* 68:883–98.

————. 1968. "Adopt a Daughter-in-Law, Marry a Sister: A Chinese Solution to the Problem of the Incest Taboo." *American Anthropologist* 70:864–74.

————. 1975. "The Women of Hai Shan." In *Women in Chinese Society*, ed. Margery Wolf and Roxane Witke. Stanford: Stanford University Press.

Wolf, Margery. 1968. *The House of Lim*. New York: Appleton Century Crofts.

————. 1972. *Women and the Family in Rural Taiwan*. Stanford: Stanford University Press.

————. 1975. "Women and Suicide in China." In *Women in Chinese Society*, ed. Margery Wolf and Roxane Witke. Stanford: Stanford University Press.

Yang, C. K. 1959a. *The Chinese Family in the Communist Revolution*. Cambridge, Mass.: Technology Press.

————. 1959b. *A Chinese Village in Early Communist Transition*. Cambridge, Mass.: Technology Press.

Yang, Martin. 1945. *A Chinese Village: Taitou, Shantung Province*. New York: Columbia University Press.

Character List

(H) = Hakka; (M) = Mandarin; Δ = no standard character

a-p'o-niouc(H)	阿婆肉	kouo-t'in(H)	過定
chang-sun-t'ien(M)	長孫田	kung-ch'in(M)	公親
chen(M)	鎮	kuo-fang(M)	過房
cheng-t'ing(M)	正廳	la ka-moun(H)	迁家門
chia[(M), 0.969 hectares]	甲	li[(M), administrative district]	里
chia[(M), family]	家	li[(M), ceremony]	禮
chia-chang (M)	家長	li-chi(M)	禮已
chia-t'ing(M)	家庭	lin(M)	鄰
chien-min(M)	賤民	Liu-tui(M)	六堆
chip-gni-gnit(H)	十二日	man-gniet(H)	滿月
chong-tsong(H)	上庄	mei-jen(M)	媒人
chou-k'ong(H)	書狂	mei-jen-li(M)	媒人禮
fan-ngoe-ka(H)	還外家	Mi-nung-ngin(H)	美濃人
fang(M)	房	moe-gnin(H)	媒人
fen-chia(M)	分家	mou(M)	畝
fo(H)	伙	nao fen-chia(M)	鬧分家
fu(H)	戶	nao hsin-niang(M)	鬧新娘
ha tsong(H)	下庄	nao oi-poun(H)	鬧愛分
hao-vi hai(H)	號位鞋	on ts'ong(H)	安床
hsiang(M)	鄉	pa-tzu(M)	八字
hsien(M)	縣	pac tze ts'ien soun, van nien fou koui(H)	百子千孫萬年福貴
hsin-fang(M)	新房	pac-koung(H)	伯公
hu(M)	戶	pat-se(H)	八字
i-k'ou tai-pi-jen(M)	依口代筆人	p'in-chin(M)	聘金
i-men(M)	義門	p'in-kim(H)	聘金
ka(H)	家	pu-hsi pan(M)	補習班
kao-koung(H)	交工	sai-khia(Hokkien)	私 Δ
kin ngoe-tsou(H)	敬外祖	se-koi(H)	私穢
k'on se-moe(H)	看細妹	se-koi-tiam(H)	私穢店
koung(H)	工	se-koi-t'ien(H)	私穢田
kouo-fong(H)	過房		

se-koi-tsiao(H)　　　　私頦蕉

sia-fa(H)　　　　　　下花

sin-niong-tsiou(H)　　　新娘酒

siong-gnin(H)　　　　相認

szu-fang-ch'ien(M)　　私房錢

tai-pi-jen(M)　　　　代筆人

tang-chia(M)　　　　當家

t'ang-ha(H)　　　　　廳下

tchon-kouc-fi(H)　　　轉穀會

tchon-moun(H)　　　　轉門

tchou-lan pac-koung(H)　豬欄伯公

tchou-p'ien(H)　　　　豬片

t'en-chou(H)　　　　　膽手

t'iap-hap(H)　　　　　牒盒

t'iap-kioc hai(H)　　　Δ 脚鞋

t'ien-kung(M)　　　　天公

t'oung-hang(H)　　　　同行

t'oung-ka-ngin(H)　　　同家人

ts'ap-fa(H)　　　　　插花

ts'ia-long(H)　　　　Δ 郎

tsu-chang(M)　　　　族長

tsu-shu(M)　　　　　族叔

tsu-ti(M)　　　　　　族弟

ts'un li-chi(M)　　　　存禮己

tsung(M)　　　　　　宗

tsung-ch'in(M)　　　　宗親

tsung-tsu(M)　　　　宗族

t'ung-tsu(M)　　　　同族

van-chin(H)　　　　　完神

yan-leou(H)　　　　　烟樓

yen-yeh kan-tsao-shih(M)　烟葉乾燥室

yuan(M)　　　　　　圓

Index

Studies of the East Asian Institute

The Ladder of Success in Imperial China, by Ping-ti Ho. New York: Columbia University Press, 1962.

The Chinese Inflation, 1937–1949, by Shun-hsin Chou. New York: Columbia University Press, 1963.

Reformer in Modern China: Chang Chien, 1853—1926, by Samuel Chu. New York: Columbia University Press, 1965.

Research in Japanese Sources: A Guide, by Herschel Webb with the assistance of Marleigh Ryan. New York: Columbia University Press, 1965.

Society and Education in Japan, by Herbert Passin. New York: Bureau of Publications, Teachers College, Columbia University, 1965.

Agricultural Production and Economic Development in Japan, 1873–1922, by James I. Nakamura. Princeton: Princeton University Press, 1966.

Japan's First Modern Novel: Ukigumo of Futabatei Shimei, by Marleigh Ryan. New York: Columbia University Press, 1967.

The Korean Communist Movement, 1918–1948, by Dae-Sook Suh. Princeton: Princeton University Press, 1967.

The First Vietnam Crisis, by Melvin Gurtov. New York: Columbia University Press, 1967.

Cadres, Bureaucracy, and Political Power in Communist China, by A. Doak Barnett. New York: Columbia University Press, 1967.

The Japanese Imperial Institution in the Tokugawa Period, by Herschel Webb. New York: Columbia University Press, 1968.

Higher Education and Business Recruitment in Japan, by Koya Azumi. New York: Teachers College Press, Columbia University, 1969.

The Communists and Chinese Peasant Rebellions: A Study in the Rewriting of Chinese History, by James P. Harrison, Jr. New York: Atheneum, 1969.

How the Conservatives Rule Japan, by Nathaniel B. Thayer. Princeton: Princeton University Press, 1969.

Aspects of Chinese Education, edited by C. T. Hu. New York: Teachers College Press, Columbia University, 1970.

Documents of Korean Communism, 1918–1948, by Dae-Sook Suh. Princeton: Princeton University Press, 1970.

Japanese Education: A Bibliography of Materials in the English Language, by Herbert Passin. New York: Teachers College Press, Columbia University, 1970.

Economic Development and the Labor Market in Japan, in Koji Taira. New York: Columbia University Press, 1970.

The Japanese Oligarchy and the Russo-Japanese War, by Shumpei Okamoto. New York: Columbia University Press, 1970.

Imperial Restoration in Medieval Japan, by H. Paul Varley. New York: Columbia University Press, 1971.

Japan's Postwar Defense Policy, 1947–1968, by Martin E. Weinstein. New York: Columbia University Press, 1971.

Election Campaigning Japanese Style, by Gerald L. Curtis. New York: Columbia University Press, 1971.

China and Russia: The "Great Game," by O. Edmund Clubb. New York: Columbia University Press, 1971.

Money and Monetary Policy in Communist China, by Katharine Huang Hsiao. New York: Columbia University Press, 1971.

The District Magistrate in Late Imperial China, by John R. Watt. New York: Columbia University Press, 1972.

Law and Policy in China's Foreign Relations: A Study of Attitudes and Practice, by James C. Hsiung. New York: Columbia University Press, 1972.

Pearl Harbor as History: Japanese-American Relations, 1931–1941, edited by Dorothy Borg and Shumpei Okamoto, with the assistance of Dale K. A. Finlayson. New York: Columbia University Press, 1973.

Japanese Culture: A Short History, by H. Paul Varley. New York: Praeger, 1973.

Doctors in Politics: The Political Life of the Japan Medical Association, by William E. Steslicke. New York: Praeger, 1973.

The Japan Teachers Union: A Radical Interest Group in Japanese Politics, by Donald Ray Thurston. Princeton: Princeton University Press, 1973.

Japan's Foreign Policy, 1868–1941: A Research Guide, edited by James William Morley. New York: Columbia University Press, 1974.

Palace and Politics in Prewar Japan, by David Anson Titus. New York: Columbia University Press, 1974.

The Idea of China: Essays in Geographic Myth and Theory, by Andrew March. Devon, England: David and Charles, 1974.

Origins of the Cultural Revolution, by Roderick MacFarquhar. New York: Columbia University Press, 1974.

Shiba Kōkan: Artist, Innovator, and Pioneer in the Westernization of Japan, by Calvin L. French. Tokyo: Weatherhill, 1974.

Insei: Abdicated Sovereigns in the Politics of Late Heian Japan, by G. Cameron Hurst. New York: Columbia University Press, 1975.

Embassy at War, by Harold Joyce Noble. Edited with an introduction by Frank Baldwin, Jr. Seattle: University of Washington Press, 1975.

Rebels and Bureaucrats: China's December 9ers, by John Israel and Donald W. Klein. Berkeley, University of California Press, 1975.

Neo-Confucianism and the Political Culture of Late Imperial China, by Thomas A. Metzger. New York: Columbia University Press, 1976.

Deterrent Diplomacy, edited by James William Morley. New York: Columbia University Press, 1976.

House United, House Divided: The Chinese Family in Taiwan, by Myron L. Cohen. New York: Columbia University Press, 1976.